Test Bank

to accompany

Statistical Techniques in Business and Economics

Eleventh Edition

Douglas A. Lind
Coastal Carolina University

William G. Marchal
The University of Toledo

Robert D. Mason
Late of The University of Toledo

Prepared by
Samuel Wathen
Coastal Carolina University

Boston Burr Ridge, IL Dubuque, IA Madison, WI New York San Francisco St. Louis
Bangkok Bogotá Caracas Kuala Lumpur Lisbon London Madrid Mexico City
Milan Montreal New Delhi Santiago Seoul Singapore Sydney Taipei Toronto

McGraw-Hill Higher Education

*A Division of The **McGraw-Hill** Companies*

Test Bank to accompany
STATISTICAL TECHNIQUES IN BUSINESS AND ECONOMICS
Douglas A. Lind, William G. Marchal and Robert D. Mason

Published by McGraw-Hill/Irwin, an imprint of the McGraw-Hill Companies, Inc., 1221 Avenue of the Americas, New York, NY 10020. Copyright © 2002, 1999, 1996, 1993, 1990, 1986, 1982, 1978, 1974, 1970, 1967 by the McGraw-Hill Companies, Inc. All rights reserved.
The contents, or parts thereof, may be reproduced in print form solely for classroom use with
STATISTICAL TECHNIQUES IN BUSINESS AND ECONOMICS
provided such reproductions bear copyright notice, but may not be reproduced in any other form or for any other purpose without the prior written consent of The McGraw-Hill Companies, Inc., including, but not limited to, in any network or other electronic storage or transmission, or broadcast for distance learning.

1 2 3 4 5 6 7 8 9 0 QSR/QSR 0 9 8 7 6 5 4 3 2 1

ISBN 0-07-248166-8

www.mhhe.com

Table of Contents

TIPS ON HOW TO USE THIS TEST MANUAL

This section is directed primarily to the new user of objective tests. It is meant to provide you with assistance in assembling valid and defensible tests for your classes. We have found objective tests and student evaluations of such tests to be hard "task masters", and we do not want you to have to experience the problems associated with defending or adjusting bad questions on an exam. Problems occur in objective testing because they are considerably more difficult to write than are problem, essay, or short answer tests. In contrast, objective tests are much more easily graded than other, more subjective tests; so easy that the computer is employed to do the grading. However, valid use of objective tests do not stop at the grading stage; there is more diagnostic work to be done by the instructor after the test has been graded.

The questions in this test bank have been classified by chapter, type (e.g., True/False, Multiple-choice, Essay), difficulty (easy, medium, hard), and learning objectives. You can select questions in each chapter using these criteria. Thus, you can build your test a number of different ways, placing emphasis on those question characteristics that are most appropriate for your class. In addition, you will find narrative questions that are sets of questions using some common information. These narrative questions may be more difficult because there is more distractor information in the question narrative.

To achieve zero-defect, zero-waste testing, we suggest the following logical steps:

1) Identify the objectives of your test before construction. Identify the chapters to be tested and the important concepts to be included on the examination.

2) Write questions or select questions from the test bank by content area. Be sure that each question selected from the test manual is appropriate in the context in which you teach statistics. That is, each of the questions included in this test bank is valid in the context of the general content of the textbook *Statistical Techniques in Business and Economics*. However, there are questions that might be inappropriate depending upon the specific approach you have taken in your class. You will need to screen each question before you actually select it for inclusion in **YOUR** test. This screening should include answers to questions such as:

    * Is this a good question in the context of my class?
    * Does this question have an appropriate level of difficulty?
    * Does this question require the use of a formula or appendix table that I do or do not need to supply the test taker?
    * Is this an important question from my perspective?
    * Do I agree with the authors' assessment of the level of difficulty?

3) Confirm that your test is balanced with respect to level of difficulty and content.

    The quality, difficulty, and mix of questions on a test determine the appropriateness and validity of a test. If any of these three factors is not correct, then the test may not be appropriate. A question might be of high quality and medium difficulty when used by one instructor. However, when used by another instructor, this same question might be low quality and very difficult. Obviously, we all teach our classes somewhat differently, emphasizing different concepts and principles, and at times even disagreeing with each other and the authors.

Objective tests are not inherently easy or hard. They can be designed to be either. Good questions are those which discriminate between students who are very good (A), good (B), average (C) etc. Consequently, questions on an exam should not be all difficult, nor should they all be easy. Only a small percentage of questions should be extremely difficult.

4) Make up the correct answer key. During this process confirm that the length of test is appropriate for your class. Most importantly, confirm that each questions is a valid one.

5) After giving the test, share the key with the students. Discuss any of the questions that are suspect or particularly hard.

6) Recognize that perfectly designed tests are not common. Adjustments are almost always necessary. Some questions might have to have double keys (e.g., A and D are both correct). If the right answer to a question is not on the test, then normally everyone should receive full credit for that question. Also, if a question is confusing, then the normal rectification is to give full credit to all.

7) At all costs, do not become defensive in discussing a bad question. Stress the validity of the test after all questions have been adjusted. The adjustment process (i.e., double keying and keying all correct) yields a valid and defensible test.

8) Avoid rushing to get the test constructed. After you have given a "bad" test, you will pay ten times more for the mistakes made during test construction. Zero defects is a difficult, but necessary goal in testing, particularly during test construction.

9) Normally, it is best to weigh true and false questions as worth one point, while multiple-choice questions are worth two points. This is logical and appropriate considering the probabilities associated with guessing. It is not recommended that you use different weights for different questions; for example, don't use 2 points for some multiple-choice questions and 3 points for other multiple-choice questions.

McGraw-Hill/Irwin
Test Bank to accompany STATISTICAL TECHNIQUES IN BUSINESS AND ECONOMICS, Eleventh Edition, by Lind, Mason, & Marchal.

We hope this manual and the text are error free and easy for you to use. Invariably, however, if there are errors, we would appreciate knowing about such errors as soon as possible so that we can correct them in subsequent printings and future editions. Please help us by using this postage-paid form to report any that you find. Thank you.

Note: Extra copies of this form appear at the end of this manual.
Attention: R. Hercher

Name________________________School____________________________

Office Phone__________________________

Please fold and seal so that our address is visible, and mail.

NO POSTAGE
NECESSARY
IF MAILED
IN THE
UNITED STATES

BUSINESS REPLY MAIL
FIRST-CLASS MAIL PERMIT NO. 204 OAKBROOK, IL

POSTAGE WILL BE PAID BY ADDRESSEE

ATTENTION: R. T. Hercher

THE McGRAW-HILL COMPANIES
RICHARD D. IRWIN
1333 BURR RIDGE PKY.
BURR RIDGE, IL 60521-0085

(fold)

(fold)

Chapter 1. What is Statistics?

TRUE/FALSE QUESTIONS

1-1 T
Easy
Goal: 2

A population is a collection of all individuals, objects, or measurements of interest.

1-2 T
Easy
Goal: 2

A sample is a portion or part of the population of interest.

1-3 T
Easy
Goal: 2

To infer something about a population, we usually take a sample from the population.

1-4 F
Easy
Goal: 2

The techniques used to find out something about a population, such as their average weight, based on a sample are referred to as descriptive statistics.

1-5 T
Easy
Goal: 6

Mutually exclusive indicates that an individual, object, or measurement is included in only one category.

1-6 F
Easy
Goal: 5

There are four levels of measurement—qualitative, quantitative, discrete, and continuous.

1-7 T
Easy
Goal: 6

Exhaustive means that each individual, object, or measurement from a sample or population must appear in at least one category.

1-8 F
Easy
Goal: 5

Ordinal level of measurement is considered the "lowest" level of measurement.

1-9 F
Easy
Goal: 5

A store asks shoppers for their zip code to identify market areas. Zip codes are an example of ratio data.

1-10 T
Easy
Goal: 5

Ordinal level of measurement implies some sort of ranking.

1-11 T
Easy
Goal: 5

Data that can only be classified into categories is nominal data.

1-12 F Easy Goal: 2	The words descriptive statistics and inferential statistics can be used interchangeably.
1-13 T Easy Goal: 5	A marketing research agency was hired to test a new pizza roll. Consumers rated it outstanding, very good, fair or poor. The level of measurement for this experiment is ordinal.
1-14 F Easy Goal: 2	The Union of Electrical Workers of America with 9,128 members polled 362 members regarding a new wage package to be submitted to management. Since 362 members is so large, it is the population.
1-15 T Easy Goal: 1	The World Almanac and Book of Facts cited these numbers for the U.S: – Birth rate is 8.7 births per 1,000 population – Average life expectancy for white females is 70.5 years – Approximately 250 million persons reside in the United States Each of these numbers is referred to as statistic.
1-16 F Easy Goal: 2	If we select 100 persons out of 25,000 registered voters and question them about candidates and issues, the 100 persons are referred to as the population.
1-17 T Easy Goal: 1	Statistics is defined as a body of techniques used to facilitate the collection, organization, presentation, analysis and interpretation of information for the purpose of making better decisions.
1-18 F Easy Goal: 2	Another name for inductive statistics is descriptive statistics.
1-19 F Easy Goal: 5	Categorizing voters as Democrats, Republicans and Independents is an example of interval level measurement.
1-20 F Med Goal: 4	The order that runners finish in a race would be an example of continuous data.
1-21 T Easy Goal: 1	Based on a sample of 3,000 people, the civilian unemployment rate in the United States was 5.5%. 5.5% is referred to as a statistic.
1-22 T Med Goal: 5	The principal difference between the interval and ratio scale is that the ratio scale has a meaningful zero point.
1-23 F Easy Goal: 1	The branch of mathematics used to facilitate the collection, organization, presentation, analysis and interpretation of numerical data is referred to as a statistic.

1-24 T
Easy
Goal: 5

The number of children in a family is discrete data.

MULTIPLE CHOICE QUESTIONS

1-25 B
Easy
Goal: 2

The main purpose of descriptive statistics is to:
A. Summarize data in a useful and informative manner.
B. Make inferences about a population.
C. Determine if the data adequately represents the population.
D. Gather or collect data.

1-26 A
Easy
Goal: 4

Which of the following is an example of continuous data?
A. Family income
B. Number of students in a statistics class
C. Zip codes of shoppers
D. Rankings of baseball teams in a league
E. None of the above

1-27 D
Easy
Goal: 5

The incomes of a group of 50 loan applicants are obtained. Which level of measurement is income?
A. Nominal
B. Ordinal
C. Interval
D. Ratio
E. None of the above

1-28 C
Med
Goal: 2

When TV advertisements report that "2 out of 3 dentists surveyed indicated they would recommend Brand X toothpaste to their patients," an informed consumer may question the conclusion because:
A. The results were incorrectly computed.
B. Dentists were not really surveyed.
C. The conclusion does not include the total number of dentists surveyed.
D. The conclusion is not illustrated with a graph

1-29 B
Easy
Goal: 5

A bank asks customers to evaluate the drive-thru service as to good, average, or poor. Which level of measurement is this classification?
A. Nominal
B. Ordinal
C. Interval
D. Ratio
E. None of the above

1-30 B
Easy
Goal: 2

What is a portion or part of a population called?
A. Random sample
B. Sample
C. Tally
D. Frequency distribution
E. None of the above

1-31 C
Med
Goal: 6

A student was studying the political party preferences of a university's student population. The survey instrument asked students to identify themselves as a democrat or a republican. This question is flawed because:

A. Students generally don't know their political preferences.
B. The categories are generally mutually exclusive.
C. The categories are not exhaustive.
D. Political preference is a continuous variable.

1-32 A
Easy
Goal: 5

If Gallup, Harris and other pollsters asked people to indicate their political party affiliation - Democrat, Republican or Independent, the data gathered would be an example of which scale of measurement?

A. Nominal
B. Ordinal
C. Interval
D. Ratio
E. None of the above

1-33 A
Easy
Goal: 5

The members of each basketball team wear numbers on the back of their jerseys. What scale of measurement are these numbers considered?

A. Nominal
B. Ordinal
C. Interval
D. Ratio
E. None of the above

1-34 C
Med
Goal: 2

A marketing class of 50 students evaluated the instructor using the following scale: superior, good, average, poor, and inferior. The descriptive summary showed the following survey results: 2% superior, 8% good, 45% average, 45% poor, and 0% inferior.

A. The instructor's performance was great!!!
B. The instructor's performance was inferior.
C. Most students rated the instructor as poor or average.
D. No conclusions can be made.

1-35 D
Easy
Goal: 5

A questionnaire contained a question regarding marital status. The respondent checked either single, married, divorced, separated or widowed. What is the scale of measurement for this question?

A. Ratio
B. Interval
C. Ordinal
D. Nominal
E. None of the above

1-36 D
Med
Goal: 5

Respondents were asked, "Do you now earn more than or less than you did five years ago?" What is this level of measurement?

A. Interval
B. Ratio
C. Nominal
D. Ordinal
E. None of the above

1-37 D
Med
Goal: 2

Which word is NOT part of the definition of descriptive statistics?

A. Organizing
B. Analyzing
C. Presenting
D. Predicting
E. None of the above

1-38 C
Med
Goal: 5

If unemployment is 5.5% of the population, what is this level of measurement?

A. Nominal
B. Ordinal
C. Interval or ratio
D. Descriptive
E. None of the above

1-39 A
Easy
Goal: 5

The Equal Employment Opportunity Act requires employers to classify their employees by gender and national origin. Which level of measurement is this?

A. Nominal
B. Ordinal
C. Interval
D. Ratio
E. None of the above

1-40 C
Med
Goal: 5

What level of measurement are the Centigrade and Fahrenheit temperature scales?

A. Nominal
B. Ordinal
C. Interval
D. Ratio
E. None of the above

1-41 B
Med
Goal: 3

What type of data is the number of gallons of gasoline pumped by a filling station during a day?

A. Qualitative
B. Continuous
C. Attribute
D. Discrete
E. None of the above

1-42 B
Med
Goal: 3

What type of data is the projected return on an investment?

A. Qualitative
B. Continuous
C. Attribute
D. Discrete
E. None of the above

1-43 C
Med
Goal: 3

What type of data is the number of robberies reported in your city?

A. Attribute
B. Continuous
C. Discrete
D. Qualitative
E. None of the above

1-44 D
Med
Goal: 5

What level of measurement is the number of auto accidents reported in a given month?

A. Nominal
B. Ordinal
C. Interval
D. Ratio
E. None of the above

1-45 A
Easy
Goal: 5

The names of the positions on a hockey team, such as forward and goalie, are examples of what level of measurement?

A. Nominal
B. Ordinal
C. Interval
D. Ratio
E. None of the above

1-46 D
Easy
Goal: 5

What level of measurement is the price of an admission ticket to a movie theater?

A. Nominal
B. Ordinal
C. Interval
D. Ratio
E. None of the above

1-47 B
Easy
Goal: 5

The final rankings of the top 20 NCAA college basketball teams are an example of which level of measurement?

A. Nominal
B. Ordinal
C. Interval
D. Ratio
E. None of the above

1-48 D
Med
Goal: 5

Your height and weight are examples of which level of measurement?

A. Nominal
B. Ordinal
C. Interval
D. Ratio
E. None of the above

1-49 B
Med
Goal: 5

Shoe sizes, such as 7B, 10D and 12EEE, are examples of what level of measurement?

A. Nominal
B. Ordinal
C. Interval
D. Ratio
E. None of the above

1-50 A
Med
Goal: 1

The general process of gathering, organizing, summarizing, analyzing, and interpreting data is called

A. Statistics.
B. Descriptive statistics.
C. Inferential statistics.
D. Levels of measurement.
E. None of the above.

1-51 C
Med
Goal: 5

The Nielsen Ratings break down the number of people watching a particular television show by age. Age is what level of measurement?

A. Nominal
B. Ordinal
C. Interval
D. Ratio
E. None of the above

1-52 C
Easy
Goal: 3

Which of the following is an example of attribute data?

A. Number of children in a family
B. Weight of a person
C. Color of ink in a pen
D. Miles between oil changes
E. None of the above

1-53 C
Med
Goal: 4

Which one of the following is NOT an example of discrete data?

A. Number of households watching the Home Improvement.
B. Number of employees reporting in sick.
C. Number of miles between New York City and Chicago.
D. Number of members of the Dobbs Ferry-Irvington Lions Club.
E. Number of family members.

1-54 D
Med
Goal: 5

What level of measurement is a bar code?

A. Ratio
B. Ordinal
C. Interval
D. Nominal
E. None of the above

1-55 B
Med
Goal: 5

A group of women tried five brands of hair spray and ranked them according to preference. What level of measurement is this?

A. Nominal
B. Ordinal
C. Interval
D. Ratio
E. None of the above

FILL-IN QUESTIONS

1-56
Easy
Goal: 1

The monthly Consumer Price Index is called a(n) ________________.

1-57
Easy
Goal: 3

Qualitative variables are also referred to as a(n) ________________.

1-58
Med
Goal: 3

Quantitative data are either ________________ or ________________.

1-59
Med
Goal: 5

Ranked data is an example of what level of measurement?
____

1-60
Med
Goal: 5

The prime rate of interest is an example of what level of measurement?
____

1-61
Easy
Goal: 2

The branch of statistics which does not involve generalizations is called ________________.

1-62
Easy
Goal: 2

When we make an estimate or prediction, we use ________________ techniques.

1-63
Easy
Goal: 2

The branch of statistics in which data is collected, analyzed and presented in a concise format is called ______________ statistics.

1-64 Easy Goal: 2	The branch of statistics from which we draw conclusions from sample data is called ________________ statistics.
1-65 Med Goal: 4	The number of workers reporting sick in any particular week is considered to be ______________ data.
1-66 Med Goal: 2	If we test a small number of light bulbs from a large group, the small group is called a _____________.
1-67 Easy Goal: 2	What is the total group being studied called? ________________
1-68 Easy Goal: 2	Among the many classes held at your college or university, your statistics class has been selected for a study. This one class is referred to as a _____________.
1-69 Med Goal: 2	Another name for inferential statistics is _____________ statistics.
1-70 Easy Goal: 5	The "lowest" level of measurement is ____________.
1-71 Easy Goal: 5	The "highest" level of measurement is _______________.
1-72 Med Goal: 5	The major advantage of ordinal data over nominal data is that it allows for __________________.
1-73 Med Goal: 5	The principal difference between the interval and ratio scale of measurement is that the ratio scale has a __________________.
1-74 Med Goal: 5 & 6	Nominal data requires that the categories be _________________ and ______________________.
1-75 Easy Goal: 5	Categorizing students as freshmen, sophomores, juniors and seniors is an example of the _____________ level of measurement.

1-76 Med Goal: 2	The collection of all possible objects of interest is referred to as the _______________.
1-77 Med Goal: 6	If an individual, object or measurement appears in at least one category, this listing of categories is said to be _____________.
1-78 Easy Goal: 5	The lowest level of measurement that has some sort of ranking is _____________.
1-79 Med Goal 4	A variable that can have any value within a specific range is called __________________.
1-80 Easy Goal 1	The collecting, organizing, presenting, analyzing, and interpreting of data is called ______________________.
1-81 Med Goal 6	Data that can be categorized into only one category is said to be ______________________________.

Answers to Fill-In Questions

Chapter 1. What is Statistics?

1-56. statistic

1-57. attribute

1-58. discrete, continuous

1-59. ordinal

1-60. ratio

1-61. descriptive statistics

1-62. inferential or inductive

1-63. descriptive

1-64. inferential

1-65. discrete

1-66. sample

1-67. population

1-68. sample

1-69. inductive

1-70. nominal

1-71. ratio

1-72. ranking or "greater than" relationship

1-73. meaningful zero point

1-74. mutually exclusive, exhaustive

1-75. ordinal

1-76. population

1-77. exhaustive

1-78. ordinal

1-79. continuous

1-80. statistics

1-81. mutually exclusive

Chapter 2. Describing Data: Frequency Distributions and Graphic Presentation

TRUE/FALSE QUESTIONS

2-1 T
Easy
Goal: 1

A frequency distribution is grouping of data into classes showing the number of observations in each class.

2-2 T
Easy
Goal: 1

The midpoint of a class, which is also called a class mark, is halfway between the lower and upper limits.

2-3 T
Easy
Goal: 1

A class interval, which is the width of a class, can be determined by subtracting the lower limit of a class from the lower limit of the next higher class.

2-4 T
Easy
Goal: 1

A suggested class interval can be determined by the formula:

$$\frac{\text{Highest value} - \text{Lowest value}}{\text{Number of classes}}$$

2-5 F
Easy
Goal: 1

In constructing a frequency distribution, you should try to have open-ended classes such as "Under $100" and "$1,000 and over".

2-6 F
Easy
Goal: 1

When constructing a frequency distribution, try to include overlapping stated class limits, such as 100 up to 201, 200 up to 301, and 300 up to 401.

2-7 T
Easy
Goal: 1

To convert a frequency distribution to a relative frequency distribution, divide each class frequency by the sum of the class frequencies.

2-8 T
Easy
Goal: 2

To construct a histogram, the class frequencies are plotted on the vertical or *Y*-axis and either the stated limits, the true limits or the midpoints are plotted on the horizontal or *X*-axis.

2-9 T
Easy
Goal: 2

A cumulative frequency distribution is used when we want to determine how many observations lie above or below certain values.

2-10 F
Easy
Goal: 1

In general, we should construct a frequency distribution so that there are either 4 or 24 classes.

2-11 F
Easy
Goal: 3

There is some loss of information when raw data is tallied into a stem-and-leaf display.

2-12 F
Easy
Goal: 3

For a stem-and-leaf display, the leaf for the value 98 is 9.

2-13 T
Easy
Goal: 3

The stem in a stem-and-leaf display is the leading digit.

2-14 T
Easy
Goal: 2

The height of a bar in a histogram represents the number of observations for a class.

2-15 F
Easy
Goal: 2

A relative frequency distribution shows the number of ~~occurrences~~ observations in each class.

2-16 T
Easy
Goal: 2

A frequency polygon is a very useful graphic technique when comparing two or more distributions.

2-17 T
Easy
Goal: 4

Simple bar charts may be constructed either horizontally or vertically.

2-18 F
Easy
Goal: 4

Simple line charts may be constructed having sales or production either on the *X*-axis or the *Y*-axis.

MULTIPLE CHOICE QUESTIONS

2-19 B
Easy
Goal: 1

Monthly commissions of first-year insurance brokers are $1,270, $1,310, $1,680, $1,380, $1,410, $1,570, $1,180 and $1,420. These figures are referred to as:

A. histogram.
B. raw data.
C. frequency distribution.
D. frequency polygon.
E. none of the above.

2-20 D
Easy
Goal: 1

The monthly incomes of a small sample of computer operators are $1,950, $1,775, $2,060, $1,840, $1,795, $1,890, $1,925 and $1,810. What are these ungrouped numbers called?

A. Histogram
B. Class limits
C. Class frequencies
D. Raw data
E. None of the above

2-21 A
Med
Goal: 1

When data is collected using a quantitative, ratio variable, what is true about a frequency distribution that summarizes the data?

A. Upper and lower class limits must be calculated.
B. A pie chart can be used to summarize the data.
C. Number of classes corresponds to variable's values.
D. The "5 to the k rule" can be applied.

2-22 C
Med
Goal: 1

When data is collected using a qualitative, nominal variable, i.e., male or female, what is true about a frequency distribution that summarizes the data?

A. Upper and lower class limits must be calculated.
B. Class midpoints can be computed.
C. Number of classes corresponds to number of the variable's values.
D. The "2 to the k rule" can be applied.

2-23 B
Med
Goal: 1

A student was interested in the cigarette smoking habits of college students and collected data from an unbiased random sample of students. The data is summarized in the following table:

Male: 50
Female: 75
Males who smoke: 20
Males who do not smoke: 30
Females who smoke: 25
Females who do not smoke: 50

Why is the table NOT a frequency distribution?

A. The number of males does not equal the sum of males that smoke and do not smoke.
B. The classes are not mutually exclusive.
C. There are too many classes.
D. Class limits cannot be computed

2-24 D
Easy
Goal: 2

The relative frequency for a class is computed as

A. Class width divided by class interval.
B. Class midpoint divided by the class frequency.
C. Class frequency divided by the class interval.
D. Class frequency divided by the total frequency.

2-25 C
Easy
Goal: 2

When a class interval is expressed as: 100 up to 200,

A. Observations with values of 100 are excluded from the class frequency.
B. Observations with values of 200 are included in the class frequency.
C. Observations with values of 200 are excluded from the class frequency.
D. The class interval is 99.

2-26 C
Easy
Goal: 3

A row of a stem-and-leaf chart appears as follows: 3 | 0 1 3 5 7 9. Assume that the data is rounded to the nearest unit.

A. The frequency of the class is seven.
B. The minimum value in the class is 0.
C. The maximum value in the class could be 39.
D. The class interval is 5.

2-27 D
Easy
Goal: 2

The relative frequency for a class is computed as

A. Class width divided by class interval.
B. Class midpoint divided by the class frequency.
C. Class frequency divided by the class interval.
D. Class frequency divided by the total frequency.

2-28 D
Med
Goal 1

A group of 100 students were surveyed about their interest in a new International Studies program. The survey asked students about their interest in the program in terms of high, medium, or low. 30 students responded high interest; 50 students responded medium interest; 40 students responded low interest. What is the relative frequency of students with high interest?

A. 30%
B. 50%
C. 40%
D. Cannot be determined.

2-29 B
Med
Goal: 1

The monthly salaries of a sample of 100 employees were rounded to the nearest ten dollars. They ranged from a low of $1,040 to a high of $1,720. If we want to condense the data into seven classes, what is the most convenient class interval?

A. $ 50
B. $100
C. $150
D. $200
E. None of the above

2-30 D
Easy
Goal: 1

What is the following table called?

Ages	*Number of Ages*
20 up to 30	16
30 up to 40	25
40 up to 50	51
50 up to 60	80
60 up to 70	20
70 up to 80	8

A. Histogram
B. Frequency polygon
C. Cumulative frequency distribution
D. Frequency distribution
E. None of the above

2-31 C
Med
Goal: 1

For the following distribution of heights, what are the limits for the class with the greatest frequency?

Heights	60" up to 65"	65" up to 70"	70" up to 75"
Number	10	70	20

A. 64 and up to 70
B. 65 and 69
C. 65 and up to 70
D. 69.5 and 74.5
E. None of the above

2-32 D
Easy
Goal: 1

In a frequency distribution, what is the number of observations in a class called?

A. Class midpoint
B. Class interval
C. Class array
D. Class frequency
E. None of the above

2-33 A
Easy
Goal: 1

Why are unequal class intervals sometimes used in a frequency distribution?

A. To avoid a large number of empty classes
B. For the sake of variety in presenting the data
C. To make the class frequencies smaller
D. To avoid the need for midpoints
E. None of the above

2-34 A
Easy
Goal: 4

In a simple line chart, where is time plotted?

A. On the *X*-axis
B. On the *Y*-axis
C. On either axis.
D. Never plotted

2-35 C
Med
Goal: 2

The age distribution of a sample of the part-time employees at Lloyd's Fast Food Emporium is:

Ages	*Cumulative Number*
18 up to 23	6
23 up to 28	19
28 up to 33	52
33 up to 38	61
38 up to 43	65

What type of chart has the data been organized to draw?

A. Histogram
B. Simple line chart
C. Cumulative Frequency Distribution
D. Pie chart
E. Frequency polygon

2-36 D
Med
Goal: 1

A sample distribution of hourly earnings in Paul's Cookie Factory is:

Hourly Earnings	$6 up to $9	$9 up to $12	$12 up to $15
Numbers	16	42	10

The limits of the class with the smallest frequency are:

A. $ 6.00 and $9.00
B. $12.00 and up to $14.00
C. $11.75 and $14.25
D. $12.00 and up to $15.00
E. None of the above

FILL-IN QUESTIONS

2-37
Easy
Goal: 2

In constructing a frequency polygon, which axis are the class frequencies scaled on? ______

2-38
Easy
Goal: 1

What is the number of observations in each class of a frequency distribution called? __________________________.

2-39
Med
Goal: 4

What is a useful chart or graph to use for illustrating relative frequencies? ______________________.

2-40
Med
Goal: 4

The midpoint of a class interval is also called a __________.

2-41
Easy
Goal: 3

For a stem-and-leaf display, what is the stem for the value 67? ____.

2-42
Easy
Goal: 3

For a stem-and-leaf display, what is the leaf for the value 123? ____.

2-43
Easy
Goal: 1

What is a table showing the number of observations that have been grouped into each of several classes called? ____________________.

2-44
Med
Goal: 2

In a cumulative frequency distribution, what percent of the total frequencies would fall below the upper limit of the highest class? ______

2-45
Easy
Goal: 4

Unorganized data is referred to as _______________.

2-46
Med
Goal: 1

What is it called when classes in a frequency table are constructed so that data will fit into only one category?___________________________

2-47
Med
Goal: 2

Calculate the suggested class interval based on number of observations given the data ranges from 100 to 200 with 50 observations.

2-48
Med
Goal: 1

If the number of observations is 124, calculate the suggested number of classes using the "2 to the k rule".

2-49
Med
Goal: 1

If you are constructing a stem-and-leaf display, the "3" in 19.3 would be the _____________.

2-50
Med
Goal: 2

If you are constructing a stem-and-leaf display, the "20" in 20.5 would be the ______________.

2-51
Med
Goal: 1

What is the best means to display data that is based on a trend over a period of time? __________________

2-52
Easy
Goal: 2 and 3

What are two advantages of a stem-and-leaf chart over a histogram? ____________________

Questions 53-54 refer to the following distribution of commissions:

Monthly commissions	*Class Frequencies*
$ 600 up to $800	3
800 up to 1,000	7
1,000 up to 1,200	11
1,200 up to 1,400	22
1,400 up to 1,600	40
1,600 up to 1,800	24
1,800 up to 2,000	9
2,000 up to 2,200	4

2-53 C
Med
Goal: 1

Referring to the table above, what is the relative frequency for those salespersons that earn between $1,600 and $1,799?

A. 2%
B. 2.4%
C. 20%
D. 24%
E. None of the above

2-54 D
Med
Goal: 2

The first plot for a cumulative frequency distribution be

A. $X = 0$, $Y = 600$.
B. $X = 600$, $Y = 3$.
C. $X = 3$, $Y = 600$.
D. $X = 600$, $Y = 0$.
E. none of the above.

Questions 55-57 refer to the following chart showing a distribution of exporting firms:

Exports ($ millions)	*Number of Firms*
$ 2 up to $5	6
5 up to 8	13
8 up to 11	20
11 up to 14	10
14 up to 17	3

2-55 D
Med
Goal: 1

Referring to the table above, what is the relative frequency of those salespersons that earn more than $1,599?

A. 25.5%
B. 27.5%
C. 29.5%
D. 30.8%
E. None of the above

2-56 B
Med
Goal: 1

For the distribution above, what is the midpoint of the class with the greatest frequency?

A. $ 6 million
B. $ 9.5 million
C. $ 15.5 million
D. The midpoint cannot be determined
E. None of the above

2-57 B
Med
Goal: 2

What is the class interval? _____

A. 2
B. 3
C. 3.5
D. 4
E. None of the above

Questions 58-60 refer to the following ages (rounded to the nearest whole year) of employees at a large company that were grouped into a distribution with class limits:

20 up to 30, 30 up to 40, 40 up to 50, 50 up to 60, and 60 up to 70.

2-58
Med
Goal: 1

The class limits for the class 50 up to 60 class are _______ and ________ .

2-59
Med
Goal: 1

What is the midpoint for the class 40 up to 50? ________

2-60
Med
Goal: 1

What is the class interval? ______

Questions 61-64 refer to the following weights of college men that were recorded to the nearest pound:

The first three class marks are 105, 115, and 125.

2-61
Easy
Goal: 1

What is the class interval? _____

2-62
Hard
Goal: 1

What is the lower limit for the third class? _______

2-63
Med
Goal: 1

What is the upper limit for the third class? _______

2-64
Hard
Goal: 1

What are the true class limits for the fourth class? _______ and _______

Questions 65-67 refer to the following wage breakdown for a garment factory.

Hourly Wages	*Number of Wage Earners*
$ 4 up to $7	18
7 up to 10	36
10 up to 13	20
13 up to 16	6

2-65 B
Easy
Goal: 1

What is the class interval for the table of wages above?
A. $2
B. $3
C. $4
D. $5
E. None of the above

2-66 B
Med
Goal: 1

What is the class midpoint for the class with the greatest frequency?
A. $ 5.50
B. $ 8.50
C. $11.50
D. $14.50
E. None of the above

2-67 C
Med
Goal: 1

What are the class limits for the class with the smallest number of frequencies?
A. 3.5 and 6.5
B. 4 and up to 7
C. 13 and up to 15
D. 12.5 and 15.5
E. None of the above

Questions 68-70 refer to the following distribution of ages:

Ages	*Number*
40 up to 50	10
50 up to 60	28
60 up to 70	12

2-68 C
Med
Goal: 1

For the distribution of ages above, what is the relative class frequency for the lowest class?
A. 50%
B. 18%
C. 20%
D. 10%
E. None of the above

2-69 B
Med
Goal: 1

What is the class interval?

A. 9
B. 10
C. 10.5
D. 11
E. None of the above

2-70 D
Med
Goal: 1

What is the class midpoint of the highest class?

A. 54
B. 55
C. 64
D. 65
E. None of the above

Questions 71-73 refer to the following heights of college women are recorded to the nearest inch:

The first two class midpoints are 62.5" and 65.5".

2-71 D
Easy
Goal: 1

What is the class interval?

A. 1"
B. 2"
C. 2.5"
D. 3"
E. None of the above

2-72 A
Hard
Goal: 1

What are the class limits for the lowest class?

A. 61 and up to 64
B. 62 and up to 64
C. 62 and 65
D. 62 and 63
E. None of the above

2-73 C
Hard
Goal: 1

What are the class limits for the third class?

A. 64 and up to 67
B. 67 and 69
C. 67 and up to 70
D. 66 and 68
E. None of the above

Questions 74-76 refer to the following distribution:

Cost of Textbooks	Number
$25 up to $35	2
35 up to 45	5
45 up to 55	7
55 up to 65	20
65 up to 75	16

2-74 B
Med
Goal: 1

What is the relative class frequency for the $25 up to $35 class?

A. 2%
B. 4%
C. 5%
D. 10%
E. None of the above.

2-75 C
Med
Goal: 1

What is the class midpoint for the $45 up to $55 class?

A. 49
B. 49.5
C. 50
D. 50.5
E. None of the above

2-76 C
Med
Goal: 1

What are the true class limits for the $55 up to $65 class?

A. 55 and 64
B. 54 and 64
C. 55 and up to 65
D. 55 and 64.5
E. None of the above

Questions 77-80 refer to the following cumulative frequency distribution on days absent during a calendar year by employees of a manufacturing company:

Days Absent	Cumulative Number of Employees
0 up to 3	60
3 up to 6	31
6 up to 9	14
9 up to 12	6
12 up to 15	2

2-77 E
Dif
Goal: 2

How many employees were absent between 3 up to 6 days?

A. 31
B. 29
C. 14
D. 2
E. 17

2-78 D
Dif
Goal: 2

How many employees were absent fewer than six days?

A. 60
B. 31
C. 91
D. 46
E. None of the above

2-79 B
Dif
Goal: 2

How many employees were absent more than five days?

A. 8
B. 4
C. 22
D. 31
E. None of the above

2-80 C
Dif
Goal: 2

How many employees were absent from 6 up to 12 days?

A. 20
B. 8
C. 12
D. 17
E. None of the above

Answers to Fill-In Questions

Chapter 2. Summarizing Data: Frequency Distributions and Graphic Presentation

2-37 Y

2-38 Class frequency

2-39 pie chart

2-40 class mark

2-41 6

2-42 3

2-43 frequency distribution

2-44 100

2-45 raw or ungrouped data

2-46 mutually exclusive

2-47 15 intervals

2-48 7 intervals

2-49 leaf

2-50 stem

2-51 line chart

2-52 1) The identity of each observation is not lost, and 2) it presents a picture of the distribution.

2-58 50 and up to 60

2-59 45

2-60 10 or ten

2-61 10

2-62 120

2-63 up to 130

2-64 130 and up to 140

Chapter 3. Describing Data: Measures of Central Tendency

TRUE/FALSE QUESTIONS

3-1 T
Easy
Goal: 1

A value that is typical or representative of the data is referred to as a measure of central tendency.

3-2 T
Easy
Goal: 1

The arithmetic mean is the sum of the observations divided by the total number of observations.

3-3 F
Easy
Goal: 1

The value of the observation in the center after they have been arranged in numerical order is called the weighted mean.

3-4 F
Easy
Goal: 2

A set of ordinal, interval or ratio level data may only have one mode.

3-5 T
Easy
Goal: 2

If the data is interval or ratio level, all the values are included in computing the mean.

3-6 F
Easy
Goal: 2

A set of interval or ratio level data can have more than one arithmetic mean.

3-7 T
Easy
Goal: 1

The mode is the value of the observation that appears most frequently.

3-8 T
Easy
Goal: 3

A distribution that has the same shape on either side of the center is said to be symmetrical.

3-9 T
Easy
Goal: 3

Negatively skewed indicates that a distribution is not symmetrical. The long tail is to the left or in the negative direction.

3-10 T
Med
Goal: 1

The geometric mean is the nth root of n observations.

3-11 F
Easy
Goal: 1

A statistic is a measurable characteristic of the population.

3-12 F
Easy
Goal: 1

A parameter is a measurable characteristic of a sample.

3-13 T
Easy
Goal: 2

The median can be determined for any set of interval-level data.

3-14 F
Easy
Goal: 2

Extremely high or low scores affect the value of the median.

3-15 T
Easy
Goal: 2

The sum of the deviations from the mean for the set of numbers 4, 9 and 5 will equal zero.

3-16 F
Easy
Goal: 2

For salaries of $102,000, $98,000, $45,000, $106,000 and $101,000, the arithmetic mean would be an appropriate average.

3-17 T
Med
Goal: 1

Three persons earn $8 an hour, six earn $9 an hour, and one earns $12 an hour. The weighted mean hourly wage is $9.

3-18 F
Easy
Goal: 2

There are always as many values above the mean as below it.

3-19 T
Easy
Goal: 1

If there are an even number of ungrouped values, the median is found by arranging them from low to high and then determining the arithmetic mean of the two middle values.

3-20 T
Easy
Goal: 1

If there are an even number of ungrouped values, then half of the values will be less than the median.

3-21 F
Easy
Goal: 3

In a negatively skewed distribution, the mean is always greater than the median.

3-22 T
Easy
Goal: 3

In a negatively skewed distribution, the mean is smaller than the median or mode and the mode occurs at the peak of the curve.

3-23 F
Med
Goal 3

In a positively skewed distribution, the mode is greater than the median.

MULTIPLE CHOICE QUESTIONS

3-24 B
Easy
Goal: 1

For which measure of central tendency will the sum of the deviations of each value from that average always be zero?

A. Mode
B. Mean
C. Median
D. Geometric mean
E. None of the above

3-25 D
Easy
Goal: 2

Which measures of central tendency always have but one value for a set of grouped or ungrouped data?

A. Mode and median
B. Mode and mean
C. Mode and geometric mean
D. Mean and median
E. None of the above

3-26 C
Easy
Goal: 2

Which measures of central tendency are not affected by extremely low or extremely high values?

A. Mean and median
B. Mean and mode
C. Mode and median
D. Geometric mean and mean
E. None of the above

3-27 A
Easy
Goal: 3

What is the relationship among the mean, median and mode in a symmetric distribution?

A. All equal
B. Mean is always the smallest value
C. Mean is always the largest value
D. Mode is the largest value
E. None of the above

3-28 A
Easy
Goal: 2

What are half of the observations always greater than?

A. Median
B. Mode
C. Mean
D. Geometric mean
E. None of the above

3-29 B
Med
Goal: 2

What must be the least scale of measurement for the median?

A. Nominal
B. Ordinal
C. Interval
D. Ratio
E. None of the above

3-30 C
Med
Goal: 1

If there is an odd number of observations in a set of ungrouped data that have been arrayed from low to high or vice versa, where is the median located?

A. n
B. $n/2$
C. $(n + 1)/2$
D. $n + 1/2$
E. None of the above.

3-31 D
Easy
Goal: 1

Which measure of central tendency is used to determine the average annual percent increase?

A. Arithmetic mean
B. Weighted mean
C. Mode
D. Geometric mean
E. Median

3-32 C
Med
Goal: 2

If a frequency distribution has open-ended intervals at the extremes, which measure of central tendency is the most difficult to estimate?

A. Median
B. Mode
C. Mean
D. All of the above
E. None of the above

3-33 B
Med
Goal: 1

Which one of the following is referred to as the population mean?

A. Statistic
B. μ
C. Sample
D. $\overline{X}$
E. None of the above

3-34 A
Med
Goal: 1

Fifteen accounting majors had an average grade of 90 on a finance exam. Seven marketing majors averaged 85, while ten finance majors averaged 93 on the same exam. What is the weighted mean for the 32 students taking the exam?

A. 89.84
B. 89.33
C. 89.48
D. Impossible to determine without more information
E. None of the above

3-35 E
Med
Goal: 2

In the calculation of the arithmetic mean for grouped data, which value is used to represent all the values in a particular class?

A. The upper limit of the class
B. The lower limit of the class
C. The frequency of the class
D. The cumulative frequency preceding the class
E. None of the above

3-36 C
Med
Goal: 1

On a survey questionnaire, students were asked to indicate their class rank in college. If there were only four choices from which to choose, which measure(s) of central tendency would be appropriate to use for the data generated by that questionnaire item?

A. Mean and median
B. Mean and mode
C. Mode and median
D. Mode only
E. Median only

3-37 D
Med
Goal: 1

What is the median of 26, 30, 24, 32, 32, 31, 27 and 29?

A. 32
B. 29
C. 30
D. 29.5
E. None of the above

3-38 C
Easy
Goal: 1

The net incomes (in $ millions) of a sample of steel fabricators are: $86, $67, $86 and $85. What is the modal net income?

A. $67
B. $85
C. $85.5
D. $86
E. None of the above

3-39 B
Hard
Goal: 1

A sample of light trucks using diesel fuel revealed the following distribution based on fuel efficiency, i.e., miles per gallon (mpg).

mpg	*No. of Trucks*
10 up to 13	2
13 up to 16	5
16 up to 19	10
19 up to 22	8
22 up to 25	3
25 up to 28	2

What is the arithmetic mean miles per gallon?

A. 16.9
B. 18.6
C. 17.0
D. 17.9
E. None of the above

3-40 E
Hard
Goal: 1

The ages of newly hired, unskilled employees were grouped into the following distribution:

Ages	*Number*
18 up to 21	4
21 up to 24	8
24 up to 27	11
27 up to 30	20
30 up to 33	7

What is the median age?

A. 25.0
B. 29.7
C. 26.8
D. 26.5
E. None of the above

3-41 A
Hard
Goal: 1

A sample of the daily production of transceivers was organized into the following distribution.

Daily Production	*Frequencies*
80 up to 90	5
90 up to 100	9
100 up to 110	20
110 up to 120	8
120 up to 130	6
130 up to 140	2

What is the median daily production?

A. 104.5
B. 119.6
C. 109.2
D. 104.8
E. None of the above

3-42 B
Hard
Goal: 1

The net sales of a sample of small stamping plants were organized into the following percent frequency distribution.

Net Sales (in $ millions)	*Percent of Total*
1 up to 4	13
4 up to 7	14
7 up to 10	40
10 up to 13	23
13 or more	10

What is the median net sales (in $ millions)?

A. $8.000
B. $8.225
C. $7.775
D. $8.325
E. Median cannot be computed

3-43 E
Hard
Goal: 1

A stockbroker placed the following order for a customer:

- 50 shares of Kaiser Aluminum preferred at $104 a share
- 100 shares of GTE preferred at $25 1/4 a share
- 20 shares of Boston Edison preferred at $9 1/8 a share

What is the weighted arithmetic mean price per share?

A. $ 25.25
B. $ 79.75
C. $ 103.50
D. $ 42.75
E. None of the above

3-44 B
Hard
Goal: 1

During the past six months, the purchasing agent bought:

Tons of Coal	1,200	3,000	500
Price per Ton	$28.50	$87.25	$88.00

What is the weighted arithmetic mean price per ton?

A. $87.25
B. $72.33
C. $68.47
D. $89.18
E. None of the above

3-45 D
Med
Goal: 1

A sample of single persons receiving social security payments revealed these monthly benefits: $826, $699, $1,087, $880, $839 and $965. How many observations are below the median?

A. 0
B. 1
C. 2
D. 3
E. None of the above

3-46 C
Med
Goal: 1

The number of work stoppages in a highly industrialized region for selected months are: 6, 0, 10, 14, 8 and 0. What is the median number of stoppages?

A. 0
B. 6
C. 7
D. 8
E. None of the above

3-47 A
Hard
Goal: 1

The U.S. Federal Aviation Administration reported that passenger revenues on international flights increased from $528 million in 1977 to $5,100 million in 2000. What is the geometric mean annual percent increase in international passenger revenues?

A. 10.4
B. 27.9
C. 103.6
D. 9.96
E. None of the above

3-48 B
Hard
Goal: 1

The Investment Company Institute reported in its Mutual Fund Fact Book that the number of mutual funds increased from 410 in 1990 to 857 in 2000. What is the geometric mean annual percent increase in the number of funds?

A. 1.12
B. 7.65
C. 19.41
D. 48.66
E. None of the above

3-49 C
Hard
Goal: 1

Assume a student received the following grades for the semester: History, B; Statistics, A; Spanish, C; and English, C. History and English are 5 credit hour courses, Statistics a 4 credit hour course and Spanish a 3 credit hour course. If 4 grade points are assigned for an A, 3 for a B and 2 for a C, what is the weighted mean for the semester grades?

A. 4.00
B. 1.96
C. 2.61
D. 3.01
E. 2.88

3-50 C
Hard
Goal: 1

Production of passenger cars in Japan increased from 3.94 million in 1990 to 6.74 million in 2000. What is the geometric mean annual percent increase?

A. 4.0
B. 1.9
C. 5.5
D. 16.6
E. 47.3

3-51 B
Hard
Goal: 1

A sample of the paramedical fees charged by clinics revealed these amounts: $55, $49, $50, $45, $52 and $55. What is the median charge?

A. $47.50
B. $51.00
C. $52.00
D. $55.00
E. None of the above

3-52 A
Hard
Goal: 1

The lengths of time (in minutes) several underwriters took to review applications for similar insurance coverage are: 50, 230, 52 and 57. What is the median length of time required to review an application?

A. 54.5
B. 141.0
C. 97.25
D. 109.0
E. None of the above

3-53 B
Hard
Goal: 1

The U.S. Department of Education reported that for the past six years 23, 19, 15, 30, 27 and 25 women received doctorate degrees in computer and information sciences. What is the mean arithmetic annual number of women receiving this degree?

A. 15.1
B. 23.2
C. 37.9
D. 22.9
E. None of the above

3-54 D
Hard
Goal: 1

A bottling company offers three kinds of delivery service – instant, same day and within five days. The profit per delivery varies according to the kind of delivery. The profit for an instant delivery is less than the other kinds because the driver has to go directly to a grocery store with a small load and return to the bottling plant. To find out what effect each type of delivery has on the profit picture, the company has made the following tabulation based on deliveries for the previous quarter.

Type of Delivery	*Number of Deliveries During the Quarter*	*Profit per Delivery*
Instant	100	$ 70
Same day	60	100
Within five days	40	160

What is the weighted mean profit per delivery?

A. $72
B. $100
C. $142
D. $97
E. None of the above

3-55 B
Hard
Goal: 1

The U.S. Department of Education reported that for the past seven years 4,033, 5,652, 6,407, 7,201, 8,719, 11,154, and 15,121 people received bachelor's degrees in computer and information sciences. What is the arithmetic mean annual number receiving this degree?

A. About 12,240
B. About 8,327
C. About 6,217
D. About 15,962
E. None of the above

3-56 B
Easy
Goal: 1

Which measure of central tendency is found by arranging the data from low to high and selecting the middle value?

A. Arithmetic mean
B. Median
C. Mode
D. Geometric mean
E. None of the above

3-57 C
Hard
Goal: 1

The number of students at a local university increased from 2,500 students 5000 students in 10 years. Based on a geometric mean, the university grew at an average percentage rate of

A. 2,500 students per year
B. 1.071 students per year
C. 7.1 percent per year
D. 250 students per year

3-58 A
Easy
Goal: 1

A question in a market survey asks for a respondent's favorite car color. Which measure of central tendency should be used to summarize this question?

A. Mode
B. Median
C. Mean
D. Geometric mean

3-59 B
Med
Goal: 2

Sometimes, data has two values that have the highest and equal frequencies. In this case, the distribution of the data can best be summarized as

A. symmetric
B. bimodal (having two modes)
C. positively skewed
D. negatively skewed

3-60 D
Easy
Goal: 1

A disadvantage of using a arithmetic mean to summarize a set of data is

A. The arithmetic mean sometimes has two values
B. It can be used for interval and ratio data
C. It is always different from the median
D. It can be biased by one or two extremely small or large values.

3-61 C
Easy
Goal: 1

The denominator for a mean of grouped data is:

A. *N*, the population size
B. *n*, the sample size
C. The sum of the group frequencies
D. The number of groups

3-62 D
Med
Goal: 2

The mean, as a measure of central tendency would be inappropriate for which one of the following?

A. Ages of adults at a senior citizen center
B. Incomes of lawyers
C. Number of pages in textbooks on statistics
D. Marital status of college students at a particular university
E. None of the above

FILL-IN QUESTIONS

3-63
Easy
Goal: 1

What is the measure of central tendency that uses all of the observations in its calculation? _______________

3-64
Easy
Goal: 1

What is the class with the largest number of observations called?
____

3-65
Med
Goal: 1

What is the most representative measure of central tendency. If a set of observations contains an extreme value and none of the observations repeat themselves? _____________

3-66
Easy
Goal: 1

The value that occurs most often in a set of data is called the _____

3-67
Med
Goal: 3

The weekly sales from a sample of ten computer stores yielded a mean of $25,900; a median $25,000 and a mode of $24,500. What is the shape of the distribution? ___________________

3-68
Med
Goal: 1

For which measure of central tendency must the data be ranked before it is possible to determine it? _____________

3-69
Med
Goal: 1

If the sum of all the values of a distribution are divided by the number of values, what is the result? _____________

3-70
Med
Goal: 3

If a distribution is highly skewed, what measure of central tendency should be avoided? _____________

3-71
Med
Goal: 1

If the n-th root is taken of the product of ""n"" values, what is the result?
____

3-72
Easy
Goal: 1

What is a characteristic of the population called? __________________

3-73
Med
Goal: 2

A sample revealed that the ages of musicians playing in small local combos are 36, 29, 37, 32, 36 and 75. What is the most appropriate measure of central tendency to represent the ages of the musicians?
____

3-74
Med
Goal 2

What measure of central tendency cannot be determined if the distribution has an open-ended class? ______________________.

3-75
Easy
Goal: 1

What is the measure of central tendency used to determine the average annual percent increase in sales from one time period to another?
____

3-76
Med
Goal: 3

What is the smallest measure of central tendency in a positively skewed distribution? ____________

3-77
Med
Goal: 2

A small manufacturing company with 52 employees has annual salaries distributed such that the mean is $25,459, the median is $24,798 and the mode is $24,000. An additional foreman is hired at an annual salary of $50,700. What is the measure of central tendency that is most affected by the addition of this salary? ____________________

3-78
Med
Goal: 3

What is the relationship between the mean and median in a negatively skewed distribution? ________________

3-79
Med
Goal: 3

What is the relationship between the median and the mode in a positively skewed distribution? ________________

3-80
Hard
Goal: 1

Five students were given a page of problems with the instructions to solve as many as they could in one hour. Five students solved the following number of problems: 12, 10, 8, 6 and 4. What is the arithmetic mean number of minutes required per problem?________

3-81
Hard
Goal: 1

David Electronics had a profit of $10 million in 1998. Profit doubled from 1998 to 1999 and profit increased eight fold from 1999 to 2000. What was the annual geometric mean rate of growth from 1998 to 2000?

____

Questions 82-92 refer to the following:
A sample of five full service gasoline stations, each carrying three grades of gasoline, was taken and the price per gallon (to the nearest cent) was recorded for each grade of gasoline, as shown in the table below.

	STATION				
Gasoline	*1*	*2*	*3*	*4*	*5*
Unleaded	$1.27	$1.27	$1.27	$1.27	$1.27
Unleaded Plus	1.36	1.37	1.38	1.38	1.40
Super Unleaded	1.47	1.49	1.50	1.50	1.59

3-82
Easy
Goal: 2

What is the mean price of Unleaded gas? ________

3-83
Med
Goal: 2

What is the mean price of Unleaded Plus gas? ________

3-84 Med Goal: 2 — What is the mean price of Super Unleaded gas? ________

3-85 Easy Goal: 2 — What is the median price of Unleaded gas? ________

3-86 Easy Goal: 2 — What is the median price of Unleaded Plus gas? ________

3-87 Easy Goal: 2 — What is the median price of Super Unleaded gas? ________

3-88 Easy Goal: 2 — What is the modal price of Unleaded gas? ________

3-89 Med Goal: 2 — What is the modal price of Unleaded Plus gas? ________

3-90 Med Goal: 3 — For Unleaded gas, which measure of central tendency would be the lowest?

3-91 Med Goal: 3 — For Super Unleaded gas, which measure of central tendency would be the highest?

3-92 Med Goal: 3 — For Unleaded Plus gas, which measure of central tendency would not be appropriate to use?

Questions 93-96 refer to the following:
The weights of a sample of 100 boxes being shipped by Air France from New York to Paris are:

Weights (pounds)	*Number*
50 up to 75	4
75 up to 100	16
100 up to 125	21
125 up to 150	46
150 up to 175	13

3-93 Med Goal: 2 — What is the approximate mode for the grouped data? ______________

3-94
Hard
Goal: 2

What is the approximate mean for the grouped data? ______________

3-95
Hard
Goal: 2

What is the approximate median for the grouped data? ____________

3-96 C
Easy
Goal 2

The mean for this data is referred to as the

A. Sample mean
B. Population mean
C. Estimated mean
D. Weighted mean

Questions 97-100 refer to the following:
A company's human resource department was interested in the average number of years that a person works before retiring. The sample of size 11 follows:

12 16 18 19 21 21 21 22 24 24 26

3-97
Easy
Goal: 1

What is the arithmetic mean? ________________

3-98
Easy
Goal: 1

What is the median? ______________________________

3-99
Easy
Goal: 1

What is the mode? _____________________

3-100
Hard
Goal: 3

Based on the values of the arithmetic mean, median, and mode, what is the most likely shape of the distribution? _________________

Answers to Fill-In Questions

Chapter 3. Describing Data-Measures of Central Tendency

3-63. mean
3-64. mode
3-65. median
3-66. mode
3-67. positively skewed
3-68. median
3-69. arithmetic mean
3-70. mean
3-71. geometric mean
3-72. parameter
3-73. median
3-74. arithmetic mean
3-75. geometric mean
3-76. mode
3-77. arithmetic mean
3-78. mean is less than the median
3-79. median is greater than the mode
3-80. 7.5 minutes (average of 8 problems in an hour)
3-81. 300% (4 fold)
3-82. $1.27
3-83. $1.38
3-84. $1.51
3-85. $1.27
3-86. $1.38
3-87. $1.50
3-88. $1.27
3-89. $1.38
3-90. all the same
3-91. Mean
3-92. mode
3-93. 137.5 lbs.
3-94. 124.5 lbs.
3-95. 129.9 lbs.
3-97. 20
3-98. 21
3-99. 21
3-100. symmetric

Chapter 4. Other Descriptive Measures

TRUE/FALSE QUESTIONS

4-1 T
Easy
Goal: 1

Dispersion is the degree of variation in the data.

4-2 F
Med
Goal: 1

The mean deviation is the mean of the actual values of the deviations from the arithmetic mean.

4-3 F
Med
Goal: 1

The variance is the mean of the sum of the squared deviations between each observation and the median.

4-4 T
Med
Goal: 1

The standard deviation is the positive square root of the variance.

4-5 T
Med
Goal: 5

The interquartile range is the difference between the values of the first and third quartile, indicating the range of the middle fifty percent of the observations.

4-6 F
Med
Goal: 5

The quartile deviation is one-fourth of the interquartile range.

4-7 T
Med
Goal: 5

A percentile divides a distribution into one hundred equal parts.

4-8 T
Med
Goal: 4

Chebyshev's Theorem gives the proportion of observations in any data set that occurs within *k* standard deviations of the mean, where *k* is greater than 1.0.

4-9 T
Med
Goal: 4

The Empirical states that about 68% of the observation will lie within one standard deviation of the mean; about 95% of the observations will lie within two standard deviations of the mean; and virtually all (99.7%) will lie within three standard deviations of the mean.

4-10 T
Med
Goal: 7

The coefficient of variation is a measure of relative dispersion, which expresses the standard deviation as a percent of the mean.

4-11 T
Med
Goal: 7

The Pearson's coefficient of skewness is a measure of the lack of symmetry of a distribution.

4-12 F
Easy
Goal: 3

The mean absolute deviation is the most widely used measure of dispersion.

4-13 T
Easy
Goal: 3

The coefficient of variation is useful for comparing distributions with different units.

4-14 F
Med
Goal: 1

For a symmetrical distribution, the variance is equal to the standard deviation.

4-15 T
Easy
Goal: 5

The three quartiles divide a set of data into four quarters.

4-16 F
Easy
Goal: 1

If the standard deviation of the ages of a female group of employees is six years and the standard deviation of the ages of a male group in the same plant is ten years, it indicates that there is more spread in the ages of the female employees.

4-17 T
Easy
Goal: 5

There are 99 percentiles that divide a distribution into 100 parts.

4-18 F
Easy
Goal: 5

A student scored in the 85 percentile on a standardized test. This means that the student scored lower than 85% of the rest of the students taking.

4-19 F
Easy
Goal: 1

If we find the deviation of each value from the median, the sum of these deviations is always zero.

4-20 F
Med
Goal: 7

The coefficient of variation is computed by dividing the standard deviation by the median and multiplying the quotient by 1,000.

4-21 T
Med
Goal: 3

If a frequency distribution is open-ended, the variance cannot be determined.

4-22 T
Med
Goal: 1

The range cannot be computed for data grouped in a frequency distribution having an open end.

4-23 F
Easy
Goal: 6

A box plot is a means to graphically depict data that is in percentiles.

4-24 T
Easy
Goal: 6

The "box" in a box plot shows the interquartile range.

4-25 F
Easy
Goal: 6

An outlier is a data point that always occurs in the first quartile.

4-26 T
Easy
Goal: 6

An outlier is a value in a data set that is inconsistent with the rest of the data.

MULTIPLE CHOICE QUESTIONS

4-27 D
Med
Goal: 3

A Pearson's coefficient of skewness of 2.48 indicates:
A. A large positive skewness
B. The tail of the distribution is to the right
C. The mean is larger than the median
D. All of the above are correct
E. None of the above are correct

4-28 A
Easy
Goal: 3

What is a disadvantage of the range as a measure of dispersion?
A. Based on only two observations
B. Can be distorted by a large mean
C. Not in the same units as the original data
D. Has no disadvantage
E. None of the above

4-29 B
Easy
Goal: 1

Rank the measures of dispersion in terms of their relative computational difficulty from least to most difficulty.
A. Mode, median, mean
B. Range, mean deviation, variance
C. Variance, mean deviation, range
D. There is no difference

4-30 C
Med
Goal: 1

A purchasing agent for a trucking company is shopping for replacement tires for their trucks from two suppliers. The suppliers' prices are the same. However, Supplier A's tires have an average life of 60,000 miles with a standard deviation of 10,000 miles. Supplier B's tires have an average life of 60,000 miles with a standard deviation of 2,000 miles. Which of the following statements is true?
A. The two distributions of tire life are the same
B. On average, Supplier A's tires have a longer life then Supplier B's tires
C. The life of Supplier B's tire is more predictable than the life of Supplier A's tires
D. The dispersion of Supplier A's tire life is less than the dispersion of Supplier B's tire life

4-31 B
Easy
Goal: 6

What statistics are needed to draw a box plot?

A. Minimum, maximum, median, first and third quartiles
B. Median, mean and standard deviation
C. A mean and a dispersion
D. A mean and a standard deviation

4-32 B
Easy
Goal: 6

A box plot shows

A. The mean and variance
B. The relative symmetry of a distribution for a set of data
C. The percentiles of a distribution
D. The deciles of a distribution

4-33 A
Easy
Goal: 1

The sum of the differences between sample observations and the sample mean is

A. Zero
B. The mean deviation
C. The range
D. The standard deviation

4-34 C
Med
Goal: 3

What disadvantage(s) are there of the mean deviation?

A. Based on only two observations
B. Based on deviations from the mean
C. Uses absolute values, which are difficult to manipulate
D. All of the above
E. None of the above

4-35 D
Med
Goal: 3

Which of the following measures of dispersion are based on deviations from the mean?

A. Variance
B. Standard deviation
C. Mean deviation
D. All of the above
E. None of the above

4-36 B
Med
Goal: 5

What do the quartile deviation and the interquartile range describe?

A. Lower 50% of the observations
B. Middle 50% of the observations
C. Upper 50% of the observations
D. Lower 25% and the upper 25% of the observations
E. None of the above

4-37 B
Med
Goal: 7

The coefficient of variation for a set of annual incomes is 18%; the coefficient of variation for the length of service with the company is 29%. What does this indicate?

A. More dispersion in the distribution of the incomes compared with the dispersion of their length of service
B. More dispersion in the lengths of service compared with incomes
C. Dispersion in the two distributions (income and service) cannot be compared using percents
D. Dispersions are equal
E. None of the above

4-38 B
Med
Goal: 3

What is the relationship between the variance and the standard deviation?

A. Variance is the square root of the standard deviation
B. Variance is the square of the standard deviation
C. Variance is twice the standard deviation
D. No constant relationship between the variance and the standard deviation
E. None of the above

4-39 B
Med
Goal: 7

Mr. and Mrs. Jones live in a neighborhood where the mean family income is $45,000 with a standard deviation of $9,000. Mr. and Mrs. Smith live in a neighborhood where the mean is $100,000 and the standard deviation is $30,000. What are the relative dispersion of the family incomes in the two neighborhoods?

A. Jones 40%, Smith 20%
B. Jones 20%, Smith 30%
C. Jones 30%, Smith 20%
D. Jones 50%, Smith 33%
E. None of the above

4-40 C
Med
Goal: 4

According to Chebyshev's Theorem, what percent of the observations lie within plus and minus 1.75 standard deviations of the mean?

A. 56%
B. 95%
C. 67%
D. Cannot compute because it depends on the shape of the distribution
E. None of the above

4-41 B
Med
Goal: 7

A large oil company is studying the number of gallons of gasoline purchased per customer at self-service pumps. The mean number of gallons is 10.0 with a standard deviation of 3.0 gallons. The median is 10.75 gallons. What is the Pearson's coefficient of skewness?

A. –1.00
B. –0.75
C. +0.75
D. +1.00
E. None of the above

4-42 C
Easy
Goal: 1

What is the range for a sample of March electric bills amounts for all-electric homes of similar sizes (to the nearest dollar): $212, $191, $176, $129, $106, $92, $108, $109, $103, $121, $175 and $194.

A. $100
B. $130
C. $120
D. $112
E. None of the above

4-43 C
Easy
Goal: 1

A survey of passengers on domestic flights revealed these miles:

Miles Flown	*Number of Passengers*
100 up to 500	16
500 up to 900	41
900 up to 1300	81
1300 up to 1700	11
1700 up to 2100	9
2100 up to 2500	6

What is the range (in miles)?

A. 2,499
B. 1,100
C. 2,400
D. 1,999
E. None of the above

4-44 B
Easy
Goal: 1

Which measure of dispersion disregards the algebraic signs (plus and minus) of each difference between X and the mean?

A. Standard deviation
B. Mean deviation
C. Arithmetic mean
D. Variance
E. None of the above

4-45 D
Easy
Goal: 1

The following are the weekly amounts of welfare payments made by the federal government to a sample of six families: $139, $136, $130, $136, $147 and $136. What is the range?

A. $0
B. $14
C. $52
D. $17
E. None of the above

4-46 A
Easy
Goal: 2

Measures of dispersion calculated from grouped data are

A. Estimates
B. Biased
C. Means
D. Skewed

4-47 A
Med
Goal: 7

What is the value of the Pearson coefficient of skewness for a distribution with a mean of 17, median of 12 and standard deviation of 6?

A. +2.5
B. –2.5
C. +0.83
D. –0.83
E. None of the above

4-48 C
Med
Goal: 5

One-half the difference between the third and first quartiles is called?

A. Variance
B. Standard deviation
C. Quartile deviation
D. Interquartile range
E. None of the above

4-49 B
Med
Goal: 7

A study of business faculty at state supported institutions in Ohio revealed that the arithmetic mean salary for nine months is $52,000 and a standard deviation of $3,000. The study also showed that the faculty had been employed an average (arithmetic mean) of 15 years with a standard deviation of 4 years. How does the relative dispersion in the distribution of salaries compare with that of the lengths of service?

A. Salaries about 100%, service about 50%
B. Salaries about 6%, service about 27%
C. Salaries about 42%, service about 81%
D. Salaries about 2%, service about 6%
E. None of the above

4-50 A
Med
Goal: 1

The ages of a sample of the typewriters used by the typists in the typing pool were organized into the following table:

Ages (in years)	*Number*
2 up to 5	2
5 up to 8	5
8 up to 11	10
11 up to 14	4
14 up to 17	2

What is the sample variance?

A. About 10.2
B. About 6.1
C. About 14.0
D. About 3.2
E. None of the above

4-51 C
Med
Goal: 7

What is the range of the coefficient of variation?

A. –1 and +1
B. –3 and +3
C. 0% and 100%
D. Unlimited values
E. None of the above

4-52 D
Med
Goal: 1

The weights of a sample of crates ready for shipment to Laos are (in kilograms): 103, 97, 101, 106 and 103. What is the mean deviation?

A. 0 kg
B. 6.9 kg
C. 102.0 kg
D. 2.4 kg
E. None of the above

4-53 C
Med
Goal: 1

The closing prices of a common stock have been 61.5, 62, 61.25, 60.875 and 61.5 for the past week. What is the range?

A. $1.250
B. $1.750
C. $1.125
D. $1.875
E. None of the above

4-54 B
Med
Goal: 1

Ten experts rated a newly developed chocolate chip cookie on a scale of 1 to 50. Their ratings were: 34, 35, 41, 28, 26, 29, 32, 36, 38 and 40. What is the mean deviation?

A. 8.00
B. 4.12
C. 12.67
D. 0.75
E. None of the above

4-55 A
Med
Goal: 1

The weights (in kilograms) of a group of crates being shipped to Panama are 95, 103, 110, 104, 105, 112 and 92. What is the mean deviation?

A. 5.43 kg
B. 6.25 kg
C. 0.53 kg
D. 52.50 kg
E. None of the above

4-56 D
Med
Goal: 1

A sample of the personnel files of eight male employees revealed that, during a six-month period, they lost the following number of days due to illness: 2, 0, 6, 3, 10, 4, 1 and 2. What is the mean deviation (in days)?

A. 1
B. 0
C. 3 1/8
D. 2 3/8
E. None of the above

4-57 D
Med
Goal: 4

A sample of the monthly amounts spent for food by families of four receiving food stamps approximates a symmetrical distribution. The sample mean is $150 and the standard deviation is $20. Using the Empirical Rule, about 95 percent of the monthly food expenditures are between what two amounts?

A. $100 and $200
B. $85 and $105
C. $205 and $220
D. $110 and $190
E. None of the above

4-58 A
Med
Goal: 1

The ages of all the patients in the isolation ward of the hospital are 38, 26, 13, 41 and 22. What is the population variance?

A. 106.8
B. 91.4
C. 240.3
D. 42.4
E. None of the above

4-59 C
Med
Goal: 4

A sample of assistant professors on the business faculty at state supported institutions in Ohio revealed the mean income to be $32,000 for 9 months with a standard deviation of $3,000. Using Chebyshev's Theorem, what is the proportion of faculty that earn more than $26,000 but less than $38,000?

A. At least 50%
B. At least 25%
C. At least 75%
D. At least 100%
E. None of the above

4-60 A
Med
Goal: 1

A population consists of all the weights of all defensive tackles on Sociable University's football team. They are: Johnson, 204 pounds; Patrick, 215 pounds; Junior, 207 pounds; Kendron, 212 pounds; Nicko, 214 pounds; and Cochran, 208 pounds. What is the population standard deviation (in pounds)?

A. About 4
B. About 16
C. About 100
D. About 40
E. None of the above

4-61 D
Med
Goal: 1

The weights (in grams) of the contents of several small bottles are 4, 2, 5, 4, 5, 2 and 6. What is the sample variance?

A. 6.92
B. 4.80
C. 1.96
D. 2.33
E. None of the above

4-62 A
Med
Goal: 1

Each person who applies for an assembly job at Robert's Electronics is given a mechanical aptitude test. One part of the test involves assembling a plug-in unit based on numbered instructions. A sample of the length of time it took 42 persons to assemble the unit was organized into the following frequency distribution.

Length of Time (in minutes)	*Number*
1 up to 4	4
4 up to 7	8
7 up to 10	14
10 up to 13	9
13 up to 16	5
16 up to 19	2

What is the standard deviation (in minutes)?

A. 3.89
B. 6.01
C. 8.78
D. 17.00
E. None of the above

4-63 B
Med
Goal: 7

A research analyst wants to compare the dispersion in the price-earnings ratios for a group of common stock with their return on investment. For the price-earnings ratios, the mean is 10.9 and the standard deviation is 1.8. The mean return on investment is 25 percent and the standard deviation 5.2 percent. What is the relative dispersion for the price-earnings ratios and return on investment?

A. Ratios = 32.0 percent, investment =19.0 percent
B. Ratios =16.5 percent, investment = 20.8 percent
C. Ratios =132.0 percent, investment =190.0 percent
D. Ratios = 50.0 percent, investment =10.0 percent
E. None of the above

4-64 C
Med
Goal: 7

A study of the scores on an in-plant course in management principles and the years of service of the employees enrolled in the course resulted in these statistics:

- Mean test score was 200 with a standard deviation of 40
- Mean number of years of service was 20 years with a standard deviation of 2 years.

In comparing the relative dispersion of the two distributions, what are the coefficients of variation?

A. Test 50%, service 60%
B. Test 100%, service 400%
C. Test 20%, service 10%
D. Test 35%, service 45%
E. None of the above

4-65 C
Med
Goal: 4

The distribution of a sample of the outside diameters of PVC gas pipes approximates a symmetrical, bell-shaped distribution. The arithmetic mean is 14.0 inches, and the standard deviation is 0.1 inches. About 68 percent of the outside diameters lie between what two amounts?

A. 13.5 and 14.5 inches
B. 13.0 and 15.0 inches
C. 13.9 and 14.1 inches
D. 13.8 and 14.2 inches
E. None of the above

4-66 A
Med
Goal: 7

A large group of inductees was given a mechanical aptitude and a finger dexterity test. The arithmetic mean score on the mechanical aptitude test was 200, with a standard deviation of 10. The mean and standard deviation for the finger dexterity test were 30 and 6 respectively. What is the relative dispersion in the two groups?

A. Mechanical 5 percent, finger 20 percent
B. Mechanical 20 percent, finger 10 percent
C. Mechanical 500 percent, finger 200 percent
D. Mechanical 50 percent, finger 200 percent
E. None of the above

4-67 A
Hard
Goal: 2

A sample of the daily number of passengers per bus riding the Bee Line commuter route yielded the following information:

No. of Passengers	Frequency
0 up to 5	4
5 up to10	9
10 up to 15	15
15 up to 20	10
20 up to 25	2

What is the standard deviation?

A. About 5.2
B. About 20.0
C. About 12.9
D. About 2.3
E. None of the above

4-68 C
Med
Goal: 1

If the sample variance for a frequency distribution consisting of hourly wages was computed to be 10, what is the sample standard deviation?

A. $1.96
B. $4.67
C. $3.16
D. $10.00
E. None of the above

4-69 D
Med
Goal: 7

A sample of experienced data entry clerks revealed that their mean typing speed is 87 words per minute and the median is 73. The standard deviation is 16.9 words per minute. What is the Pearson's coefficient of skewness?

A. –2.5
B. –4.2
C. +4.2
D. +2.5
E. None of the above

4-70 D
Med
Goal: 4

Based on the Empirical Rule, what percent of the observations will lie above the mean plus two standard deviations?

A. 95%
B. 5%
C. 68%
D. 2.5%
E. None of the above

4-71 E
Med
Goal: 7

A study of the net sales of a sample of small corporations revealed that the mean net sales is $2.1 million, the median $2.4 million, the modal sales $2.6 million and the standard deviation of the distribution is $500,000. What is the Pearson's coefficient of skewness?

A. –9.1
B. +6.3
C. –3.9
D. +2.4
E. None of the above

4-72 A
Easy
Goal: 5

The test scores for a class of 147 students are computed. What is the location of the test score associated with the third quartile?

A. 111
B. 37
C. 74
D. 75%

4-73 C
Med
Goal: 4

Samples of the wires coming off the production line were tested for tensile strength. The statistical results (in PSI) were:

Arithmetic mean	500	Median	500
Mode	500	Standard deviation	40
Mean deviation	32	Quartile deviation	25
Range	240	Number is sample	100

According to the Empirical Rule, the middle 95 percent of the wires tested between approximately what two values?

A. 450 and 550
B. 460 and 540
C. 420 and 580
D. 380 and 620
E. None of the above

FILL-IN QUESTIONS

4-74
Easy
Goal: 1

What is the difference between the highest and the lowest value in a set of data? __________

4-75
Med
Goal: 5

The percentile range is the distance between any two _______________.

4-76
Med
Goal: 7

If the mean of a frequency distribution is smaller than the median and mode, what is the sign of Pearson's coefficient of skewness? _______________

4-77
Med
Goal: 3

When is the only time the variance equals the standard deviation? ________________

4-78
Med
Goal: 4

According to the Empirical Rule, what percent of the observations lie within plus and minus one standard deviation of the mean? ________

4-79
Med
Goal: 5

A frequency distribution may be divided into how many percentiles? ___

4-80
Easy
Goal: 1

What is the standard deviation the positive square root of? _________

4-81
Med
Goal: 5

For a set of data, how many quartiles are there? _____

4-82
Easy
Goal: 1

The capacities of several metal containers are: 38, 20, 37, 64, and 27 liters. What is the range in liters? _____

4-83
Easy
Goal: 1

What does the sum of the deviations of each value from the mean equal? ______________________________________

4-84
Med
Goal: 7

If two sets of data are in different units, we can compare the dispersion by using? ___________________________________

4-85
Med
Goal: 7

What is the coefficient of variation expressed in terms of? _________

4-86
Med
Goal: 1

A study is made of the commissions paid to furniture salespersons. If the variance is computed, what would it be measured in? ____________

4-87
Med
Goal: 7

The coefficient of variation is a measure of _______________.

4-88
Hard
Goal: 7

The research director of a large oil company conducted a study of the buying habits of consumers with respect to the amount of gasoline purchased at full-service pumps. The arithmetic mean amount is 11.5 gallons and the median amount is 11.95 gallons. The standard deviation of the sample is 4.5 gallons. What is the Pearson's coefficient of skewness? __________

4-89
Hard
Goal: 7

Rainbow Trout, Inc., feeds fingerling trout in special ponds and markets them when they attain a certain weight. A group of 9 trout (considered the population) were isolated in a pond and fed a special food mixture called Grow Em Fast. At the end of the experimental period, the weights of the trout were (in grams): 124, 125, 123, 120, 124, 127, 125, 126 and 121. Another special mixture, Fatso 1B, was used in another pond. The mean of the population was computed to be 126.9 grams and the standard deviation was 1.20 grams. Which food results in a more uniform weight? ___________

4-90
Hard
Goal: 7

The annual incomes of the five vice presidents of Elly's Industries are: $41,000, $38,000, $32,000, $33,000 and $50,000. The annual incomes of Unique, another firm similar to Elly's Industries, were also studied and found to have a mean of $38,900 and a standard deviation of $6,612. What company has the greater coefficient of variation?

____

4-91
Hard
Goal: 7

The spread in the annual prices of stocks selling under $10 and those selling over $60 are to be compared. The mean price of the stocks selling under $10 is $5.25 and the standard deviation is $1.52. The mean price of those stocks selling over $60 is $92.50 and the standard deviation is $5.28. Why should the coefficient of variation be used to compare the dispersion in the prices? ____________________

4-92
Med
Goal: 7

The lengths of stay on the cancer floor of Community Hospital were organized into a frequency distribution. The mean length was 28 days, the median 25 days and the modal length 23 days. The standard deviation was computed to be 4.2 days. What is the Pearson's coefficient of skewness? __________

4-93
Med
Goal: 7

A sample of the homes currently offered for sale revealed that the mean asking price is $75,900, the median $70,100 and the modal price is $67,200. The standard deviation of the distribution is $5,900. What is the Pearson's coefficient of skewness? __________

4-94
Med
Goal: 3

A study has been made of the number of hours a light bulb will operate before it burns out. If the variance of this distribution were computed, what would it be measured in? ____________________

4-95
Hard
Goal: 7

The Pearson's coefficient of skewness (Sk) measures the amount of skewness and may range from –3.0 to +3.0. It is computed by subtracting the median from the mean, multiplying the result by 3 and dividing by? ________________

Questions 96-105 refer to the following:
A sample of five full service gasoline stations, each carrying three grades of gasoline, was taken and the price per gallon (to the nearest cent) was recorded for each grade of gasoline, as shown in the table below.

	STATION				
Gasoline	*1*	*2*	*3*	*4*	*5*
Unleaded	$1.27	$1.27	$1.27	$1.27	$1.27
Unleaded Plus	1.36	1.37	1.38	1.38	1.40
Super Unleaded	1.47	1.49	1.50	1.50	1.59

4-96
Easy
Goal: 1

What is the range for Unleaded gas? _______

4-97
Easy
Goal: 1

What is the range for Unleaded Plus gas? _______

4-98
Easy
Goal: 1

What is the range for Super Unleaded gas? _______

4-99
Easy
Goal: 1

What is the mean deviation for Unleaded gas? _______

4-100
Easy
Goal: 1

What is the mean deviation for Unleaded Plus gas? _______

4-101
Easy
Goal: 1

What is the mean deviation for Super Unleaded gas? _______

4-102
Easy
Goal: 1

What is the variance for Unleaded gas? ____________

4-103
Med
Goal: 1

What is the standard deviation for Super Unleaded gas? ______

4-104
Easy
Goal: 1

What is the standard deviation for Unleaded gas? ______

4-105
Med
Goal: 1

What is the standard deviation for Unleaded Plus gas? ______

Questions 106-108 refer to the following:
The weights of a sample of 100 boxes being shipped by Air France from New York to Paris are:

Weights (pounds)	*Number*
50 up to 75	4
75 up to 100	16
100 up to 125	21
125 up to 150	46
150 up to 175	13

4-106
Hard
Goal: 2

Estimate the sample standard deviation. ______________

4-107
Hard
Goal: 2

Estimate the sample variance. ___________________

4-108
Med
Goal: 2

Estimate the range. ____________

Questions 109-113 refer to the following:
A telemarketing firm is monitoring the performance of its employees based on the number of sales per hour. One employee had the following sales for the last 20 hours.

9	5	2	6	5	6	4	4	4	7
4	4	7	8	4	4	5	5	4	8

4-109

What is the median for the distribution of number of sales per hour?
____

4-110 What is the first quartile for the distribution of number of sales per hour?

____

4-111 What is the third quartile for the distribution of number of sales per hour?

____

4-112 For the distribution of number of sales per hour, 50% are greater than

____

4-113 For the distribution of number of sales per hour, 50% of the observations are between ___________ and ____________.

4-114 Compute the Software Coefficient of Skewness for the following data:

5 5 7 7 7

____

Answers to Fill-In Questions

Chapter 4. Measures of Dispersion and Skewness

4-74. range
4-75. percentiles
4-76. negative
4-77. both equal 1
4-78. 68
4-79. 100
4-80. variance
4-81. three
4-82. 44 liters
4-83. zero
4-84. coefficient of variation
4-85. percent
4-86. dollars squared
4-87. relative dispersion
4-88. - 0.30
4-89. Fatso 1B
4-90. Elly (19.0) > Unique (17.0)
4-91. means differ vastly
4-92. 2.14
4-93. 2.95
4-94. hours squared
4-95. standard deviation
4-96. 0 or none
4-97. $0.04 or 4 cents
4-98. $0.12 or 12 cents
4-99. 0 or none
4-100. 1.0 cents
4-101. 3.2 cents
4-102. 0 or none
4-103. 4.64 cents
4-104. 0 or none
4-105. 1.48 cents
4-106. Approx. $25.98
4-107. Approx. $675.25
4-108. Approx. $125
4-109. Median = 5 sales per hour
4-110. Q1 = 4 sales per hour
4-111. Q3 = 6.5 sales per hour
4-112. The median or 5 sales per hour
4-113. Q1 (4) and Q3 (6.5)
4-114. – 0.61

Chapter 5. A Survey of Probability Concepts

TRUE/FALSE QUESTIONS

5-1 T
Med
Goal: 2
The probability of an event, based on a classical approach, is defined as the number of favorable outcomes divided by the total number of possible outcomes.

5-2 T
Med
Goal: 2
If among several events only one can occur at a time, we refer to these events as being mutually exclusive events.

5-3 F
Med
Goal: 2
The classical approach to probability requires that the outcomes of an experiment are not equally likely.

5-4 F
Med
Goal: 4
The probability of rolling a 3 or 2 on a single die is an example of conditional probability.

5-5 F
Med
Goal: 3
A particular outcome of an experiment is referred to as a sample space.

5-6 F
Med
Goal: 3
The Cunard luxury liner, Queen Elizabeth 2, cannot be docked in Hong Kong and Bangkok at the same time. Events such as these that cannot occur simultaneously are said to be outcomes.

5-7 F
Med
Goal: 1
The probability assigned to an event that is certain not to occur is 1.0.

5-8 T
Med
Goal: 3
If an experiment, such as a die-tossing experiment, has a set of events that includes every possible outcome, the set of events is called collectively exhaustive.

5-9 T
Med
Goal: 2
A subjective probability can be assigned to an event by an individual based on the individual's knowledge about the event.

5-10 T
Med
Goal: 5
To apply the special rule of addition, the events must be mutually exclusive.

5-11 F
Med
Goal: 2
The probability that you would assign to the likelihood that the New York Jets will be in the Super Bowl this season must be between 0 and 10.

5-12 T Med Goal: 4	A joint probability is a probability that measures the likelihood that two or more events will happen concurrently.
5-13 T Med Goal: 5	If there are two independent events *A* and *B*, the probability that *A* and *B* will occur is found by multiplying the two probabilities. Thus for two events *A* and *B*, the special rule of multiplication shown symbolically is: $P(A \text{ and } B) = P(A)\,P(B)$.
5-14 T Med Goal: 5	The general rule of multiplication is used to find the joint probability that two events will occur. Symbolically, the joint probability $P(A \text{ and } B)$ is found by: $P(A \text{ and } B) = P(A)\,P(B/A)$.
5-15 T Med Goal: 6	A tree diagram is very useful for portraying conditional and joint probabilities.
5-16 F Med Goal: 5	A coin is tossed four times. The probability is ¼ or 0.25 that all four tosses will result in a head face up.
5-17 T Med Goal: 5	If there are 'm' ways of doing one thing and 'n' ways of doing another thing, the multiplication formula states that there are (m) • (n) ways of doing both.
5-18 T Med Goal: 5	A permutation is an arrangement of a set of objects in which there is an order from the first through the last.
5-19 T Med Goal: 3	Two coins are tossed. The tossing of the coins is called an experiment, and one possible event is two heads.
5-20 T Med Goal: 2	A joint probability indicates the likelihood that two events occur concurrently.
5-21 T Med Goal: 5	The complement rule states that the probability of an event not occurring is equal to one minus the probability of its occurrence.
5-22 F Med Goal: 3	If two events are mutually exclusive, then $P(A \text{ or } B) = P(A)\,P(B)$.
5-23 F Med Goal: 5	The combination formula is: $n!\,/\,(n-r)!$

5-24 F
Med
Goal: 2

A probability is a number from –1 to +1 inclusive that measures one's belief that an event resulting from an experiment will occur.

5-25 T
Med
Goal: 3

An experiment is an activity that is either observed or measured.

5-26 T
Med
Goal: 3

An illustration of an experiment is turning the ignition key of an automobile as it comes off the assembly line to determine whether or not the engine will start

5-27 T
Med
Goal: 1

A probability is usually expressed as a decimal, such as 0.70 or 0.27, but it may be given as a fraction, such as 7/10 or 27/100.

5-28 F
Med
Goal: 6

A tree diagram portrays outcomes that are not mutually exclusive.

5-29 F
Med
Goal: 1

The closer a probability is to 0, the more likely that an event will happen. The closer the probability is to 1.00, the more likely an event will not happen.

5-30 F
Med
Goal: 2

It was announced that the probability of rain tomorrow is –1.0. Such a low probability of –1.0 indicates that there is no chance of rain.

5-31 T
Med
Goal: 7

Bayes' theorem is a method to revise the probability of an event given additional information.

5-32 F
Med
Goal: 7

Bayes' theorem is used to calculate subjective probability.

MULTIPLE CHOICE QUESTIONS

5-33 A
Med
Goal: 2

The National Center for Health Statistics reported that of every 883 deaths in recent years, 24 resulted from an automobile accident, 182 from cancer and 333 from heart disease. Using the relative frequency approach, what is the probability that a particular death is due to an automobile accident?

A. 24/883 or 0.027
B. 539/883 or 0.610
C. 24/333 or 0.072
D. 182/883 or 0.206
E. None of the above

5-34 A
Med
Goal: 5

If two events A and B are mutually exclusive, what does the special rule of addition state?

A. $P(A \text{ or } B) = P(A) + P(B)$
B. $P(A \text{ and } B) = P(A) + P(B)$
C. $P(A \text{ and/or } B) = P(A) + P(B)$
D. $P(A \text{ or } B) = P(A) - P(B)$
E. None of the above

5-35 B
Med
Goal: 5

What does the complement rule state?

A. $P(A) = P(A) - P(B)$
B. $P(A) = 1 - P(\text{not } A)$
C. $P(A) = P(A) \bullet P(B)$
D. $P(A) = P(A)X + P(B)$
E. None of the above

5-36 B
Med
Goal: 2

Which approach to probability is exemplified by the following formula?

$$\text{Probability of Event Happening} = \frac{\text{Number of times event occurred in past}}{\text{Total number of observations}}$$

A. Classical approach
B. Relative frequency approach
C. Subjective approach
D. None of the above

5-37 C
Med
Goal: 2

A study of 200 stamping firms revealed these incomes after taxes:

Income After Taxes	*Number of Firms*
Under \$1 million	102
\$1 million up to \$20 million	61
\$20 million and more	37

What is the probability that a particular firm selected has \$1 million or more in income after taxes?

A. 0.00
B. 0.25
C. 0.49
D. 0.51
E. None of the above

5-38 A
Med
Goal: 5

Routine physical examinations are conducted annually as part of a health service program for the employees. It was discovered that 8% of the employees needed corrective shoes, 15% needed major dental work and 3% needed both corrective shoes and major dental work. What is the probability that an employee selected at random will need either corrective shoes or major dental work?

A. 0.20
B. 0.25
C. 0.50
D. 1.00
E. None of the above

5-39 D
Med
Goal: 5

A survey of top executives revealed that 35% of them regularly read Time magazine, 20% read Newsweek and 40% read U.S. News & World Report. Ten percent read both Time and U.S. News & World Report. What is the probability that a particular top executive reads either Time or U.S. News & World Report regularly?

A. 0.85
B. 0.06
C. 1.00
D. 0.65
E. None of the above

5-40 C
Med
Goal: 5

A study by the National Park Service revealed that 50% of the vacationers going to the Rocky Mountain region visit Yellowstone Park, 40% visit the Tetons and 35% visit both. What is the probability that a vacationer will visit at least one of these magnificent attractions?

A. 0.95
B. 0.35
C. 0.55
D. 0.05
E. None of the above

5-41 D
Med
Goal: 5

A tire manufacturer advertises "the median life of our new all-season radial tire is 50,000 miles. An immediate adjustment will be made on any tire that does not last 50,000 miles." You purchased four of these tires. What is the probability that all four tires will wear out before traveling 50,000 miles?

A. 1/10, or 0.10
B. ¼, or 0.25
C. 1/64, or 0.0156
D. 1/16, or 0.0625
E. None of the above

5-42 B
Med
Goal: 5

A sales representative calls on four hospitals in Westchester County. It is immaterial what order he calls on them. How many ways can he organize his calls?

A. 4
B. 24
C. 120
D. 37
E. None of the above

5-43 D
Med
Goal: 5

There are 10 rolls of film in a box and 3 are defective. Two rolls are to be selected, one after the other. What is the probability of selecting a defective roll followed by another defective roll?

A. 1/2, or 0.50
B. 1/4, or 0.25
C. 1/120, or about 0.0083
D. 1/15, or about 0.07
E. None of the above

5-44 C
Med
Goal: 5

Giorgio offers the person who purchases an 8 ounce bottle of Allure two free gifts, either an umbrella, a 1 ounce bottle of Midnight, a feminine shaving kit, a raincoat or a pair of rain boots. If you purchased Allure what is the probability you selected at random an umbrella and a shaving kit in that order?

A. 0.00
B. 1.00
C. 0.05
D. 0.20
E. None of the above

5-45 D
Med
Goal: 5

A board of directors consists of eight men and four women. A four-member search committee is to be chosen at random to recommend a new company president. What is the probability that all four members of the search committee will be women?

A. 1/120 or 0.00083
B. 1/16 or 0.0625
C. 1/8 or 0.125
D. 1/495 or 0.002
E. None of the above

5-46 D
Med
Goal: 5

A lamp manufacturer has developed five lamp bases and four lampshades that could be used together. How many different arrangements of base and shade can be offered?

A. 5
B. 10
C. 15
D. 20
E. None of the above

5-47 B
Med
Goal: 5

The machine has just been filled with 50 black, 150 white, 100 red and 100 yellow gum balls that have been thoroughly mixed. Sue and Jim approached the machine first. They both said they wanted red gum balls. What is the likelihood they will get their wish?

A. 0.50
B. 0.062
C. 0.33
D. 0.75
E. None of the above

5-48 C
Med
Goal: 5

What does $\frac{6!\,2!}{4!\,3!}$ equal?

A. 640
B. 36
C. 10
D. 120
E. None of the above

5-49 B
Med
Goal: 5

In a management trainee program, 80 percent of the trainees are female, 20 percent male. Ninety percent of the females attended college, 78 percent of the males attended college. A management trainee is selected at random. What is the probability that the person selected is a female who did NOT attend college?

A. 0.20
B. 0.08
C. 0.25
D. 0.80
E. None of the above

5-50 D
Med
Goal: 5

Three defective electric toothbrushes were accidentally shipped to a drugstore by the manufacturer along with 17 nondefective ones. What is the probability that the first two electric toothbrushes sold will be returned to the drugstore because they are defective?

A. 3/20 or 0.15
B. 3/17 or 0.176
C. 1/4 or 0.25
D. 3/190 or 0.01579
E. None of the above

5-51 C
Med
Goal: 5

An electronics firm manufacturers three models of stereo receivers, two cassette decks, four speakers and three turntables. When the four types of components are sold together, they form a "system." How many different systems can the electronic firm offer?

A. 36
B. 18
C. 72
D. 144
E. None of the above

5-52 A
Med
Goal: 5

The numbers 0 through 9 are to be used in code groups of four to identify an item of clothing. Code 1083 might identify a blue blouse, size medium. The code group 2031 might identify a pair of pants, size 18, and so on. Repetitions of numbers are not permitted, i.e., the same number cannot be used more than once in a total sequence. As examples, 2256, 2562 or 5559 would not be permitted. How many different code groups can be designed?

A. 5,040
B. 620
C. 10,200
D. 120
E. None of the above

5-53 C
Med
Goal: 5

There are two letters C and D. If repetitions such as CC are permitted, how many permutations are possible?

A. 1
B. 0
C. 4
D. 8
E. None of the above

5-54 B
Hard
Goal: 5

You have the assignment of designing color codes for different parts. Three colors are to be used on each part, but a combination of three colors used for one part cannot be rearranged and used to identify a different part. This means that if green, yellow and violet were used to identify a camshaft, yellow, violet and green (or any other combination of these three colors) could not be used to identify a pinion gear. If there are 35 combinations, how many colors were available?

A. 5
B. 7
C. 9
D. 11
E. None of the above

5-55 C
Med
Goal: 5

A builder has agreed not to erect all "look alike" homes in a new subdivision. Five exterior designs are offered to potential homebuyers. The builder has standardized three interior plans that can be incorporated in any of the five exteriors. How many different ways can the exterior and interior plans be offered to potential homebuyers?

A. 8
B. 10
C. 15
D. 30
E. None of the above

5-56 D
Hard
Goal: 5

Six basic colors are to be used in decorating a new condominium. They are to be applied to a unit in groups of four colors. One unit might have gold as the principal color, blue as a complementary color, red as the accent color and touches of white. Another unit might have blue as the principal color, white as the complimentary color, gold as the accent color and touches of red. If repetitions are permitted, how many different units can be decorated?

A. 7,825
B. 25
C. 125
D. 1,296
E. None of the above

5-57 A
Med
Goal: 5

Consideration is being given to forming a Super Ten Football Conference. The top 10 football teams in the country, based on past records, would be members of the Super Ten Conference. Each team would play every other team in the conference during the season and the team winning the most games would be declared the national champion. How many games would the conference commissioner have to schedule each year? (Remember, Oklahoma versus Michigan is the same as Michigan versus Oklahoma.)

A. 45
B. 50
C. 125
D. 14
E. None of the above

5-58 B
Hard
Goal: 5

A rug manufacturer has decided to use 7 compatible colors in her rugs. However, in weaving a rug, only 5 spindles can be used. In advertising, the rug manufacturer wants to indicate the number of different color groupings for sale. How many color groupings using the seven colors taken five at a time are there? (This assumes that 5 different colors will go into each rug, i.e., there are no repetitions of color.)

A. 120
B. 2,520
C. 6,740
D. 36
E. None of the above

5-59 B
Med
Goal: 2

The first card selected from a standard 52-card deck was a king. If it is returned to the deck, what is the probability that a king will be drawn on the second selection?

A. 1/4 or 0.25
B. 1/13, or 0.077
C. 12/13, or 0.923
D. 1/3 or 0.33
E. None of the above

5-60 A
Med
Goal: 2

According to which classification or type of probability are the events equally likely?

A. Classical
B. Relative frequency
C. Subjective
D. Mutually exclusive
E. None of the above

5-61 C
Med
Goal: 3

An experiment may have:

A. Only one result
B. Only two results
C. Two or more results
D. None of the above

5-62 B
Med
Goal: 1

When are two events mutually exclusive?

A. They overlap on a Venn diagram
B. If one event occurs, then the other cannot
C. Probability of one affects the probability of the other
D. Both (a) and (b)
E. None of the above

5-63 B
Med
Goal: 1

Calculating the probability of an outcome is useful in the following except

A. inferential statistics.
B. descriptive statistics.
C. predicting a future outcome.
D. relative frequency.
E. none of the above.

5-64 D
Easy
Goal: 3

The result of a particular experiment is called a(n)

A. observation.
B. conditional probability.
C. event.
D. outcome.
E. none of the above.

5-65 C
Easy
Goal: 4

When two or more events can occur concurrently it is called

A. conditional probability.
B. empirical probability.
C. joint probability.
D. Bayes' theorem
E. none of the above.

5-66 A
Easy
Goal: 6

A visual means useful in calculating joint and conditional probability is

A. a tree diagram.
B. a Venn diagram.
C. Bayes' theorem.
D. inferential statistics.
E. none of the above.

5-67 A
Easy
Goal: 7

Using the terminology of Bayes Theorem, a posterior probability can also be defined as a:

A. conditional probability
B. joint probability
C. 1
D. 0

5-68 D
Easy
Goal: 4

When an experiment is conducted "without replacement",

A. events are independent
B. events are equally likely
C. the experiment can be illustrated with a Venn Diagram
D. the probability of two or more events is computed as a joint probability

5-69 B
Easy
Goal: 4

If two events are independent, then their joint probability is
A. computed with the special rule of addition
B. computed with the special rule of multiplication
C. computed with the general rule of multiplication
D. computed with Bayes theorem

5-70 C
Easy
5

When applying the special rule of addition for mutually exclusive events, the joint probability is:
A. 1
B. .5
C. 0
D. unknown

5-71 A
Easy
Goal: 4

When an event's probability depends on the likelihood of another event, the probability is
A. conditional probability.
B. empirical probability.
C. joint probability.
D. Bayes' theorem
E. none of the above

5-72 A
Easy
Goal: 7

The process used to calculate the probability of an event given additional information has been obtained is
A. Bayes's theorem.
B. classical probability.
C. permutation.
D. subjective probability.
E. none of the above.

FILL-IN QUESTIONS

5-73
Med
Goal: 2

If the set of events are collectively exhaustive and mutually exclusive, what does the sum of the probabilities equal? ___

5-74
Med
Goal: 3

A particular outcome of an experiment is called a sample point. What does the total of all sample points equal? _______________

5-75
Med
Goal: 5

What does the special rule of multiplication requires events *A* and *B* to be? _________________

5-76
Med
Goal: 2

Suppose four heads did appear face up on the toss of a coin four times. What is the probability that a head will appear face up in the next toss of the coin? _____

5-77
Med
Goal: 2

What approach to probability is based on a person's degree of belief and hunches that a particular event will happen? _________

5-78
Med
Goal: 5

If there are five vacant parking places and five automobiles arrive at the same time, in how many different ways they can park? _____

5-79
Med
Goal: 3

An experiment that may result in one or more possible outcomes is statistically referred to as ______________.

5-80
Med
Goal: 2

A new computer game has been developed and its market potential is to be tested by 80 veteran game players. If sixty players liked the game, what is the probability that veteran game players will like the new computer game? _______

5-81
Med
Goal: 1

A company has warehouses in four regions: South, Midwest, Rocky Mountain and Far West. One warehouse is to be selected at random to store a seldom used item. What is the probability that the warehouse selected would be the one in the Far West region? _____

5-82
Med
Goal: 2

One card from a standard 52-card deck of cards is to be selected at random. What is the probability that it will be the jack of hearts? _____

5-83
Med
Goal: 2

The number of times an event occurred in the past is divided by the total number of occurrences. What is this approach to probability called? ___________________

5-84
Med
Goal: 1

If there is absolutely no chance a person will recover from 50 bullet wounds, what is the probability assigned to this event? ______

5-85
Med
Goal: 2

What is the probability that a one-spot or a two-spot or a six-spot will appear face up on the throw of one die? ______

5-86
Med
Goal: 3

What is an activity called that is measured or observed? ________________

5-87
Med
Goal: 2

What is a probability that is based on someone's opinion, guess or hunch called? ___________________

5-88
Med
Goal: 3

What is a particular result of an experiment called? __________

5-89
Med
Goal: 3

What is it called when one or more basic outcomes are combined?
____

5-90
Med
Goal: 5

To apply the special rule of addition, what must the events be?
____

5-91
Med
Goal: 4

What are the two events called when the occurrence of one event does not affect the occurrence of the other event? ____________________.

5-92
Med
Goal: 5

What is it called if the order of a set of objects is important? _________

5-93
Med
Goal: 7

The method for calculating probability of an event given there is additional information is called ________________________.

5-94
Med
Goal: 7

Calculating the likelihood that a specific event will occur given that a specific other has occurred is what type of probability?
____

Questions 95-98 refer to the following:
A group of employees of Unique Services is to be surveyed with respect to a new pension plan. In-depth interviews are to be conducted with each employee selected in the sample. The employees are classified as follows.

Classification	*Event*	*Number of Employees*
Supervisors	A	120
Maintenance	B	50
Production	C	1,460
Management	D	302
Secretarial	E	68

5-95 C
Med
Goal: 5

What is the probability that the first person selected is classified as a maintenance employee?
A. 0.20
B. 0.50
C. 0.025
D. 1.00
E. None of the above

5-96 C
Med
Goal: 5

What is the probability that the first person selected is either in maintenance or in secretarial?

A. 0.200
B. 0.015
C. 0.059
D. 0.001
E. None of the above

5-97 A
Med
Goal: 5

What is the probability that the first person selected is either in management and in supervision?

A. 0.00
B. 0.06
C. 0.15
D. 0.21
E. None of the above

5-98 A
Med
Goal: 5

What is the probability that the first person selected is a supervisor and in management?

A. 0.00
B. 0.06
C. 0.15
D. 0.21
E. None of the above

Questions 99-101 refer to the following:
Each salesperson in a large department store chain is rated with respect to sales potential for advancement. These traits for the 500 salespeople were cross classified into the following table.

Sales Ability	*Fair*	*Good*	*Excellent*
Below average	16	12	22
Average	45	60	45
Above average	93	72	135

5-99 C
Med
Goal: 5

What is the probability that a salesperson selected at random has above average sales ability and is an excellent potential for advancement?

A. 0.20
B. 0.50
C. 0.27
D. 0.75
E. None of the above

5-100 B
Med
Goal: 5

What is the probability that a salesperson selected at random will have average sales ability and good potential for advancement?

A. 0.09
B. 0.12
C. 0.30
D. 0.525
E. None of the above

5-101 A
Med
Goal: 5

What is the probability that a salesperson selected at random will have below average sales ability and fair potential for advancement?

A. 0.032
B. 0.10
C. 0.16
D. 0.32
E. None of the above

Questions 102-104 refer to the following:
A study of the opinion of designers with respect to the primary color most desirable for use in executive offices showed that:

Primary Color	*Number of Opinions*
Red	92
Orange	86
Yellow	46
Green	91
Blue	37
Indigo	46
Violet	2

5-102 B
Med
Goal: 5

What is the probability that a designer does not prefer red?

A. 1.00
B. 0.77
C. 0.73
D. 0.23
E. None of the above

5-103 C
Med
Goal: 5

What is the probability that a designer does not prefer yellow?

A. 0.000
B. 0.765
C. 0.885
D. 1.000
E. None of the above

5-104 B
Med
Goal: 5

What is the probability that a designer does not prefer blue?

A. 1.0000
B. 0.9075
C. 0.8850
D. 0.7725
E. None of the above

Questions 105-106 refer to the following:
An automatic machine inserts mixed vegetables into a plastic bag. Past experience revealed that some packages were underweight and some were overweight, but most of them had satisfactory weight.

Weight	*% of Total*
Underweight	2.5
Satisfactory	90.0
Overweight	7.5

5-105 B
Med
Goal: 5

What is the probability of selecting and finding that all three of them are overweight?

A. 0.0000156
B. 0.0004218
C. 0.0000001
D. 0.075
E. None of the above

5-106 C
Med
Goal: 5

What is the probability of selecting and finding that all three of them are satisfactory?

A. 0.900
B. 0.810
C. 0.729
D. 0.075
E. None of the above

Questions 107-109 refer to the following:
A mortgage holding company has found that 2% of its mortgage holders default on their mortgage and lose the property. Furthermore, 90% of those who default are late on at least two monthly payments over the life of their mortgage as compared to 45% of those who do not default.

5-107 A
Hard
Goal: 7

What is the joint probability that a mortgagee has two or more late monthly payments and does not default on the mortgage?

A. 0.432
B. 0.441
C. 0.018
D. 0.039
E. None of the above

5-108 A
Hard
Goal: 7

What is the joint probability that a mortgagee has one or less late monthly payments and does not default on the mortgage?

A. 0.528
B. 0.539
C. 0.002
D. 0.039
E. None of the above

5-109 A Hard Goal: 7		Based on Bayes Theorem, what is the posterior probability that a mortgagee will not default given one or less payments over the life of the mortgage?

A. Nearly 1
B. Nearly 0
C. 0.538
D. 0.98
E. Cannot be computed

Answers to Fill-In Questions

Chapter 5. A Survey of Probability Concepts

5-73 1

5-74 sample space

5-75 independent

5-76 ½ or 0.5

5-77 subjective

5-78 120

5-79 events

5-80 ¾ or 0.75

5-81 ¼ or 0.25

5-82 1/52 or 0.0192

5-83 relative frequency or empirical

5-84 zero

5-85 ½ or 0.5

5-86 experiment

5-87 subjective

5-88 outcome

5-89 event

5-90 mutually exclusive

5-91 independent

5-92 permutation

5-93 Bayes' theorem

5-94 conditional probability

Chapter 6. Discrete Probability Distributions

TRUE/FALSE QUESTIONS

6-1 F
Easy
Goal: 6

The Poisson probability distribution is always negatively skewed.

6-2 T
Easy
Goal: 1

A random variable is assigned numerical values based on the outcomes of an experiment.

6-3 T
Easy
Goal: 1

A random variable represents the outcomes of an experiment.

6-4 F
Easy
Goal: 1

The probability of a particular outcome, designated X, must always be between 0 and 100 inclusive.

6-5 T
Easy
Goal: 1

A random variable is a quantity resulting from a random experiment that can assume different values by chance.

6-6 T
Easy
Goal: 2

If we toss two coins and count the number of heads, there could be 0, 1 or 2 heads. Since the exact number of heads resulting from this experiment is due to chance, the number of heads appearing is a random variable.

6-7 F
Easy
Goal: 2

If Unique Buying Services has 100 employees, there might be 0, 1, 2, 3 up to 100 employees absent on Monday. In this case, the day of the week is the random variable.

6-8 F
Easy
Goal: 2

A discrete random variable is one, which can have only certain clearly separated values resulting from a count of some item of interest.

6-9 T
Easy
Goal: 2

A discrete variable may assume fractional or decimal values, but they must have distance between them.

6-10 T
Easy
Goal: 4

For a binomial distribution, each trial has a known number of successes. For example, a four question multiple-choice test can only have zero, one, two, three and four successes (number correct).

6-11 T Easy Goal: 6	The random variable for a Poisson probability distribution can assume an infinite number of values.
6-12 T Easy Goal: 1	A probability distribution is a mutually exclusive listing of experimental outcomes that can occur by chance and their corresponding probabilities.
6-13 T Easy Goal: 4	To construct a binomial probability distribution, the number of trials and the probability of success must be known.
6-14 F Easy Goal: 6	The Poisson probability distribution is a continuous probability distribution.
6-15 F Easy Goal: 2	If we measure the weight of an eggnog carton, the variable is referred to as being a discrete random variable.
6-16 T Easy Goal: 4	A binomial distribution has a characteristic that the trials are independent, which means that the outcome of one trial does not affect the outcome of any other trial.
6-17 T Easy Goal: 4	A binomial distribution has a characteristic that an outcome of an experiment is classified into one of two mutually exclusive categories (a success or a failure).
6-18 F Easy Goal: 4	A binomial distribution has the characteristic that the probability of a success stays the same for each trial, but the probability of a failure varies from trial to trial.
6-19 T Easy Goal: 4	A binomial distribution has the characteristic that the data collected are the result of counts.
6-20 T Easy Goal: 5	If the probability of success does not remain the same from trial to trial when sampling is done without replacement, the hypergeometric distribution should be applied.
6-21 T Easy Goal: 6	A Poisson distribution is a discrete probability distribution. It has the same four characteristics as the binomial, but in addition, the probability of a success (π) is small and the number of trials (n) is relatively large.
6-22 T Easy Goal: 2	A random variable may be either discrete or continuous.

6-23 F
Med
Goal: 4

The mean of a binomial probability distribution can be determined by multiplying the probability of a failure by the number of trials.

6-24 F
Easy
Goal: 4

A binomial distribution is a continuous probability distribution.

6-25 T
Easy
Goal: 4

To construct a binomial distribution, it is necessary to know the total numbers of trials and the probability of success on each trial.

6-26 T
Med
Goal: 4

If the probability of success (π) remains the same, but n increases, the shape of the binomial distribution becomes more symmetrical.

6-27 T
Easy
Goal: 1

The mean of a probability distribution is referred to as its expected value, $E(X)$.

6-28 T
Easy
Goal: 3

The mean of a binomial distribution is the product of n and π.

6-29 T
Med
Goal: 3

The variance of a binomial distribution is found by $n\pi(1 - \pi)$.

6-30 T
Med
Goal: 5

As a general rule of thumb, if the items selected for a sample are not replaced and the sample size is less than 5 percent of the population, the binomial distribution can be used to approximate the hypergeometric distribution.

6-31 F
Easy
Goal: 6

In a Poisson distribution, the probability of success may vary from trial to trial.

6-32 T
Hard
Goal: 6

A mail-order house, advertising "same day" service, received a large number of complaints. A change in the handling of orders was made with a goal of less than 5 unfilled orders on hand (per picker) at the end of 95 out of every 100 working days. Frequent checks of unfilled orders at the end of the day revealed that the distribution of unfilled orders approximated a Poisson distribution; that is, most of the days there were no unfilled orders; some of the days there was one order, and so on. Since the average number of unfilled orders per picker was 2.0, the mail-order house lived up to its goal.

6-33 F
Easy
Goal: 4

The binomial probability distribution is always negatively skewed.

MULTIPLE CHOICE QUESTIONS

6-34 B
Easy
Goal: 3

If the variance of a probability was computed to be 3.6 grams, what is the standard deviation?
A. 0.6
B. 1.9
C. 6.0
D. 12.96
E. None of the above

6-35 C
Med
Goal: 4

Sixty percent of the customers of a fast food chain order the Whopper, french fries and a drink. If a random sample of 15 cash register receipts is selected, what is the probability that 10 or more will show that the above three food items were ordered?
A. 1,000
B. 0.186
C. 0.403
D. 0.000
E. None of the above

6-36 C
Hard
Goal: 4

Judging from recent experience, 5 percent of the worm gears produced by an automatic, high-speed machine are defective. What is the probability that out of six gears selected at random, exactly zero gears will be defective?
A. 0.001
B. 0.167
C. 0.735
D. 0.500
E. None of the above

6-37 C
Med
Goal: 3

The probabilities and the number of automobiles lined up at a Lakeside Olds at opening time (7:30 a.m.) for service are:

Number	*Probability*
1	0.05
2	0.30
3	0.40
4	0.25

On a typical day, how many automobiles should Lakeside Olds expect to be lined up at opening?
A. 10.00
B. 1.00
C. 2.85
D. 1.96
E. None of the above

6-38 C
Hard
Goal: 4

On a very hot summer day, 5 percent of the production employees at Midland States Steel are absent from work. The production employees are to be selected at random for a special in-depth study on absenteeism. What is the probability of selecting 10 production employees at random on a hot summer day and finding that none of them are absent?

A. 0.002
B. 0.344
C. 0.599
D. 0.100
E. None of the above

6-39 A
Hard
Goal: 5

The marketing department of a nationally known cereal maker plans to conduct a national survey to find out whether or not consumers of flake cereals can distinguish one of their favorite flake cereals. To test the questionnaire and procedure to be used, eight persons were asked to cooperate in an experiment. Five very small bowls of flake cereals were placed in front of a person. The bowls were labeled A, B, C, D and E. The person was informed that only one bowl contained his or her favorite flake cereal. Suppose that the eight persons in the experiment were unable to identify their favorite cereal and just guessed which bowl it was in. What is the probability that none of the eight guessed correctly?

A. 0.168
B. 0.009
C. 0.788
D. 0.125
E. None of the above

6-40 D
Med
Goal: 5

An insurance agent has appointments with four prospective clients tomorrow. From past experience the agent knows that the probability of making a sale on any appointment is 1 out of 5. Using the rules of probability, what is the likelihood that the agent will sell a policy to 3 of the 4 prospective clients?

A. 0.250
B. 0.500
C. 0.410
D. 0.026
E. None of the above

6-41 C
Med
Goal: 6

Sweetwater & Associates write weekend trip insurance at a very nominal charge. Records show that the probability that a motorist will have an accident during the weekend and file a claim is 0.0005. Suppose they wrote 400 policies for the coming weekend, what is the probability that exactly two claims will be filed?

A. 0.8187
B. 0.2500
C. 0.0164
D. 0.0001
E. None of the above

6-42 C
Med
Goal: 5

In which of the following discrete distribution does the probability of a success vary from one trial to the next?

A. Binomial
B. Poisson
C. Hypergeometric
D. All of the above
E. None of the above

6-43 A
Med
Goal: 5

Which of the following is a requirement for use of the hypergeometric distribution?

A. Only 2 possible outcomes
B. Trials are independent
C. Probability of a success is greater than 1.0
D. All of the above
E. None of the above is correct

6-44 B
Easy
Goal: 1

What is a listing of all possible outcomes of an experiment and their corresponding probability of occurrence called?

A. Random variable
B. Probability distribution
C. Subjective probability
D. Frequency distribution
E. None of the above

6-45 D
Med
Goal: 4

Which one of the following is NOT a condition of the binomial distribution?

A. Independent trials
B. Only two outcomes
C. Probability of success remains constant from trial to trial
D. At least 10 observations
E. None of the above

6-46 B
Med
Goal: 4

Which is true for a binomial distribution?

A. There are three or more possible outcomes
B. Probability of success remains the same from trial to trial
C. Value of p is equal to 1.50
D. All of the above are correct
E. None of the above are correct

6-47 A
Easy
Goal: 6

How is a Poisson distribution skewed?

A. Positively
B. Negatively
C. Symmetrical
D. All of the above
E. None of the above

6-48 B
Hard
Goal: 4

Sponsors of a local charity decided to attract wealthy patrons to its $500-a-plate dinner by allowing each patron to buy a set of 20 tickets for the gaming tables. The chance of winning a prize for each of the 20 plays is 50-50. If you bought 20 tickets, what is the chance of winning 15 or more prizes?

A. 0.250
B. 0.021
C. 0.006
D. 0.750
E. None of the above

6-49 A
Easy
Goal: 2

What kind of distribution are the binomial and Poisson distributions?

A. Discrete
B. Continuous
C. Both discrete and continuous
D. Neither discrete or continuous

6-50 D
Easy
Goal: 1

Which of the following is correct about a probability distribution?

A. Sum of all possible outcomes must equal 1
B. Outcomes must be mutually exclusive
C. Probability of each outcome must be between 0 and 1 inclusive
D. All of the above
E. None of the above

6-51 A
Easy
Goal: 2

The weight of an offensive linesman may be 210 pounds, 210.1 pounds, 210.13 pounds or 210.137 pounds depending on the accuracy of the scale. What is this an illustration of?

A. Continuous random variable
B. Discrete random variable
C. Complement rule
D. All of the above
E. None of the above

6-52 C
Hard
Goal: 4

Carlson Jewelers permits the return of their diamond wedding rings, provided the return occurs within two weeks of the purchase date. Their records reveal that 10 percent of the diamond wedding rings are returned. Five different customers buy five rings. What is the probability that none will be returned?

A. 0.250
B. 0.073
C. 0.590
D. 0.500
E. 0.372

6-53 A
Hard
Goal: 4

In a large metropolitan area, past records revealed that 30 percent of all the high school graduates go to college. From 20 graduates selected at random, what is the probability that exactly 8 will go to college?

A. 0.114
B. 0.887
C. 0.400
D. 0.231
E. None of the above

6-54 B
Hard
Goal: 4

Chances are 50-50 that a newborn baby will be a girl. For families with five children, what is the probability that all the children are girls?

A. 0.100
B. 0.031
C. 0.001
D. 0.250
E. None of the above

6-55 D
Hard
Goal: 6

A new chassis was put into production. It involved soldering, inserting transistors, and so on. Each chassis was inspected at the end of the assembly line and the number of defects per unit was recorded. For the first 100 chassis produced, there were 40 defects. Some of the chassis had no defects; a few had one defect, and so on. The distribution of defects followed a Poisson distribution. Based on the first 100 produced, about how many out of every 1,000 chassis assembled should have one or more defects?

A. About 660
B. About 165
C. About 630
D. About 330
E. None of the above

6-56 A
Hard
Goal: 6

The production department has installed a new spray machine to paint automobile doors. As is common with most spray guns, unsightly blemishes often appear because of improper mixture or other problems. A worker counted the number of blemishes on each door. Most doors had no blemishes; a few had one; a very few had two, and so on. The average number was 0.5 per door. The distribution of blemishes followed the Poisson distribution. Out of 10,000 doors painted, about how many would have no blemishes?

A. About 6,065
B. About 3,935
C. About 5,000
D. About 500
E. None of the above

6-57 D
Hard
Goal: 6

A manufacturer of headache medicine claims it is 70 percent effective within a few minutes. That is, out of every 100 users 70 get relief within a few minutes. A group of 12 patients are given the medicine. If the claim is true, what is the probability that 8 have relief within a few minutes?

A. 0.001
B. 0.168
C. 0.667
D. 0.231
E. None of the above

6-58 B
Easy
Goal: 4

A true-false test consists of six questions. If you guess the answer to each question, what is the probability of getting all six questions correct?

A. 0
B. 0.016
C. 0.062
D. 0.250
E. None of the above

6-59 B
Hard
Goal: 6

A hybrid-grower is experiencing trouble with corn borers. A random check of 5,000 ears revealed the following: many of the ears contained no borers. Some ears had one borer; a few had two borers; and so on. The distribution of the number of borers per ear approximated the Poisson distribution. The grower counted 3,500 borers in the 5,000 ears. What is the probability that an ear of corn selected at random will contain no borers?

A. 0.3476
B. 0.4966
C. 1.000
D. 0.0631
E. None of the above

6-60 C
Hard
Goal: 1

A tennis match requires that a player win three of five sets to win the match. If a player wins the first two sets, what is the probability that the player wins the match, assuming that each player is equally likely to win each match?

A. 0.5
B. 1/8 or 0.125
C. 7/8 or 0.875
D. Cannot be computed.

6-61 D
Hard
Goal: 6

A machine shop has 100 drill presses and other machines in constant use. The probability that a machine will become inoperative during a given day is 0.002. During some days no machines are inoperative, but during some days, one, two, three or more are broken down. What is the probability that fewer than two machines will be inoperative during a particular day?

A. 0.0200
B. 0.1637
C. 0.8187
D. 0.9824
E. None of the above

6-62 A
Easy
Goal: 1

What is the following table called?

Number of Heads	*Probability of Outcome*
0	1/8 = 0.125
1	3/8 = 0.375
2	3/8 = 0.375
3	1/8 = 0.125
Total	8/8 = 1.000

A. Probability distribution
B. Ogive
C. Standard deviation
D. Frequency table
E. None of the above

6-63 B
Med
Goal: 6

What is the only variable in the Poisson probability formula?

A. μ
B. x
C. e
D. P
E. None of the above

6-64 D
Easy
Goal: 4

Which of the following is NOT a characteristic of a binomial probability distribution?

A. Each outcome is mutually exclusive
B. Each trial is independent
C. Probability of success remains constant from trial to trial
D. Each outcome results from two trials
E. All of the above are characteristics of the binomial distribution

6-65 D
Med
Goal: 4

What must you know to develop a binomial probability distribution?

A. Probability of success
B. Number of trials
C. Number of successes
D. "a" and "b" only
E. "a" and "c" only

6-66 A
Easy
Goal: 6

In a Poisson distribution the mean is equal to

A. $n\pi$.
B. $\frac{\Sigma x}{n}$.
C. e^{n-x}
D. $\frac{\mu^x e^{-\mu}}{x!}$.
E. zero.

FILL-IN QUESTIONS

6-67
Easy
Goal: 1

What is the total of the probabilities of all possible events? ____

6-68
Easy
Goal: 6

How many possible experimental outcomes do the binomial distribution and the Poisson distribution have? _______

6-69
Med
Goal: 1

What type of population consists of a fixed number of individuals, objects, or measurements? ___________

6-70
Easy
Goal: 1

A probability distribution is a listing of the expected outcomes of an experiment and the probability of each outcome occurring. What must the probability of all events sum to? _____

6-71
Easy
Goal: 4

To construct a binomial distribution we need to know the total number of ___________ and the probability of a success.

6-72
Easy
Goal: 1

A probability distribution relates the expected outcomes of an experiment to the ___________________ of each one occurring.

6-73
Easy
Goal: 1

What must the sum of the probabilities of the mutually exclusive outcomes of a probability distribution equal? ______

6-74
Easy
Goal: 4

In a binomial experiment, what probability remains constant from one trial to another? _____________

6-75
Easy
Goal: 4

In a binomial experiment, what does the probability of a failure equal?
____

6-76 Med Goal: 4	A binomial probability distribution approaches a greater degree of symmetry as probability of success remains constant and the number of trials becomes ______________
6-77 Med Goal: 6	The Poisson distribution or, the law of improbable events, has ______________ skewed shape.
6-78 Med Goal: 3	If $\pi = 1/3$ and $n = 900$, what is the mean of this binomial distribution? ____________
6-79 Hard Goal: 3	If $\pi = 1/5$ and $n = 100$, what is the standard deviation of this binomial distribution? ______
6-80 Med Goal: 3	If $n = 900$ and $\pi = 1/3$, what is the variance of this binomial distribution? _______
6-81 Med Goal: 2	A ______________ random variable can assume only a certain number of separated values.
6-82 Med Goal: 2	A continuous random variable can assume one of an ___________ number of values within a specific range.
6-83 Med Goal: 5	In the ______________________ distribution the probability of a success is not the same on each trail.
6-84 Med Goal: 5	For the hypergeometric distribution there are ________________ possible outcomes.
6-85 Med Goal: 6	A random variable with a Poisson distribution has one of _______ mutually exclusive values.
6-86 Med Goal: 6	In a Poisson distribution each trail is ____________________.

Questions 87-88 refer to the following:
The arrival of customers at a service desk follows a Poisson distribution.

6-87
Hard
Goal: 6

If they arrive at the rate of two every five minutes, what is the probability that no customers arrive in a five minute period? ______

6-88
Hard
Goal: 6

If they arrive at the rate of four every five minutes, what is the probability that more than four customers arrive in a five minute period?_________

Questions 89-92 refer to the following:
Elly's hot dog emporium is famous for its chilidogs. Some customers order the hot dogs with hot peppers, while many do not care for that added bit of zest. Elly's latest sales indicate that 30% of the customers ordering her chilidogs order it with hot pepper. Suppose 18 customers are selected at random.

6-89
Hard
Goal: 4

What is the probability that exactly ten customers will ask for hot pepper? _______

6-90
Hard
Goal: 4

What is the probability that between two and six people inclusive want hot peppers? ________

6-91
Hard
Goal: 4

What is the probability that fifteen or more customers will want hot peppers? ____________

6-92
Med
Goal: 4

This situation is an example of what type of discrete probability distribution? _______________________

Questions 93-96 refer to the following;
David's gasoline station offers 4 cents off per gallon if the customer pays in cash and does not use a credit card. Past evidence indicates that 40% of all customers pay in cash. During a one-hour period twenty-five customers buy gasoline at this station.

6-93 B
Hard
Goal: 4

What is the probability that at least ten pay in cash?

A. 0.416
B. 0.575
C. 0.586
D. 0.425
E. None of the above

6-94 D
Med
Goal: 4

What is the probability that no more than twenty pay in cash?

A. 0.0
B. 0.1
C. 0.9
D. 1.0
E. None of the above

6-95 C
Hard
Goal: 4

What is the probability that more than ten and less than fifteen customers pay in cash?

A. 0.541
B. 0.401
C. 0.380
D. 0.562
E. None of the above

6-96 C
Med
Goal: 4

This situation is an example of what type of discrete probability distribution?

A. Continuous probability distribution
B. Poisson probability distribution
C. Binomial probability distribution
D. Hypergeometric probability distribution

Questions 97-100 refer to the following:
Affirmative action commitments by industrial organizations have led to an increase in the number of women in executive positions. Satellite Office Systems has vacancies for two executives that it will fill from among four women and six men.

6-97 B
Hard
Goal: 5

What is the probability that no woman is selected?
A. 1/5
B. 1/3
C. 2/15
D. 8/15
E. None of the above

6-98 C
Hard
Goal: 5

What is the probability that at least one woman is selected?
A. 8/15
B. 3/5
C. 2/3
D. ¾
E. None of the above

6-99
Hard
Goal: 5

What is the probability that exactly one woman is selected? ________

6-100
Med
Goal 6

This is an example of what type of probability distribution? ___________

Questions 101-103 refer to the following:
A statistic professor finds she averages five e-mail messages per day from students. Assume the number of messages approximates a Poisson distribution.

6-101 A
Hard
Goal: 6

What is the probability that on a randomly selected day she will have no messages?
A. 0.0067
B. zero
C. 0.0335
D. Impossible to have no messages
E. None of the above

6-102 C
Hard
Goal: 6

What is the probability that on a randomly selected day she will have five messages?

A. 0.0067
B. 0.875
C. 0.175
D. 1.0
E. None of the above

6-103 D
Med
Goal: 6

What is the probability that on a randomly selected day she will have two messages?

A. 0.0067
B. 0.0014
C. 0.420
D. 0.084
E. None of the above

Questions 104-106 refer to the following information.

A company is studying the number of monthly absences among its 125 employees. The following probability distribution shows the likelihood that people were absent 0, 1, 2, 3, 4, or 5 days last month.

Number of days absent	Probability
0	0.60
1	0.20
2	0.12
3	0.04
4	0.04
5	0

6-104 C
Easy
Goal: 3

What is the mean number of days absent?

A. 1.00
B. 0.40
C. 0.72
D. 2.5

6-105 A
Med
Goal: 3

What is the variance of the number of days absent?

A. 1.99
B. 1.41
C. 5.00
D. 55.52

6-106 C
Easy
Goal: 1

Given the probability distribution, which of the following predictions is correct?

A. 60% of the employees will have more than one day absent for a month
B. There is a 0.04 probability that an employee will be absent 1 day during a month
C. There is a 0.12 probability that an employee will be absent 2 days during a month
D. There is a 0.50 probability that an employee will be absent 0.72 days during a month.

Answers to Fill-In Questions

Chapter 6. Discrete Probability Distribution

6-67 one

6-68 two

6-69 finite

6-70 one

6-71 trials

6-72 probability

6-73 one

6-74 success or failure

6-75 1 – probability of success

6-76 larger or greater

6-77 positively

6-78 300

6-79 four

6-80 200

6-81 discrete

6-82 infinite

6-83 hypergeometric

6-84 only 2

6-85 two

6-86 independent

6-87 0.1353

6-88 0.3711

6-89 0.015

6-90 0.708

6-91 0.0000

6-92 binomial probability distribution

6-99 8/15 or 0.5333

6-100 hypergeometric

Chapter 7. The Normal Probability Distribution

TRUE/FALSE QUESTIONS

7-1 T
Easy
Goal: 1

Asymptotic means that the normal curve gets closer and closer to the *X*-axis but never actually touches it.

7-2 T
Easy
Goal: 6

A continuity correction compensates for estimating a discrete distribution with a continuous distribution.

7-3 T
Easy
Goal: 1

The normal curve falls off smoothly in either direction from the central value. Since it is asymptotic, the curve gets closer and closer to the *X*-axis, but never actually touches it.

7-4 T
Easy
Goal: 1

When referring to the normal probability function, there is not just one of them; there is a "family" of them.

7-5 T
Easy
Goal: 1

Some normal probability distributions have equal arithmetic means, but their standard deviations may be different.

7-6 T
Easy
Goal: 1

Some normal probability distributions have different arithmetic means and different standard deviations.

7-7 T
Easy
Goal: 3

For a normal probability distribution, about 95 percent of the area under normal curve is within plus and minus two standard deviations of the mean and practically all (99.73 percent) of the area under the normal curve is within three standard deviations of the mean.

7-8 T
Easy
Goal: 3

The area under the normal curve within plus and minus one standard deviation of the mean is about 68.26%.

7-9 T
Easy
Goal: 3

The total area under the normal curve is 100%.

7-10 T
Easy
Goal: 2

A *z*-score is the distance between a selected value (X) and the population mean (μ) divided by the population standard deviation (σ).

7-11 T
Easy
Goal: 2

In terms of a formula the standardized value of z is found by $z = (X - \mu)/\sigma$.

7-12 T
Easy
Goal: 1

The mean (μ) divides the normal curve into two identical halves.

7-13 T
Med
Goal: 6

The normal probability distribution is generally deemed a good approximation for the binomial probability distribution when $n\pi$ and $n(1 - \pi)$ are both greater than five.

7-14 T
Easy
Goal: 1

The number of different normal distributions is unlimited.

7-15 T
Easy
Goal: 2

A *z*-score is also referred to as the standard normal deviate or just the normal deviate.

7-16 F
Easy
Goal: 2

The mean of a normal distribution is represented by σ.

7-17 T
Med
Goal: 2

The standard normal distribution is a special normal distribution with a mean of 0 and a standard deviation of 1.

7-18 F
Med
Goal: 2

A computed z for X values to the right of the mean is negative.

7-19 F
Med
Goal: 2

A computed z for X values to the left of the mean is positive.

7-20 F
Med
Goal: 3

Disaster Airlines determined that the mean number of passengers per flight is 152 with a standard deviation of ten passengers. Practically all flights have between 142 and 162 passengers.

7-21 F
Med
Goal: 6

The binomial can be used to approximate the normal distribution.

MULTIPLE CHOICE QUESTIONS

7-22 B
Med
Goal: 6

What is the value of the continuity correction factor?

A. 1.00
B. 0.50
C. 100
D. 1.96
E. None of the above

7-23 C
Hard
Goal: 4

A new drug has been developed that is found to relieve nasal congestion in 90 percent of those with the condition. The new drug is administered to 300 patients with the condition. What is the probability that more than 265 will be relieved of nasal congestion?

A. 0.0916
B. 0.1922
C. 0.8078
D. 0.3078
E. None of the above

7-24 D
Med
Goal: 1

Which of the following is NOT true regarding the normal distribution?

A. Mean, median and mode are all equal
B. It has a single peak
C. It is symmetrical
D. The points of the curve meet the *X*-axis at $z = -3$ and $z = 3$
E. None of the above

7-25 C
Med
Goal: 3

For the normal distribution, the mean plus and minus 1.96 standard deviations will include about what percent of the observations?

A. 50%
B. 99.7%
C. 95%
D. 68%
E. None of the above

7-26 A
Med
Goal: 4

For a standard normal distribution, what is the probability that z is greater than 1.75?

A. 0.0401
B. 0.0459
C. 0.4599
D. 0.9599
E. None of the above

7-27 A
Hard
Goal: 4

What is the area under the normal curve between z = 0.0 and z = 1.79?

A. 0.4633
B. 0.0367
C. 0.9599
D. 0.0401
E. None of the above

7-28 C
Hard
Goal: 3

What is the area under the normal curve between $z = -1.0$ and $z = -2.0$?
A. 0.0228
B. 0.3413
C. 0.1359
D. 0.4772
E. None of the above

7-29 D
Hard
Goal: 3

What is the area under the normal curve between $z = 0.0$ and $z = 2.0$?
A. 1.0000
B. 0.7408
C. 0.1359
D. 0.4772
E. None of the above

7-30 D
Hard
Goal: 4

The mean amount spent by a family of four on food per month is $500 with a standard deviation of $75. Assuming that the food costs are normally distributed, what is the probability that a family spends less than $410 per month?
A. 0.2158
B. 0.8750
C. 0.0362
D. 0.1151
E. None of the above

7-31 A
Easy
Goal: 1

Which of the following is NOT a characteristic of the normal probability distribution?
A. Positively-skewed
B. Bell-shaped
C. Symmetrical
D. Asymptotic
E. All of the above

7-32 C
Easy
Goal: 3

What is the proportion of the total area under the normal curve within plus and minus two standard deviations of the mean?
A. 68%
B. 99.7%
C. 34%
D. 95%
E. None of the above are correct

7-33 D
Hard
Goal: 4

The mean score of a college entrance test is 500; the standard deviation is 75. The scores are normally distributed. What percent of the students scored below 320?
A. About 50.82%
B. About 34.13%
C. About 7.86%
D. About 0.82%
E. None of the above

7-34 A
Med
Goal: 2

The mean of a normally distributed group of weekly incomes of a large group of executives is $1,000 and the standard deviation is $100. What is the *z*-score for an income of $1,100?

A. 1.00
B. 2.00
C. 1.683
D. -0.90
E. None of the above

7-35 D
Med
Goal: 3

A new extended-life light bulb has an average service life of 750 hours, with a standard deviation of 50 hours. If the service life of these light bulbs approximates a normal distribution, about what percent of the distribution will be between 600 hours and 900 hours?

A. 95%
B. 68%
C. 34%
D. 99.7%
E. None of the above

7-36 A
Hard
Goal: 4

A study of a company's practice regarding the payment of invoices revealed that on the average an invoice was paid 20 days after it was received. The standard deviation equaled five days. Assuming that the distribution is normal, what percent of the invoices were paid within 15 days of receipt?

A. 15.87%
B. 37.91%
C. 34.13%
D. 86.74%
E. None of the above

7-37 D
Med
Goal: 3

An accelerated life test on a large number of type-D alkaline batteries revealed that the mean life for a particular use before they failed is 19.0 hours. The distribution of the lives approximated a normal distribution. The standard deviation of the distribution was 1.2 hours. About 95.44 percent of the batteries failed between what two values?

A. 8.9 and 18.9
B. 12.2 and 14.2
C. 14.1 and 22.1
D. 16.6 and 21.4
E. None of the above

7-38 C
Med
Goal: 3

The mean of a normal distribution is 400 pounds. The standard deviation is 10 pounds. What is the area between 415 pounds and the mean of 400 pounds?

A. 0.5000
B. 0.1932
C. 0.4332
D. 0.3413
E. None of the above

7-39 B
Med
Goal: 3

The distribution of the annual incomes of a group of middle management employees approximated a normal distribution with a mean of $37,200 and a standard deviation of $800. About 68 percent of the incomes lie between what two incomes?

A. $30,000 and $40,000
B. $36,400 and $38,000
C. $34,800 and $39,600
D. $35,600 and $38,800
E. None of the above

7-40 D
Med
Goal: 1

Which of the following is true in a normal distribution?

A. Mean equals the mode and the median
B. Mode equals the median
C. Mean divides the distribution into two equal parts
D. All of the above are correct
E. None of the above

7-41 D
Easy
Goal: 3

Tables of normal distribution probabilities are found in many statistics books. These probabilities are calculated from a normal distribution with

A. a mean of 1 and a standard deviation of 1
B. a mean of 100 and a standard deviation of 15
C. a mean of 0 and a standard deviation of 15
D. a mean of 0 and a standard deviation of 1

7-42 C
Easy
Goal: 3

Two normal distributions are compared. One has a mean of 10 and a standard deviation of 10. The second normal distribution has a mean of 10 and a standard deviation of 2. Which of the following it true?

A. the locations of the distributions are different
B. the distributions are from two different families
C. the dispersions of the distributions are different
D. the dispersions of the distributions are the same

7-43 A
Easy
Goal: 3

A random variable from an experiment where outcomes are normally distributed

A. can have any value between $-\infty$ and $+\infty$
B. can have only a few discrete values
C. can have a mean of 0 and a standard deviation of 1
D. can have no values

7-44 B
Easy
Goal: 3

The total area of a normal probability distribution is

A. between –3.0 and 3.0
B. 1.00
C. dependent on a value of 'z'.
D. approximated by the binomial distribution.

7-45 C
Easy
Goal: 3

An area of a normal probability distribution represents

A. a permutation
B. a combination
C. a likelihood
D. a shaded area

7-46 D
Easy
Goal: 2

The standard normal probability distribution is one which has:

A. A mean of 1 and any standard deviation
B. Any mean and a standard deviation of 1
C. A mean of 0 and any standard deviation
D. A mean of 0 and a standard deviation of 1
E. None of the above are correct

7-47 D
Hard
Goal: 4

The weekly mean income of a group of executives is $1000 and the standard deviation of this group is $100. The distribution is normal. What percent of the executives have an income of $925 or less?

A. About 15%
B. About 85%
C. About 50%
D. About 23%
E. None of the above

7-48 C
Hard
Goal: 4

The weights of cans of fruit are normally distributed with a mean of 1,000 grams and a standard deviation of 50 grams. What percent of the cans weigh 860 grams or less?

A. 0.0100
B. 0.8400
C. 0.0026
D. 0.0001
E. None of the above

7-49 C
Easy
Goal: 2

What is the distribution with a mean of 0 and a standard deviation of 1 called?

A. Frequency distribution
B. z-score
C. Standard normal distribution
D. Binomial probability distribution
E. None of the above

7-50 B
Hard
Goal: 3

The seasonal output of a new experimental strain of pepper plants was carefully weighed. The mean weight per plant is 15.0 pounds, and the standard deviation of the normally distributed weights is 1.75 pounds. Of the 200 plants in the experiment, how many produced peppers weighing between 13 and 16 pounds?

A. 100
B. 118
C. 197
D. 53
E. None of the above

7-51 C
Hard
Goal: 4

Ball-Bearings, Inc. produces ball bearings automatically on a Kronar BBX machine. For one of the ball bearings, the mean diameter is set at 20.00 mm (millimeters). The standard deviation of the production over a long period of time was computed to be 0.150 mm. What percent of the ball bearings will have diameters 20.27 mm or more?

A. 41.00%
B. 12.62%
C. 3.59%
D. 85.00%
E. None of the above

7-52 D
Hard
Goal: 3

A national manufacturer of unattached garages discovered that the distribution of the lengths of time it takes two construction workers to erect the Red Barn model is approximately normally distributed with a mean of 32 hours and a standard deviation of 2 hours. What percent of the garages take between 32 and 34 hours to erect?

A. 16.29%
B. 76.71%
C. 3.14%
D. 34.13%
E. None of the above

7-53 D
Hard
Goal: 4

Past experience of a large manufacturing firm with administering a test to recent college graduates who had applied for a job revealed that the mean test score was 500, and the standard deviation was 50. The distribution of the test scores was normal. Based on this experience, management is considering placing a person whose score is in the upper 6 percent of the distribution directly into a responsible position. What is the lowest score a college graduate must earn to qualify for a responsible position?

A. 50
B. 625
C. 460
D. 578
E. None of the above

7-54 B
Hard
Goal: 4

An analysis of the grades on the first test in History 101 revealed that they approximate a normal curve with a mean of 75 and a standard deviation of 8. The instructor wants to award the grade of A to the upper 10 percent of the test grades. What is the dividing point between an A and a B grade?

A. 80
B. 85
C. 90
D. 95
E. None of the above

7-55 A
Hard
Goal: 3

The annual commissions per salesperson employed by a manufacturer of light machinery averaged $40,000 with a standard deviation of $5,000. What percent of the sales persons earn between $32,000 and $42,000?

A. 60.06%
B. 39.94%
C. 34.13%
D. 81.66%
E. None of the above

7-56 B
Med
Goal: 3

The mean of a normal probability distribution is 500 and the standard deviation is 10. About 95 percent of the observations lie between what two values?

A. 475 and 525
B. 480 and 520
C. 400 and 600
D. 350 and 650
E. None of the above

7-57 A
Hard
Goal: 4

A cola-dispensing machine is set to dispense a mean of 2.02 liters into a container labeled 2 liters. Actual quantities dispensed vary and the amounts are normally distributed with a standard deviation of 0.015 liters. What is the probability a container will have less than 2 liters?

A. 0.0918
B. 0.3413
C. 0.1926
D. 0.8741
E. None of the above

7-58 B
Med
Goal: 3

The employees of Cartwright Manufacturing are awarded efficiency ratings. The distribution of the ratings approximates a normal distribution. The mean is 400, the standard deviation 50. What is the area under the normal curve between 400 and 482?

A. 0.5000
B. 0.4495
C. 0.3413
D. 0.4750
E. None of the above

7-59 A
Hard
Goal: 3

Suppose a tire manufacturer wants to set a mileage guarantee on its new XB 70 tire. Life test revealed that the mean mileage is 47,900 and the standard deviation of the normally distributed distribution of mileage is 2,050 miles. The manufacturer wants to set the guaranteed mileage so that no more than 5 percent of the tires will have to be replaced. What guaranteed mileage should the manufacturer announce?

A. 44,528
B. 32,960
C. 49,621
D. 40,922
E. None of the above

7-60 B
Hard
Goal: 3

The mean amount of gasoline and services charged by Key Refining Company credit customers is $70 per month. The distribution of amounts spent is approximately normal with a standard deviation of $10. What is the probability of selecting a credit card customer at random and finding the customer charged between $70 and $83?

A. 0.1962
B. 0.4032
C. 0.3413
D. 0.4750
E. None of the above

7-61 D
Hard
Goal: 4

Management is considering adopting a bonus system to increase production. One suggestion is to pay a bonus on the highest 5 percent of production based on past experience. Past records indicate that, on the average, 4,000 units of a small assembly are produced during a week. The distribution of the weekly production is approximately normally distributed with a standard deviation of 60 units. If the bonus is paid on the upper 5 percent of production, the bonus will be paid on how many units or more?

A. 6255
B. 5120
C. 3196
D. 4099
E. None of the above

FILL-IN QUESTIONS

7-62
Easy
Goal: 3

About what percent of the area under the normal curve is within plus two and minus two standard deviation of the mean? ________

7-63
Med
Goal: 1

What is a graph of a normal probability distribution called? _________

7-64
Med
Goal: 2

In a standard normal distribution, μ = ______ and σ = ______ .

7-65
Med
Goal: 1

What type of probability distribution is the normal distribution?
____

7-66
Hard
Goal: 2

What is the formula to convert any normal distribution to the standard normal distribution? ______________________

7-67
Med
Goal: 2

In what units does the standardized z value measures distance from the mean? ______________________

7-68
Med
Goal: 4

What proportion of the area under a normal curve is to the right of a z-score of zero? _________

7-69
Med
Goal: 3

The mean of a normal probability distribution is 60 and the standard deviation is 5. What percent of observations lying between 50 and 70?
_______ %

7-70
Med
Goal: 2

What does a z value of –2.00 indicate about the corresponding X value?
____

7-71
Med
Goal: 1

One of the properties of the normal curve is that it gets closer to the horizontal axis, but never touches it. What is this property of the normal curve called? _________________

7-72
Med
Goal: 4

What proportion of the area under a normal curve is to the right of $z = -1.21$? ________

7-73
Med
Goal: 4

What proportion of the area under a normal curve is to the left of $z = 0.50$? ________

7-74
Med
Goal: 4

What proportion of the area under a normal curve is to the left of $z = -2.10$? _________

7-75
Hard
Goal: 4

A statistics student receives a grade of 85 on a statistics midterm. If the corresponding z-score equals +1.5 and the standard deviation equals 7, what is the average grade on this exam? _______

Questions 76-81 refer to the following:
A sample of 500 evening students revealed that their annual incomes from employment in industry during the day were normally distributed with a mean income of $30,000 and a standard deviation of $3,000.

7-76
Hard
Goal: 4

How many students earned more than $30,000? _______

7-77
Hard
Goal: 3

How many students earned between $27,000 and $33,000? ______

7-78
Hard
Goal: 3

How many students earned between $24,000 and $30,000? ______

7-79
Med
Goal: 3

How many students earned between $20,000 and $40,000? ______

7-80
Hard
Goal: 4

How many students earned less than $22,500? _______

7-81
Hard
Goal: 4

How many students earned more than $36,000? _______

Questions 82-88 refer to the following:
A loaf of bread is normally distributed with a mean of 22 ounces and a standard deviation of ½ ounces.

7-82
Med
Goal: 4

What is the probability that a loaf of bread is < 20 ounces? _____

7-83
Med
Goal: 4

What is the probability that a loaf of bread is > 21 ounces? _____

7-84
Med
Goal: 4

What is the probability that a loaf of bread is > 23 ounces? _____

7-85
Med
Goal: 4

What is the probability that a loaf of bread is < 24 ounces? _____

7-86
Med
Goal: 3

What is the probability that a loaf of bread is between 20.75 and 23.25 ounces? _____

7-87
Med
Goal: 4

What is the probability that a loaf of bread is 22.25 ounces? _____

7-88
Med
Goal: 3

What is the probability that a loaf of bread is between 21.75 and 22.25 ounces? _____

Questions 89-91 refer to the following:
Two business major students, in two different sections of economics, were comparing test scores. The following gives the students scores, class mean, and standard deviation for each section.

Section	*Score*	μ	σ
1	84	75	7
2	75	60	8

7-89
Med
Goal: 5

Which student scored better compared to the rest of the section?
____

7-90
Med
Goal: 5

What is the *z*-score of the student from section 1? ____________

7-91
Med
Goal: 5

What is the *z*-score of the student from section 2? ____________

Questions 92-94 refer to the following:
The average score of 100 students taking a statistics final was 70 with a standard deviation of 7.

7-92 B
Med
Goal: 4

Assuming a normal distribution, approximately how many scored 90 or higher?

A. 0.4979
B. 0.0021
C. 0.9979
D. 2.86
E. None of the above

7-93 E
Med
Goal: 4

Assuming a normal distribution, approximately how many scored less than 60?

A. 0.2271
B. 0.3729
C. 0.8929
D. – 1.14
E. None of the above

7-94 C
Med
Goal: 4

Assuming a normal distribution, approximately how many scored greater than 65?

A. 0.2611
B. 0.2389
C. 0.7611
D. –0.714
E. None of the above

Questions 95-98 refer to the following:
Bottomline Ink, a forms management company, fills 100 orders a day with a 2% error rate in the completed orders. Assume this to be a binomial distribution.

7-95 C
Med
Goal: 6

What is the mean for this distribution?

A. 0.02
B. 1.4
C. 2
D. There is no mean for this type of distribution.
E. None of the above

7-96 B
Med
Goal: 6

What is the standard deviation for this distribution?

A. 0.02
B. 4
C. 2
D. There is no standard deviation for this type of distribution.
E. None of the above

7-97 A
Med
Goal: 6

What is the probability that there will be more than 5 order errors in a given day?

A. 0.1894
B. 0.4838
C. 0.9838
D. 2.1428
E. None of the above

7-98 B
Med
Goal: 6

The probability of less than 1 order error in a given day is

A. 0.7143.
B. 0.3520
C. 0.2611.
D. 2.7611.
E. none of the above.

Answers to Fill-In Questions

Chapter 7. The Normal Probability Distribution

7-62 95% (95.5%)

7-63 normal curve

7-64 zero and one

7-65 Continuos

7-66 $z = (X - \mu) / \sigma$

7-67 standard deviation

7-68 50

7-69 95.44

7-70 less than or to the left of the mean

7-71 asymptotic

7-72 0.8461

7-73 0.6914

7-74 0.0179

7-75 74.5

7-76 250

7-77 341

7-78 239

7-79 500

7-80 3

7-81 11

7-82 0.0

7-83 0.9772

7-84 0.0228

7-85 1.0

7-86 0.9876

7-87 0.0

7-88 0.3830

7-89 student from section 2

7-90 1.28

7-91 1.87

Chapter 8. Sampling Methods and the Central Limit Theorem

TRUE/FALSE QUESTIONS

8-1 T
Easy
Goal: 2

A simple random sample assumes that each item or person in the population has an equal chance of being included.

8-2 T
Easy
Goal: 2

If nonprobability methods are used, not all items or people in a population have a chance of being included in the sample.

8-3 T
Easy
Goal: 3

If 40 samples of size 21 were selected from a population of 22,493, we would expect the mean of the sample means and the population mean to be close but not exactly equal.

8-4 T
Easy
Goal: 2

If probability sampling is done, each item in the population has a chance of being chosen.

8-5 F
Easy
Goal: 2

The items or individuals of the population are arranged in a file drawer alphabetically by date received. A random starting point is selected and then every nth member of the population is selected for the sample. This sampling method is called simple random sampling.

8-6 T
Med
Goal: 2

If the size of a sample equals the size of the population, we would not expect any error in estimating the population parameter.

8-7 T
Easy
Goal: 2

In a nonproportional stratified sample, the number of items studied in each stratum is disproportionate to their number in the population. We then weight the sample results according to the stratum's proportion of the total population.

8-8 T
Easy
Goal: 2

We can expect some difference between sample statistics and the corresponding population parameters. This difference is called the sampling error.

8-9 T
Easy
Goal: 2

A sampling distribution of the means is a probability distribution consisting of a list of all possible sample means of a given sample size selected from a population and the probability of occurrence associated with each sample mean.

8-10 T
Easy
Goal: 3

If nonprobability sampling methods are used, the results may be biased.

8-11 T
Easy
Goal: 4

If a population is not normally distributed, the sampling distribution of the sample means tends to approximate a normal distribution.

8-12 F
Med
Goal: 4

The Central Limit Theorem states that for a sufficiently large sample the sampling distribution of the means of all possible samples of size *n* generated from the population will be approximately normally distributed with the mean of the sampling distribution equal to σ^2 and the variance equal to σ^2/n.

8-13 T
Med
Goal: 4

The Central Limit Theorem states that if the sample size n is sufficiently large, the sampling distribution of the means will be approximately normal no matter whether the population is normally distributed, skewed, or uniform.

8-14 T
Easy
Goal: 2

Fish and game wardens estimate the average weight of the fish or game population by using creel checks and other devices. Based on this sample data, a warden might estimate that the mean weight of Coho salmon caught in Lake Michigan is 2.5 pounds. This single number is called a point estimate of the unknown population parameter.

8-15 T
Easy
Goal: 1

It is often not feasible to study the entire population because it is impossible to check all the items in the population.

8-16 T
Easy
Goal: 4

Based on the sampling distribution of the means and the central limit theorem, the sample mean can be used as a good estimator of the population mean, assuming that the size of the sample is sufficiently large.

8-17 F
Easy
Goal: 3

An estimate of the population mean based on a large sample is less reliable than an estimate made using a small sample.

8-18 T
Easy
Goal: 2

If the sample size keeps getting larger and larger and finally equals the size of the population, there would be no error in predicting the population mean because the sample size and the size of the population would be the same.

8-19 T
Easy
Goal: 3

The standard error of the mean will vary according to the size of the sample that is in the denominator. As the sample size *n* gets larger, the variability of the sample means gets smaller.

8-20 T
Easy
Goal: 1

There are several misconceptions about the number to sample. One fallacy is that a sample consisting of 5 percent or any other similar constant percent is adequate for all problems.

8-21 T
Easy
Goal: 2

One misconception about the number to sample is that a larger sample of voters must be selected from a heavily populated state, such as New York, than from a small state such as Nevada.

8-22 F
Easy
Goal: 2

A larger sample of consumers, or voters, must be selected from a heavily populated state such as California than from a small state such as Wyoming.

8-23 F
Med
Goal: 3

To determine the value of the standard error of the mean, the total error is divided by the sample size.

8-24 T
Easy
Goal: 1

Sampling a population is often necessary because the cost of studying all the items in the population is prohibitive.

MULTIPLE CHOICE QUESTONS

8-25 A
Easy
Goal: 2

What is it called when all the items in a population have a chance of being selected in a sample?
A. Probability sampling
B. *z*-score
C. Sampling error
D. Nonprobability sampling
E. None of the above

8-26 B
Easy
Goal: 2

What is it called when all the items in the population have the same chance of being selected for the sample?
A. Nonprobability sampling
B. Random sampling
C. Judgment sampling
D. Cluster sampling
E. None of the above

8-27 B
Easy
Goal: 2

What is the difference between a sample mean and the population mean called?
A. Standard error of the mean
B. Sampling error
C. Interval estimate
D. Point estimate
E. None of the above

8-28 C
Easy
Goal: 5

What sample statistic is used to estimate a population parameter?
A. Parameter
B. Sampling error
C. Point estimate
D. Interval estimate
E. None of the above

8-29 D
Easy
Goal: 2

Suppose we select every fifth invoice in a file. What type of sampling is this?

A. Random
B. Cluster
C. Stratified
D. Systematic
E. None of the above

8-30 A
Med
Goal: 3

All possible samples of size n are selected from a population and the mean of each sample is determined. What is the mean of the sample means?

A. Exactly the same as the population mean
B. Larger than the population mean
C. Smaller than the population mean
D. Cannot be estimated in advance
E. None of the above

8-31 B
Med
Goal: 4

As the size of the sample increases, what happens to the shape of the sampling means?

A. Cannot be predicted in advance
B. Approaches a normal distribution
C. Positively skewed
D. Negatively skewed
E. None of the above

8-32 B
Easy
Goal: 2

Manufacturers were subdivided into groups by volume of sales. Those with more than $100 million in sales were classified as Class A large; those from $50 to $100 million as Class A medium size; and those between $25 and $50 million..., and so on. Samples were then selected from each of these groups. What is this type of sampling called?

A. Simple random
B. Stratified random
C. Panel
D. Convenience
E. None of the above

8-33 A
Med
Goal: 5

An experiment involves selecting a random sample of 256 middle managers at random for study. One item of interest is their mean annual income. The sample mean is computed to be $35,420 and the sample standard deviation is $2,050. What is the standard error of the mean?

A. $128.125
B. $138.36
C. $2,050
D. $8.01
E. None of the above

8-34 B
Med
Goal: 5

The wildlife department has been feeding a special food to rainbow trout fingerlings in a pond. A sample of the weights of 40 trout revealed that the mean weight is 402.7 grams and the standard deviation 8.8 grams. What is the probability that the mean weight for a sample of 40 trout exceeds 405.5 grams?

A. 0.3783
B. 0.0228
C. 1.0
D. 0.5
E. None of the above

8-35 C
Med
Goal: 5

Suppose a research firm conducted a survey to determine the average amount of money steady smokers spend on cigarettes during a week. A sample of 100 steady smokers revealed that the sample mean is $20 and the sample standard deviation is $5. What is the probability that a sample of 100 steady smokers spend between $19 and $21?

A. 0.4772
B. 0.0228
C. 0.9544
D. $20
E. None of the above

8-36 A
Hard
Goal: 5

The mean weight of trucks traveling on a particular section of I-475 is not known. A state highway inspector needs an estimate of the mean. He selects a random sample of 49 trucks passing the weighing station and finds the mean is 15.8 tons, with a standard deviation of the sample of 4.2 tons. What is probability that a truck will weigh less than 14.3 tons?

A. 0.0062
B. 0.3632
C. 0.1368
D. 0.4938
E. None of the above

8-37 C
Med
Goal: 2

A statewide sample survey is to be made. First, the state is subdivided into counties. Seven counties are selected at random and further sampling is concentrated on these seven counties. What type of sampling is this?

A. Simple random
B. Nonproportional
C. Cluster
D. Stratified
E. None of the above

8-38 E
Med
Goal: 3

Which of the following is the standard error of the mean?
A. σ
B. x/n
C. $\overline{X}$
D. s
E. None of the above

8-39 A
Med
Goal: 5

Mileage tests were conducted on a randomly selected sample of 100 newly developed automobile tires. The average tread wear was found to be 50,000 miles with a standard deviation of 3,500 miles. What is the best estimate of the average tread life in miles for the entire population of these tires?
A. 50,000
B. 3,500
C. (50,000/100)
D. (3,500/100)
E. None of the above

8-40 D
Med
Goal: 3

The mean of all possible sample means is equal to the
A. population variance.
B. σ^2/n.
C. sample variance.
D. population mean.
E. none of the above.

8-41 C
Med
Goal: 2

Sampling error is the difference between a corresponding sample statistic and the
A. sample mean.
B. biased sample.
C. population parameter.
D. chance error.
E. none of the above.

8-42 B
Med
Goal: 4

For a population that is not normally distributed, the distribution of the sample means will
A. be negatively skewed.
B. approach the normal distribution.
C. be positively skewed.
D. take the same shape as the population.
E. none of the above.

FILL-IN QUESTIONS

8-43
Med
Goal: 2

All probability sampling methods have a similar goal, namely, to allow ____________ to determine the items or persons to be included in the sample.

8-44
Med
Goal: 2

What type of sampling is it when a population is first divided into subgroups and then a sample is selected from each subgroup?
____

8-45
Med
Goal: 2

Auditors may select every 20th file starting with say, the 5th file in the top drawer. Then file numbers 25, 45, 65, 85, . . . are audited. What type of sampling is this? ________________ sampling.

8-46
Easy
Goal: 4

What will the sampling distribution of the mean be if a population is normally distributed? ________________________

8-47
Med
Goal: 3

What is the standard deviation of the sampling distribution of the sample means? ____________________

8-48
Med
Goal: 5

What is reasoning from a sample or small group to the entire group or population? ____________________

8-49
Easy
Goal: 2

What is the mean of a population called? ______________

8-50
Easy
Goal: 3

What is the relationship of the standard deviation of the sampling distribution of the mean to the standard deviation of the population under study? __________

8-51
Med
Goal: 3

For a sampling distribution of the means, what percent of the means would be between ± 1.96 standard deviations?

8-52
Easy
Goal: 3

As the sample size (n) increases, what happens to the spread in the distribution of the sample means? __________

8-53
Med
Goal: 3

If the sampling size equals the population size, what is the sampling error? ________

8-54
Easy
Goal: 2

For populations scattered in a wide area, what is the preferred technique for sampling? ___________

8-55
Med
Goal: 2

Which sampling method would be best to use if the population can be divided into homogeneous subgroups? ____________________

8-56
Med
Goal: 2

Which sampling method would you use if every n-th item in the population sequence is selected? ______________________

Questions 57-60 refer to the following:
An accounting firm is planning for the next tax preparation season. From last year's returns, the firm collects a systematic random sample of 100 filings. The 100 filings showed an average preparation time of 90 minutes with a standard deviation of 140 minutes.

8-57 D
Med
Goal: 4

What assumptions do you need to make about the shape of the population distribution of all possible tax preparation times to make inferences about the average time to complete a tax form?
A. The population distribution is skewed to the right.
B. The population distribution is skewed to the left.
C. The population distribution is normal.
D. The shape of the population distribution does not matter.
E. None of the above

8-58 A
Med
Goal: 3

What is the standard error of the mean?
A. 14 minutes
B. 140 minutes
C. 1.4 minutes
D. 90 minutes
E. None of the above

8-59 D
Med
Goal: 5

What is the probability that the mean completion time will be more than 120 minutes?
A. Approximately zero
B. 0.0832
C. 0.4168
D. 0.0162
E. None of the above

8-60 D
Med
Goal: 5

What is the probability that the mean completion time is between 1 and 2 hours, i.e., 60 and 120 minutes?
A. Approximately 1.
B. 0.1664
C. 0.8336
D. 0.9676
E. None of the above

Questions 61-64 refer to the following:
A group of statistics students decided to conduct a survey at their university to find the mean average (mean) amount of time students spent studying per week. Based on a simple random sample, they surveyed 144 students. The statistics showed that students studied an average of 20 hours per week with a standard deviation of 10 hours.

8-61 A
Med
Goal: 3

What is the standard error of the mean?

A. 0.83
B. 10
C. 0.5
D. 2
E. None of the above

8-62 B
Hard
Goal: 5

What is the probability that a sample mean would exceed 20 hours per week?

A. 1.0
B. 0.5
C. 1.96
D. Cannot be calculated based on the given information.
E. None of the above

8-63 C
Hard
Goal: 5

What is the probability of finding a sample mean less than 18 hours?

A. 0.4820
B. 0.4920
C. 0.0080
D. 0.0180
E. None of the above

8-64 D
Hard
Goal: 5

What is the probability that average student study time is between 18 and 22 hours?

A. 0.9640
B. 0.0160
C. 0.0360
D. 0.9840
E. None of the above

Questions 65-68 refer to the following:

The Intelligence Quotient (IQ) test scores are normally distributed with a mean of 100 and a standard deviation of 15.

8-65 A
Hard
Goal: 5

What is the probability that a person would score 130 or more on the test?

A. 0.0228
B. 0.9772
C. 0.4772
D. 0.9544
E. None of the above

8-66 B
Hard
Goal: 5

What is the probability that a person would score between 85 and 115?

A. 0.3413
B. 0.6826
C. 1.00
D. very likely
E. None of the above

8-67 C
Hard
Goal: 5

You enrolled in a class of 25 students. What is the probability that the class' average IQ exceeds 130?

A. 0.0228
B. 0.9772
C. Approximately zero
D. 0.9544
E. None of the above

8-68 D
Hard
Goal: 5

Given a class with 25 students, what is the probability that the class' average IQ score is between 85 and 115?

A. 0.4987
B. 3.00
C. 0.0026
D. 0.9974
E. None of the above

Answers to Fill-In Questions

Chapter 8. Sampling Methods and Sampling Distributions

8-43 chance
8-44 stratified random
8-45 systematic
8-46 normally distributed
8-47 standard error of the mean
8-48 statistical inference
8-49 parameter
8-50 smaller
8-51 95%
8-52 decreases
8-53 zero
8-54 cluster
8-55 stratified random sampling
8-56 systematic random sampling

Chapter 9. Estimation and Confidence Intervals

TRUE/FALSE QUESTIONS

9-1 F
Med
Goal: 5

A sample of union members was selected and their opinions regarding the proposed management union contract were recorded with 1,600 out of the 2,000 members in favor of it. Using a 95% confidence level, the interval estimate for the population proportion was computed to be 0.78 and 0.82. This indicates that about 68 out of 100 similarly constructed intervals would include the population proportion.

9-2 T
Med
Goal: 1

If the size of a sample equals the size of the population, we would not expect any error in estimating the population parameter.

9-3 T
Easy
Goal: 1

We can expect some difference between sample statistics and the corresponding population parameters. This difference is called the sampling error.

9-4 T
Easy
Goal: 2

The Central Limit Theorem proves that the sampling distribution of sample means tends to approximate a normal distribution when the sample size is ≥ 30

9-5 T
Easy
Goal: 2

The 95 percent confidence interval states that 95 percent of the sample means of a specified sample size selected from a population will lie within plus and minus 1.96 standard deviations of the hypothesized population mean.

9-6 T
Easy
Goal: 6

One factor in determining the size of a sample is the degree of confidence selected. This is usually 0.95 or 0.99, but it may be any degree of confidence you specify.

9-7 T
Easy
Goal: 6

One factor in determining the size of a sample is the maximum allowable error that you must decide on. It is the maximum error you will tolerate at a specified level of confidence.

9-8 F
Easy
Goal: 6

The variation in the population as measured by the standard deviation has little or no effect in determining the size of a sample selected from the population.

9-9 T
Med
Goal: 6

The higher the degree of confidence, the larger the sample required to give a certain precision.

9-10 F
Med
Goal: 3

To determine the value of the standard error of the mean, the total error is divided by the sample size.

9-11 T
Easy
Goal: 2

A distribution of sample means is normally distributed with a mean equal to the population mean and a standard deviation equal to the standard error of the mean.

9-12 T
Med
Goal: 6

To determine the size of a sample, the standard deviation of the population must be estimated by either taking a pilot survey or by approximating it based on knowledge of the population.

9-13 T
Easy
Goal: 4

The *t* distribution is based on the assumption that the population of interest is normal or nearly normal.

9-14 T
Easy
Goal: 4

The *t* distribution is a continuous distribution.

9-15 T
Easy
Goal: 4

There is not one *t* distribution, but rather a "family" of *t* distributions.

9-16 F
Easy
Goal: 4

The *t* distribution is positively skewed.

9-17 F
Easy
Goal: 4

All *t* distributions have the same mean of zero and a standard deviation of 1.

9-18 T
Easy
Goal: 4

The *t* distribution is more spread out and flatter at the center than is the standard normal distribution. However, as the sample size increases, the *t* distribution curve approaches the standard normal distribution.

9-19 T
Easy
Goal: 4

The Student *t* distribution has a greater spread than does the z distribution. As a result, the critical values of *t* for a given level of significance are larger in magnitude than the corresponding *z* critical values.

9-20 T
Easy
Goal: 4

The test statistic *t* has $n - 1$ degrees of freedom.

9-21 T
Easy
Goal: 4

William S. Gosset, a brewmaster, developed the t test for the Guiness Brewery in Ireland, who published it in 1908 using the pen name "Student."

9-22 T
Easy
Goal: 4

The test statistic for a problem involving a small sample of under 30 and the population standard deviation is unknown is the Student's *t* distribution.

MULTIPLE CHOICE QUESTIONS

9-23 A
Hard
Goal: 6

The mean number of travel days per year for the outside salespeople employed by hardware distributors is to be estimated. The 0.90 degree of confidence is to be used. The mean of a small pilot study was 150 days, with a standard deviation of 14 days. If the population mean is to be estimated within two days, how many outside salespeople should be sampled?

A. 134
B. 452
C. 511
D. 2100
E. None of the above

9-24 C
Hard
Goal: 6

The proportion of junior executives leaving large manufacturing companies within three years is to be estimated within 3 percent. The 0.95 degree of confidence is to be used. A study conducted several years ago revealed that the percent of junior executives leaving within three years was 21. To update this study, the files of how many junior executives should be studied?

A. 594
B. 612
C. 709
D. 897
E. None of the above

9-25 E
Hard
Goal: 5

There are 2,000 eligible voters in a precinct. Despite protests from knowledgeable persons that a sample size of 500 was too large in relation to the total, the 500 selected at random were asked to indicate whether they planned to vote for the Democratic incumbent or the Republican challenger. Of the 500 surveyed, 350 said they were going to vote for the Democratic incumbent. Using the 0.99 confidence coefficient, what are the confidence limits for the proportion that plan to vote for the Democratic incumbent?

A. 0.060 and 0.700
B. 0.612 and 0.712
C. 0.397 and 0.797
D. 0.826 and 0.926
E. None of the above

9-26 C
Hard
Goal: 3

A random sample of 85 group leaders, supervisors, and similar personnel revealed that on the average a person spent 6.5 years on the job before being promoted. The standard deviation of the sample was 1.7 years. Using the 0.95 degree of confidence, what is the confidence interval within which the population mean lies?

A. 6.99 and 7.99
B. 4.15 and 7.15
C. 6.14 and 6.86
D. 6.49 and 7.49
E. None of the above

9-27 A
Hard
Goal: 3

The mean weight of trucks traveling on a particular section of I-475 is not known. A state highway inspector needs an estimate of the mean. He selects a random sample of 49 trucks passing the weighing station and finds the mean is 15.8 tons, with a standard deviation of the sample of 3.8 tons. What is the 95 percent interval for the population mean?

A. 14.7 and 16.9
B. 13.2 and 17.6
C. 10.0 and 20.0
D. 16.1 and 18.1
E. None of the above

9-28 D
Hard
Goal: 6

A bank wishes to estimate the mean balances owed by customers holding MasterCard. The population standard deviation is estimated to be $300. If a 98 percent confidence interval is used and an interval of $75 is desired, how many cardholders should be sampled?

A. 44
B. 212
C. 629
D. 87
E. None of the above

9-29 C
Med
Goal: 1

Which of the following would be used as a point estimate for the population mean (μ)?

A. σ
B. x/n
C. $\overline{X}$
D. s
E. None of the above

9-30 A
Med
Goal: 1

Mileage tests were conducted on a randomly selected sample of 100 newly developed automobile tires. The average tread life was found to be 50,000 miles with a standard deviation of 3,500 miles. What is the best estimate of the average tread life in miles for the entire population of these tires?

A. 50,000
B. 3,500
C. (50,000/100)
D. (3,500/100)
E. None of the above

9-31 B
Med
Goal: 2

For a given confidence interval, what is the interpretation of a 96% confidence level?

A. 96% chance that the given interval includes the true value of the population parameter
B. Approximately 96 out of 100 such intervals would include the true value of the population parameter
C. 4% chance that the given interval does not include the true value of the population parameter
D. Both "a" and "c" are true
E. None of the above is correct

9-32 D
Med
Goal: 4

Which statement(s) is/are correct about the *t* distribution?

A. Mean = 0
B. Symmetric
C. Based on degrees of freedom
D. All of the above are correct
E. None of the above are correct

9-33 A
Med
Goal: 4

What kind of distribution is the *t* distribution?

A. Continuous
B. Discrete
C. Subjective
D. None of the above

9-34 C
Easy
Goal: 4

How does the *t* distribution differ from the standard *z* distribution?

A. Continuous distribution
B. Bell-shaped
C. Family of distributions
D. Symmetrical
E. None of the above

9-35 E
Med
Goal: 4

What does the appropriate use of the *t* distribution for hypothesis testing assume about the population?

A. Near normal in shape
B. Standard deviation is known
C. Positively skewed
D. Standard deviation is unknown
E. Both "a" and "d" are correct

9-36 B
Med
Goal: 4

A sample of 20 is selected from the population. What is the number of degrees of freedom used to determine the appropriate critical *t*-value?

A. 20
B. 19
C. 21
D. 25
E. None of the above

9-37 D
Med
Goal: 4

The *t* distribution is similar to the *z* distribution in all BUT one of the following characteristics. Which one is it?

A. Continuous
B. Symmetrical
C. Bell-shaped
D. Only one for a given mean
E. None of the above

9-38 A
Hard
Goal: 5

Suppose 1,600 of 2,000 registered voters sampled said they planned to vote for the Republican candidate for president. Using the 0.95 degree of confidence, what is the interval estimate for the population proportion (to the nearest tenth of a percent)?

A. 78.2% to 81.8%
B. 69.2% to 86.4%
C. 76.5% to 83.5%
D. 77.7% to 82.3%
E. None of the above

9-39 B
Med
Goal: 6

Which of the following is NOT necessary to determine how large a sample to select from a population?

A. Level of confidence in estimating the population parameter
B. Size of the population
C. Maximum allowable error in estimating the population parameter
D. Estimate of the population variation
E. All of the above are necessary

9-40 C
Easy
Goal: 1

A sample mean is the best point estimate of the

A. population standard deviation
B. population median
C. population mean
D. the sample standard deviation

9-41 D
Easy
Goal: 1

A sample standard deviation is the best point estimate of the
A. population range
B. population skewness
C. population mode
D. population standard deviation

9-42 B
Easy
Goal: 2

A confidence interval for a population mean
A. estimates the population range
B. estimates a likely interval for a population mean
C. estimates a likelihood or probability
D. estimates the population standard deviation

9-43 C
Easy
Goal: 2

A 95% confidence interval infers that the population mean
A. is between 0 and 100%
B. is within ± 1.96 standard deviations of the sample mean
C. is within ± 1.96 standard errors of the sample mean
D. is too large

9-44 C
Easy
Goal: 2

When a confidence interval for a population mean is constructed from sample data,
A. we can conclude that the population mean is in the interval
B. we can conclude that the population mean is not in the interval
C. we can conclude, with a stated level of confidence, that the population mean is in the interval
D. we cannot make any inferences.

9-45 A
Easy
Goal: 4

Student's t is used when
A. the sample is less than 30 observations
B. the sample size is ≤ 5% of the population
C. the population standard deviation is unknown
D. any time

9-46 C
Easy
Goal: 4

The distribution of Student's t has
A. a mean of zero and a standard deviation of one
B. a mean of one and a standard deviation of one
C. a mean of zero and a standard deviation that depends on the sample size
D. a mean that depends on the sample size and a standard deviation of one

9-47 A
Easy
Goal: 4

The distribution of Student's t is
A. symmetrical
B. negatively skewed
C. positively skewed
D. a discrete probability distribution.

9-48 D
Easy
Goal: 4

When using Student's t to compute an interval estimate,

A. we assume that the samples are collected from normally distributed populations
B. we estimate the population standard deviation based on the sample standard deviation
C. use the z distribution
D. A and B only

FILL-IN QUESTIONS

9-49
Easy
Goal: 2

What estimate states the range within which a population parameter probably lies? ____________

9-50
Med
Goal: 2

What is the interval within which a population parameter is expected to lie? ________________

9-51
Med
Goal: 5

In order to construct the 99 percent confidence interval, how many standard errors of the mean from the hypothesized population mean must you go? _________

9-52
Med
Goal: 2

What is the measure of confidence that one has in the interval estimate called? ___________________

9-53
Med
Goal: 2

What is reasoning from a sample or small group to the entire group or population? ____________________

9-54
Med
Goal: 2

A 95 percent confidence interval implies that about 95 out of 100 similarly constructed intervals will include the ____________ being estimated.

9-55
Med
Goal: 2

For a sampling distribution of the means, what percent of the means would be between ± 1.96 standard deviations?

9-56
Med
Goal: 3

Other things being equal, a smaller sample size would result in a wider confidence interval because there would be more _________ in estimation.

9-57
Med
Goal: 4

What does the *t* distribution approach as the sample size increases?
____

9-58
Hard
Goal: 4

What happens to the computed value of *t* as the sample size increases?
____

Questions 59-61 refer to the following:
Recently, a university surveyed recent graduates of the English Department for their starting salaries. Four hundred graduates returned the survey. The average salary was $25,000 with a standard deviation of $2,500.

9-59 A
Easy
Goal: 1

What is the best point estimate of the population mean?
A. $25,000
B. $2,500
C. 400
D. $62.5

9-60 B
Med
Goal: 3

What is the 95% confidence interval for the mean salary of all graduates from the English Department?
A. [$22,500, $27,500]
B. [$24,755, $25,245]
C. [$24,988, $25,012]
D. [$24,600, $25,600]

9-61 C
Med
Goal: 3

What do the results mean?
A. The population mean is in the interval
B. The population mean is not in the interval
C. The likelihood that any confidence interval based on a sample of 400 graduates will contain the population mean is 0.95
D. There is a 5% chance that the computed interval does not contain the population mean.

Questions 62-64 refer to the following:
A survey of an urban university (population of 25,450) showed that 870 of 1100 students sampled supported a fee increase to fund improvements to the student recreation center.

9-62 A
Hard
Goal: 5

Using the 95% level of confidence, what is the confidence interval?
A. [0.767, 0.814]
B. [0.759, 0.822]
C. [0.771, 0.811]
D. [0.714, 0.866]
E. None of the above

9-63 B
Hard
Goal: 5

Using the 99% level of confidence, what is the confidence interval?

A. [0.751, 0.829]
B. [0.758, 0.822]
C. [0.767, 0.814]
D. [0.771, 0.811]
E. None of the above

9-64 C
Hard
Goal: 5

If university officials say that at least 70% of the voting student population supporting the fee increase, what conclusion can be drawn based on a 95% level of confidence?

A. 70% is not in the interval, need to take another sample.
B. 70% is not in the interval, so assume it will not be supported.
C. 70% is below the interval, so assume it will be supported.
D. Since this was not based on population, cannot make conclusion.
E. None of the above

Questions 65-66 refer to the following:
A group of statistics students decided to conduct a survey at their university to find the mean average (mean) amount of time students spent studying per week.

9-65 A
Hard
Goal: 6

Assuming a standard deviation of 6 hours, what is the required sample size if the error is to be less than ½ hour with a 95% level of confidence?

A. 554
B. 130
C. 35
D. 393
E. None of the above

9-66 B
Hard
Goal: 6

Assuming a standard deviation of 3 hours, what is the required sample size if the error is to be less than ½ hour with a 99% level of confidence

A. 196
B. 240
C. 15
D. 16
E. None of the above

Questions 67-70 refer to the following:
A survey of 144 retail stores revealed that the average price of a DVD was $375 with a standard error of $20.

9-67 D
Med
Goal: 3

What is the 95% confidence interval to estimate the true cost of the DVD?

A. $323.40 to $426.60
B. $328.40 to $421.60
C. $335.00 to $415.00
D. $335.80 to $414.20
E. None of the above

9-68 A
Med
Goal: 3

What is the 99% confidence interval to estimate the true cost of the DVD?
A. $323.40 to $426.60
B. $328.40 to $421.60
C. $335.00 to $415.00
D. $335.80 to $414.20
E. None of the above

9-69 D
Med
Goal: 3

If 90% and 95% confidence intervals were developed to estimate the true cost of the DVD, what similarities would they have?
A. Point estimates
B. Z-variates
C. Standard errors
D. Both "a" and "c"
E. None of the above

9-70 D
Med
Goal: 3

If 95% and 98% confidence intervals were developed to estimate the true cost of the DVD, what differences would they have?
A. Standard errors
B. Interval widths
C. Z-variates
D. Both "b" and "c"
E. None of the above

Questions 71-73 refer to the following:
A student wanted to quickly construct a 95% confidence interval for the average age of students in her statistics class. She randomly selected 9 students. Their average age was 19.1 years with a standard deviation of 1.5 years.

9-71 C
Med
Goal: 4

What is the best point estimate for the population mean?
A. 2.1 years
B. 1.5 years
C. 19.1 years
D. 9 years

9-72 D
Med
Goal: 4

What is the 95% confidence interval for the population mean?
A. [0.97, 3.27]
B. [15.64, 22.56]
C. [17.97, 20.23]
D. [17.95, 20.25]

9-73 A
Med
Goal: 4

What is the 99% confidence interval for the population mean?
A. [17.42, 20.78]
B. [17.48, 20.72]
C. [14.23, 23.98]
D. [0.44, 3.80]

Questions 74-76 refer to the following:
A survey of 25 grocery stores revealed that the average price of a gallon of milk was $2.98 with a standard error of $0.10.

9-74 C
Med
Goal: 4

What is the 95% confidence interval to estimate the true cost of a gallon of milk?

A. $2.81 to $3.15
B. $2.94 to $3.02
C. $2.77 to $3.19
D. $2.95 to $3.01
E. None of the above

9-75 A
Med
Goal: 4

What is the 98% confidence interval to estimate the true cost of a gallon of milk?

A. $2.73 to $3.23
B. $2.85 to $3.11
C. $2.94 to $3.02
D. $2.95 to $ 3.01
E. None of the above

9-76 D
Easy
Goal: 4

If 90% and 95% confidence intervals are developed to estimate the true cost of a gallon of milk, what similarities would they have?

A. Point estimates
B. t-statistics
C. Standard errors
D. Both "a" and "c"
E. None of the above

9-77 C
Med
Goal: 3

A sample of 25 is selected from a known population of 100 elements. What is the finite population correction factor?

A. 8.66
B. 75
C. 0.87
D. Cannot be determined

9-78 B
Med
Goal: 3

A sample of 50 is selected from a known population of 250 elements. The population standard deviation is 15. What is the standard error of the sample means using the finite population correction factor?

A. 2.89
B. 1.90
C. 2.12
D. Cannot be determined

9-79 A
Easy
Goal: 4

A sample of 100 students is selected from a known population of 1000 students to construct a 95% confidence interval for the average SAT score. What correction factor should be used to computer the standard error?

A. 0.949
B. 0.901
C. 1.96
D. Cannot be determined

9-80 B
Med
Goal: 4

A pharmaceutical company wanted to estimate the population mean of monthly sales for their 250 sales people. Forty sales people were randomly selected. Their mean monthly sales were $10,000 with a standard deviation of $1000. Construct a 95% confidence interval for the population mean.

A. [9,690.1, 10,309.9]
B. [9,715.5, 10,284.5]
C. [8,040, 11,960]
D. [8,000, 12,000]

Answers to Fill-In Questions

Chapter 9. Estimation and Confidence Intervals

9-49 Interval

9-50 Confidence interval

9-51 3

9-52 degree of level of confidence

9-53 statistical inference

9-54 parameter

9-55 95%

9-56 variability

9-57 Z distribution

9-58 decreases

Chapter 10. One Sample Tests of Hypothesis

TRUE/FALSE QUESTIONS

10-1 T
Easy
Goal: 1

Two examples of a hypothesis are: 1) mean monthly income from all sources for senior citizens is $841 and 2) twenty percent of juvenile offenders ultimately are caught and sentenced to prison.

10-2 T
Easy
Goal: 1

Hypothesis testing is a procedure based on sample evidence and probability theory to decide whether the hypothesis is a reasonable statement.

10-3 F
Easy
Goal: 2

Generally speaking, the alternate hypothesis is set up for the purpose of either accepting or rejecting it.

10-4 F
Easy
Goal: 4

For one-tailed test using the 0.05 level of significance, the critical value for the z test is 1.645, but for t it is 1.96.

10-5 F
Easy
Goal: 1

Since there is more variability in sample means computed from smaller samples, we have more confidence in the resulting estimates and are less apt to reject null hypothesis.

10-6 T
Easy
Goal: 1

The test statistic for a problem involving a small sample of under 30 and the population standard deviation is unknown is the Student's t distribution.

10-7 F
Easy
Goal: 2

The hypothesis to be tested for reasonableness is referred to as the level of significance.

10-8 T
Easy
Goal: 2

An alternate hypothesis is a statement about a population parameter that is accepted when the null hypothesis is rejected.

10-9 T
Easy
Goal: 2

The level of significance is the risk we assume of rejecting the null hypothesis when it is actually true.

10-10 F
Easy
Goal: 2

There is only one level of significance that is applied to all studies involving sampling.

10-11 T
Med
Goal: 4

Records on a fleet of trucks reveal that the average life of a set of spark plugs is normally distributed with a mean of 22,100 miles. A manufacturer of spark plugs claims that its plugs have an average life in excess of 22,100 miles. The fleet owner purchased 18 sets and found that the sample average life was 23,400 miles, the sample standard deviation was 1,500 miles and the computed $t = 3.677$. Based on these findings, there is enough evidence to accept the manufacturer's claim at the 0.05 level.

10-12 T
Easy
Goal: 2

The researcher must decide on the level of significance before formulating a decision rule and collecting sample data.

10-13 F
Easy
Goal: 6

Type II error is the probability or risk assumed by rejecting null hypothesis when it is actually true.

10-14 T
Easy
Goal: 6

Two types of possible errors always exist when testing hypotheses—a Type I error, in which the null hypothesis is rejected when it should not have been rejected, and a Type II error in which the null hypothesis is not rejected when it should have been rejected.

10-15 T
Easy
Goal: 2

A test statistic is a value determined from sample information collected to test the null hypothesis.

10-16 T
Med
Goal: 2

The region or area of rejection defines the location of all those values that are so large or so small that the probability of their occurrence under a true null hypothesis is rather remote.

10-17 T
Easy
Goal: 2

To set up a decision rule, the sampling distribution is divided into two regions - a region of non-rejection and a region where the null hypothesis is rejected.

10-18 T
Med
Goal: 2

If the null hypothesis is true and the researchers do not reject it, then a correct decision has been made.

10-19 F
Easy
Goal: 2

If the null hypothesis is false and the researchers do not reject it, then a Type I error has been made.

10-20 T
Easy
Goal: 6

The probability of a Type I error is also referred to as alpha.

10-21 F
Easy
Goal: 3

If the null hypothesis is $\mu \geq 200$ and the alternate hypothesis states that μ is less than 200, then, a two-tail test is being conducted.

10-22 F
Easy
Goal: 6

A Type I error is the probability of accepting a true null hypothesis.

10-23 T
Easy
Goal: 6

A Type I error is the probability of rejecting a true null hypothesis.

10-24 T
Easy
Goal: 2

The fifth and final step in testing a hypothesis is taking a sample and, based on the decision rule, deciding if the null hypothesis should be rejected.

10-25 T
Easy
Goal: 2

When the null hypothesis is not rejected, the conclusion is that our sample data does not allow us to reject the null hypothesis.

10-26 F
Easy
Goal: 2

If we do not reject the null hypothesis based on sample evidence, we have proven beyond doubt that the null hypothesis is true.

10-27 F
Easy
Goal: 2

The level of significance is selected after setting up a decision rule and sampling the population.

10-28 F
Easy
Goal: 6

If the null hypothesis is false and the researcher rejects it, then a Type II error has been committed.

10-29 T
Easy
Goal: 2

To prevent bias, the level of significance is selected before setting up the decision rule and sampling the population.

10-30 T
Easy
Goal: 3

For a one-tailed test of hypothesis, the area of rejection is only in one tail of the curve.

10-31 F
Easy
Goal: 2

The first step in testing a hypothesis is to state the decision rule.

10-32 T
Med
Goal: 5

One assumption in testing a hypothesis about a proportion is that the data collected are the result of counting something.

10-33 T
Med
Goal: 5

One assumption in testing a hypothesis about a proportion is that an outcome of an experiment can be classified into two mutual categories, namely, a success or a failure.

10-34 T
Med
Goal: 2

The level of significance is the probability that a true hypothesis is rejected.

10-35 T
Med
Goal: 2

If the critical values of the test statistic z are ±1.96, they are the dividing points between the areas of rejection and non-rejection.

10-36 T
Easy
Goal: 5

A proportion is a fraction, ratio or probability that gives the part of the population or sample that has a particular trait of interest.

10-37 T
Easy
Goal: 5

A sample proportion is found by dividing the number of successes in the sample by the number sampled.

10-38 T
Easy
Goal: 5

The standard normal distribution is the appropriate distribution when testing a hypothesis about a population proportion.

10-39 T
Med
Goal: 5

For one proportion, in order to safely use the z test statistic, make sure the $n\pi$ and $n(1 - \pi)$ are greater than five.

10-40 T
Easy
Goal: 5

To conduct a test of proportions, the assumptions required for the binomial distribution must be met.

MULTIPLE CHOICE QUESITIONS

10-41 D
Med
Goal: 1

Which of the following does NOT hold true for the *t* distribution?

A. Confidence intervals will be wider than for large samples.
B. The region of acceptance will be larger than for large samples.
C. A larger computed *t* value will be needed to reject the null hypothesis than for large samples using *z*.
D. There is only one *t* distribution.
E. None of the above.

10-42 A
Easy
Goal: 2

What value does the null hypothesis make a claim about?

A. Population parameter
B. Sample statistic
C. Sample mean
D. Type II error
E. None of the above

10-43 A
Med
Goal: 5

Test at the 0.01 level the statement that 55% of those families who plan to purchase a vacation residence in Florida want a condominium. The null hypothesis is $\pi = 0.55$ and the alternate is $\pi \neq 0.55$. A random sample of 400 families who planned to buy a vacation residence revealed that 228 families want a condominium. What decision should be made regarding the null hypothesis?

A. Do not reject it
B. Reject it
C. Cannot accept nor reject it based on the information given
D. None of the above

10-44 B
Easy
Goal: 2

What is the level of significance?

A. Probability of a Type II error
B. Probability of a Type I error
C. z-value of 1.96
D. Beta error
E. None of the above

10-45 A
Med
Goal: 4

The mean length of a small counter balance bar is 43 millimeters. There is concern that the adjustments of the machine producing the bars have changed. Test the claim at the 0.02 level that there has been no change in the mean length. The alternate hypothesis is that there has been a change. Twelve bars ($n = 12$) were selected at random and their lengths recorded. The lengths are (in millimeters) 42, 39, 42, 45, 43, 40, 39, 41, 40, 42, 43 and 42. The mean of the sample is 41.5 and the standard deviation 1.784. Computed $t = -2.193$. Has there been a statistically significant change in the mean length of the bars?

A. Yes, because the computed t lies in the area beyond the critical.
B. No, because the information given is not complete.
C. No, because the computed t lies in the area to the right of –2.913.
D. None of the above

10-46 E
Hard
Goal: 4

From past records it is known that the average life of a battery used in a digital clock is 305 days. The battery life is normally distributed. The battery was recently modified to last longer. A sample of 20 of the modified batteries was tested. It was discovered that the mean life was 311 days and the sample standard deviation was 12 days. We want to test at the 0.05 level of significance whether the modification increases the life of the battery. What is our decision rule?

A. Do not reject the null hypothesis if computed t is 1.96 or greater
B. Reject the null hypothesis if computed t is less than 1.96
C. Do not reject the null hypothesis if computed t is 1.729 or greater
D. Reject the null hypothesis if computed t is 2.494 or greater
E. None of the above

10-47 A
Hard
Goal: 4

A manufacturer wants to increase the shelf live of a line of cake mixes. Past records indicate that the average shelf life of the mix is 216 days. After a revised mix has been developed, a sample of nine boxes of cake mix gave these shelf lives (in days): 215, 217, 218, 219, 216, 217, 217, 218 and 218. At the 0.025 level, has the shelf life of the cake mix increased?

A. Yes, because computed t is greater than the critical value.
B. Yes, because computed *t* is less than the critical value.
C. No, because computed *t* lies in the region of acceptance.
D. No, because 217.24 is quite close to 216.
E. None of the above.

10-48 B
Hard
Goal: 4

A manufacturer wants to increase the absorption capacity of a sponge. Based on past data, the average sponge could absorb 3.5 ounces. After the redesign, the absorption amounts of a sample of sponges were (in ounces): 4.1, 3.7, 3.3, 3.5, 3.8, 3.9, 3.6, 3.8, 4.0, and 3.9. What is the decision rule at the 0.01 level of significance to test if the new design increased the absorption amount of the sponge?

A. Do not reject null hypothesis if computed *t* is less than 2.580
B. Do not reject null hypothesis if computed *t* is less than 2.821
C. Reject null hypothesis if computed *z* is 1.96 or larger
D. Reject null hypothesis if computed *t* is less than 2.764
E. None of the above

10-49 D
Med
Goal: 4

A machine is set to fill the small size packages of M&M candies with 56 candies per bag. A sample revealed: 3 bags of 56, 2 bags of 57, 1 bag of 55, and 2 bags of 58. How many degrees of freedom are there?

A. 9
B. 1
C. 8
D. 7
E. None of the above

10-50 C
Med
Goal: 4

A random sample of size 15 is selected from a normal population. The population standard deviation is unknown. Assume that a two-tailed test at the 0.10 significance level is to be used. For what value of *t* will the null hypothesis not be rejected?

A. To the left of –1.282 or to the right of 1.282
B. To the left of –1.345 or to the right of 1.345
C. To the left of –1.761 or to the right of 1.761
D. To the left of –1.645 or to the right of 1.645
E. None of the above

10-51 B
Med
Goal: 4

What is the critical value for a one-tailed hypothesis test in which a null hypothesis is tested at the 5% level of significance based on a sample size of 25?

A. 1.708
B. 1.711
C. 2.060
D. 2.064
E. None of the above

10-52 D
Med
Goal: 4

To conduct a test of hypothesis with a small sample, we need to be able to make the following assumption that:

A. a larger computed value of *t* will be needed to reject the null hypothesis
B. the region of acceptance will be wider than for large samples
C. the confidence interval will be wider than for large samples
D. the population is normally distributed.
E. None of the above

10-53 A
Easy
Goal: 2

What do we call the statement that determines if the null hypothesis is rejected?

A. Decision rule
B. Test statistic
C. Alternate hypothesis
D. Critical value
E. None of the above

10-54 A
Med
Goal: 6

What is a Type II error?

A. Accepting a false null hypothesis
B. Rejecting a false null hypothesis
C. Accepting a false alternate hypothesis
D. Rejecting a false alternate hypothesis
E. None of the above

10-55 A
Med
Goal: 3

If the alternate hypothesis states that μ does not equal 4,000, what is the rejection region for the hypothesis test?

A. Both tails
B. Lower or left tail
C. Upper or right tail
D. Center
E. None of the above

10-56 C
Med
Goal: 3

What are the two rejection areas in using a two-tailed test and the 0.01 level of significance when n is large?

A. Above 1.96 and below –1.96
B. Above 1.65 and below –1.65
C. Above 2.58 and below –2.58
D. Above 1.00 and below –1.00
E. None of the above

10-57 B
Med
Goal: 4

If the 1% level of significance is used and the computed value of z is +6.00, what is our decision?

A. Do not reject H_0
B. Reject H_0
C. Reject H_1
D. None of the above

10-58 D
Med
Goal: 2

What is another name for the alternate hypothesis?

A. Null hypothesis
B. Hypothesis of no difference
C. Rejected hypothesis
D. Research hypothesis
E. None of the above

10-59 C
Med
Goal: 4

For a two-tailed test at the 0.05 significance level, what is the rejection region when n if large?

A. Between ± 1.96
B. Between ± 1.65
C. Greater than +1.96 and less than – 1.96
D. Greater than +1.65 and less than –1.65
E. None of the above

10-60 D
Med
Goal: 4

What is the critical z-value for a one-tailed lower test at the 1% level of risk?

A. + 2.58
B. – 2.58
C. + 2.33
D. – 2.33
E. None of the above

10-61 D
Med
Goal: 5

The sample size and the population proportion are respectively represented by what symbols?

A. p and n
B. α and β
C. z and t
D. n and π
E. None of the above

10-62 C
Med
Goal: 5

What is the probability of making a Type II error if the null hypothesis is actually true?

A. α
B. 1
C. 0
D. 0.05
E. None of the above

10-63 D
Med
Goal: 4

Which of the following is a test statistic used to test a hypothesis about a population?

A. α
B. β
C. μ
D. z
E. None of the above

10-64 C
Med
Goal: 4

If $\alpha = 0.05$ for a two-tailed test, how large is the acceptance area?

A. 0.050
B. 0.025
C. 0.950
D. 0.975
E. None of the above

10-65 C
Med
Goal: 4

If the alternative hypothesis states that $\mu > 6{,}700$, what is the rejection region for the hypothesis test?

A. Both tails
B. Lower tail
C. Upper tail
D. Center
E. None of the above

10-66 C
Med
Goal: 4

What are the critical z-values for a two-tailed hypothesis test if $\alpha = 0.01$?

A. $\pm$ 1.96
B. $\pm$ 2.33
C. $\pm$ 2.58
D. $\pm$ 1.65
E. None of the above

10-67 E
Med
Goal: 7

In a hypothesis test with $\alpha = 0.02$, the decision is to reject the null hypothesis. What is the probability that a Type II error has been committed?

A. 0.95
B. 0.05
C. 1.00
D. 0.00
E. Cannot be determined.

10-68 B
Med
Goal: 4

If the critical z-value for a test statistic equals 2.45, what value of the test statistic would guarantee no chance of making a Type I error?

A. 3.74
B. 10,000
C. 2.46
D. 4.56
E. None of the above

10-69 B
Med
Goal: 4

For a one-tailed hypothesis test, the critical z-value of the test statistic is –2.33. Which of the following is true about the hypothesis test?

A. $\alpha = 0.05$ for a lower-tailed test
B. $\alpha = 0.01$ for a lower-tailed test
C. $\alpha = 0.05$ for an upper-tailed test
D. $\alpha = 0.01$ for an upper-tailed test
E. None of the above

10-70 A
Med
Goal: 2

If we reject the null hypothesis what can we conclude subject to the α risk?

A. Null hypothesis is false
B. Alternative hypothesis is false
C. Null hypothesis is true
D. Both the null hypothesis and the alternative hypothesis are true
E. Both the null hypothesis and the alternative hypothesis are false

10-71 C
Easy
Goal: 2

Which of the following is NOT one of the five steps in the hypothesis testing procedure?

A. Formulate a decision rule
B. State the null and alternate hypotheses
C. Select a level for β
D. Identify the test statistic
E. All of the above are part of the five steps

10-72 D
Med
Goal: 6

As the alternative mean approaches the hypothesized mean, what can we say about the risk?

A. Smaller risk of a Type I error
B. Smaller risk of a Type II error
C. Greater risk of a Type I error
D. Greater risk of a Type II error
E. None of the above

10-73 A
Med
Goal: 5

What must both $n\pi$ and $n(1 - \pi)$ exceed in testing a hypothesis involving one proportion?

A. 5
B. 30
C. 100
D. 2000
E. None of the above

10-74 B
Hard
Goal: 4

A manufacturer of stereo equipment introduces new models in the fall. Retail dealers are surveyed immediately after the Christmas selling season regarding their stock on hand of each piece of equipment. It has been discovered that unless 40% of the new equipment ordered by the retailers in the fall had been sold by Christmas, immediate production cutbacks are needed. The manufacturer has found that contacting all of the dealers after Christmas by mail is frustrating as many of them never respond. This year 80 dealers were selected at random and telephoned regarding a new receiver. It was discovered that 38% of those receivers had been sold. Since 38% is less than 40%, does this mean that immediate production cutbacks are needed or can this difference of 2 percentage points be attributed to sampling? Test at the 0.05 level. Computed $z = -0.37$.

A. Cut back production
B. Do not cut back production
C. Cannot determine based on information given
D. None of the above

10-75 B
Med
Goal: 4

If 20 out of 50 students sampled live in a college dormitory, what is the estimated proportion of students at the University living in a dormitory?

A. 0.20
B. 0.40
C. 0.50
D. 0.60
E. None of the above

10-76 B
Med
Goal: 4

What does z equal for an $\alpha = 0.01$ and a lower level test?

A. +2.33
B. –2.33
C. +2.58
D. –2.58
E. None of the above

10-77 B
Med
Goal: 4

What do tests of proportions require of both $n\pi$ and $n(1 - \pi)$?

A. Exceed 30
B. Exceed 5
C. Exceed 100
D. Be equal
E. None of the above

10-78 B
Med
Goal: 6

If $\alpha = 0.05$, what is the probability of making a Type I error?

A. 0
B. 1/20
C. 19/20
D. 20/20
E. None of the above

10-79 A
Hard
Goal: 4

The claim that "40% of those persons who retired from an industrial job before the age of 60 would return to work if a suitable job was available," is to be investigated at the 0.02 level of risk. If 74 out of the 200 workers sampled said they would return to work, what is our decision?

A. Do no reject the null hypothesis because –0.866 lies in the region between 0 and –2.33
B. Do not reject the null hypothesis because –0.866 lies in the region between 0 and –2.58
C. Reject the null hypothesis because 37% is less than 40%
D. Do not reject the null hypothesis because 37% lies in the area between 0% and 40%
E. None of the above

10-80 E
Med
Goal: 6

In hypothesis testing, what is the level of significance?

A. Risk of rejecting the null hypothesis when it is true
B. Symbolized by the Greek letter "α"
C. Value between 0 and 1
D. Selected before a decision rule can be formulated
E. All of the above are true

10-81 D
Med
Goal: 5

Which symbol represents a population proportion?

A. p_c
B. z
C. α
D. π
E. None of the above

10-82 B
Med
Goal: 5

What is the sample proportion defined as?

A. $n\pi$
B. x/n
C. $n!$
D. π
E. None of the above

FILL-IN QUESTONS

10-83
Easy
Goal: 6

As the probability of making a Type I error decreases, what happens to the risk of not rejecting the null hypothesis when it is actually false (Type II error)? ____________________

10-84
Med
Goal: 2

What is the first step in hypothesis testing? ______________________

10-85
Med
Goal: 4

What is the critical value of t for a two-tailed test with a null hypothesis $\mu = 25$, $\alpha = 0.05$ and $n = 17$? ___________

10-86
Med
Goal: 4

What is the critical value of *t* for an alternative hypothesis of $\mu > 30$, a 1% level of significance and a sample size of 8? ___________

10-87
Med
Goal: 4

What is the critical value of *t* for the alternative hypothesis $\mu < 12$, a level of significance of 0.005 and a sample size of 20? _______

10-88
Med
Goal: 4

What is the critical value of *t* for the null hypothesis μ equal to 50, α = 0.20 and a sample size of 5? _________

10-89
Med
Goal: 3

As the sample size increases, the curve of the *t*-distribution approaches the ______________________________

10-90
Med
Goal: 2

What is another name for the alternate hypothesis? _____________

10-91
Easy
Goal: 2

What is the level of risk also referred to as? __________________

10-92
Easy
Goal: 6

What is the probability of Type I error often referred to as? ____________

10-93
Med
Goal: 2

If the null hypothesis is true and the researchers reject it, what error has been made? __________

10-94
Med
Goal: 2

If the null hypothesis is false and the researchers accept it, what error has been made? ____________

10-95
Med
Goal: 2

What value is the dividing point separating the region of rejection from the region of non-rejection? ___________________________

10-96
Easy
Goal: 4

If the critical value is 1.96 and the computed value of the test statistic is 2.64, what is the decision? ________________

10-97
Easy
Goal: 3

What is the test of hypothesis when the alternate hypothesis states a direction? ________________________

10-98
Easy
Goal: 3

What is the test of hypothesis if no direction is specified under the alternate hypothesis? ____________

10-99
Med
Goal: 1

What do we call a statement about the value of a population parameter?
____

10-100
Easy
Goal: 2

The alternate hypothesis can be accepted only if the null hypothesis is shown to be? __________

10-101
Med
Goal: 2

If the absolute value of the computed value of the test statistic exceeds the critical value of the test statistic, what is our decision?
____

10-102
Easy
Goal: 5

Among one hundred people surveyed, sixty-six people or 0.33 preferred the product. What is the 0.33 called? ________________

10-103
Easy
Goal: 5

What is a ratio, fraction or percent of the sample or the population that has a particular trait called? ______________________

10-104
Easy
Goal: 5

A survey indicates that among eighty people surveyed sixty or 75% prefer SOS cereal. What do the sixty people represent?
____

Questions 105-107 refer to the following;
The average cost of tuition, room and board at small private liberal arts colleges is reported to be \$8,500 per term, but a financial administrator believes that the average cost is higher. A study conducted using 150 small liberal arts colleges showed that the average cost per term is \$9,000 with a standard deviation of \$1,200. Let $\alpha = 0.05$.

10-105 C
Med
Goal: 2

What is the null and alternative hypotheses for this study?

A. Null: $\mu \leq \$9,000$; alternative: $\mu > \$9,000$
B. Null: $\mu \geq \$9,000$; alternative: $\mu < \$9,000$
C. Null: $\mu \leq \$8,500$; alternative: $\mu > \$8,500$
D. Null: $\mu \geq \$8,500$; alternative: $\mu < \$8,500$
E. None of the above

10-106 C
Med
Goal: 4

What is the critical *z*-value for this test?

A. + 1.96
B. – 1.96
C. + 1.65
D. – 1.65
E. None of the above

10-107 B
Med
Goal: 4

Given the z-statistic is 5.1, what is our decision about the average cost?

A. Equal to $8,500
B. Greater than $8,500
C. Less than $8,500
D. Not equal to $8,500
E. None of the above

Questions 108-116 refer to the following:
A manufacturer claims that at least 99% of all his products meet the minimum government standards. A survey of 500 products revealed ten did not meet the standard.

10-108
Med
Goal: 2

What is the null hypothesis?____________________

10-109
Med
Goal: 2

What is the alternate hypothesis? ____________________

10-110
Med
Goal: 2

What is the critical value if $\alpha = .01$? ____________

10-111
Hard
Goal: 4

What is the z-statistic? ______________

10-112
Hard
Goal: 4

What is the critical value if the level of significance is 2%? ______

10-113
Med
Goal: 4

What is your decision if the z-statistic is –1.96 and the level of significance is 0.01? ________________

10-114
Hard
Goal: 4

What is your decision if the z-statistic is –2.58 and the level of significance is 0.02? ___________________________

10-115
Hard
Goal: 4

What is your decision if the z-statistic is –2.054 and the level of significance is 0.03? ______________________

10-116
Med
Goal: 2

What would you do if the computed value of $z = -2.25$ and the level of significance is 0.03? ________________________________

Questions 117-123 refer to the following:
Based on the Nielsen ratings, the local CBS affiliate claims its 11:00 PM newscast reaches 41% of the viewing audience in the area. In a survey of 100 viewers, 36% indicated that they watch the late evening news on this local CBS station.

10-117 B
Med
Goal: 4

What is the null hypothesis?
A. $\pi = 0.36$
B. $\pi = 0.41$
C. $\pi \neq 0.36$
D. $\mu = 0.41$
E. None of the above

10-118 C
Med
Goal: 4

What is the alternate hypothesis?
A. $\pi = 0.36$
B. $\pi = 0.41$
C. $\pi \neq 0.41$
D. $\mu \neq 0.41$
E. None of the above

10-119 D
Med
Goal: 4

What is the sample proportion?
A. 0.41
B. 0.36%
C. 0.41%
D. 0.36
E. None of the above

10-120 C
Med
Goal: 4

What is the critical value if $\alpha = 0.01$?
A. 2.58
B. 2.33
C. ± 2.58
D. -2.33
E. None of the above

10-121 C
Hard
Goal: 4

What is the z-statistic?
A. 1.02
B. 1.22
C. -1.02
D. -1.22
E. None of the above

10-122 B
Med
Goal: 4

What is the critical value if the level of significance is 0.10?
A. -1.282
B. ± 1.65
C. -2.58
D. 2.58
E. None of the above

10-123 A
Med
Goal: 4

What is your decision if $\alpha = 0.01$?

A. Fail to reject the null hypothesis and concluded about 41%.
B. Reject the null hypothesis and conclude different from 41%.
C. Fail to reject the alternate and conclude different from 41%.
D. Reject the alternate and conclude it is 41%.
E. None of the above

Questions 124-129 refer to the following:
It is claimed that in a bushel of peaches less than ten percent are defective. A sample of 400 peaches are examined and 50 are found to be defective.

10-124 B
Med
Goal: 4

What is the null hypothesis?

A. $\pi \neq 0.10$
B. $\pi \geq 0.10$
C. $\pi \leq 0.10$
D. $\pi < 0.10$
E. $\pi = 0.10$

10-125 E
Med
Goal: 4

What is the alternate hypothesis for a one-sided test?

A. $\pi \neq 0.10$
B. $\pi > 0.10$
C. $\pi \leq 0.10$
D. $\pi = 0.10$
E. $\pi < 0.10$

10-126 C
Med
Goal: 4

What is the critical value for $\alpha = 0.025$?

A. 1.96
B. ± 1.65
C. – 1.96
D. –1.65
E. None of the above

10-127 B
Med
Goal: 4

What is the sample proportion?

A. 0.10
B. 0.125
C. 40
D. 0.40
E. None of the above

10-128 D
Hard
Goal: 2

What is the z-statistic?

A. 0.025
B. 0.278
C. –1.65
D. 1.67
E. None of the above

10-129 A
Med
Goal: 2

If $\alpha = 0.025$, what will be the decision?
A. Fail to reject the null and conclude the defects are not greater than 10%
B. Reject the null and conclude the defects are not greater than 10%
C. Reject the null and conclude the defects are greater than 10%
D. Fail to reject the null and conclude the defects are not less than 10%
E. None of the above

Questions 130-132 refer to the following:
The mean gross annual incomes of certified tack welders are normally distributed with the mean of $20,000 and a standard deviation of $2,000. The ship building association wishes to find out whether their tack welders earn more or less than $20,000 annually. The alternate hypothesis is that the mean is not $20,000.

10-130 A
Hard
Goal: 4

If the level of significance is 0.10, what is the decision rule?
A. Do no reject the null hypothesis if computed z lies between –1.65 and +1.65; otherwise, reject it
B.. Do not reject the null hypothesis if computed z is greater than 1.65; otherwise, reject it
C. Do not reject the null hypothesis if computed z lies between –1.96 and +1.96; otherwise, reject it
D. Reject the null hypothesis if computed z is below –1.96; otherwise, reject it
E. None of the above

10-131 B
Med
Goal: 2

Which of the following is the alternate hypothesis?
A. $\pi \neq \$20,000$
B. $\mu \neq \$20,000$
C. $\mu < \$20,000$
D. $\mu = \$20,000$
E. $\pi = \$20,000$

10-132 E
Med
Goal: 4

If the level of significance is 0.10, what is the critical value?
A. 1.65
B. 2.58
C. 1.28
D. ± 1.28
E. ± 1.65

Questions 133-142 refer to the following:
The mean weight of newborn infants at a community hospital is 6.6 pounds. A sample of seven infants is randomly selected and their weights at birth are recorded as 9.0, 7.3, 6.0, 8.8, 6.8, 8.4, and 6.6 pounds.

10-133 A
Med
Goal: 4

The null hypothesis is
A. $\mu = 6.6$
B. $\mu \neq 6.6$
C. $\mu \geq 6.6$
D. $\mu > 7.6$
E. $\mu \neq 7.6$

10-134 B
Med
Goal: 4

What is the alternate hypothesis?
A. $\mu = 6.6$
B. $\mu \neq 6.6$
C. $\mu \geq 6.6$
D. $\mu > 7.6$
E. $\mu \neq 7.6$

10-135 C
Med
Goal: 4

What is the degrees of freedom?
A. 7
B. 8
C. 6
D. 6.6
E. 7.6

10-136 D
Med
Goal: 4

If $\alpha = 0.05$, what is the critical t value?
A. -2.365
B. ± 1.96
C. ± 2.365
D. ± 2.447
E. -2.447

10-137 B
Med
Goal: 4

What is the sample mean?
A. 6.6
B. 7.6
C. 1.177
D. 2.447
E. None of the above

10-138 C
Hard
Goal: 4

What is the sample variance?
A. 1.177
B. 6.6
C. 1.385
D. 7.6
E. None of the above

10-139 A
Hard
Goal: 4

What is the sample standard deviation?
A. 1.177
B. 6.6
C. 1.385
D. 7.6
E. None of the above

10-140 D
Hard
Goal: 4

What is the t critical value?

A. + 2.447
B. + 1.177
C. – 2.248
D. + 2.248
E. – 2.447

10-141 A
Hard
Goal: 4

What is the decision for a statistical significant change in average weights at birth at the 5% level of significance?

A. Fail to reject the null hypothesis and conclude the mean is 6.6 lb.
B. Reject the null hypothesis and conclude the mean is higher than 6.6 lb.
C. Reject the null hypothesis and conclude the mean is lower than 6.6 lb.
D. Cannot calculate because population standard deviation is unknown.
E. None of the above

10-142 C
Med
Goal: 4

What is the decision for a significant change in the average birthrate if a 5% level of significance?

A. Fail to reject the null hypothesis and conclude the mean is 6.6 lb.
B. Reject the null hypothesis and conclude the mean is lower than 6.6 lb.
C. Reject the null hypothesis and conclude the mean is not 6.6 lb.
D. Cannot calculate because population standard deviation is unknown.
E. None of the above

Question 143-148 refer to the following:
A restaurant that bills its house account monthly is concerned that the average monthly bill exceeds $200 per account. A random sample of twelve accounts is selected, resulting in a sample mean of $220 and a standard deviation of $12. The *t*-test is to be conducted at the 5% level of significance.

10-143
Med
Goal: 4

What is H_0 ? ____________________

10-144
Med
Goal: 4

What is H_1? ____________________

10-145
Med
Goal: 4

What is the critical value of t? ______________

10-146
Hard
Goal: 4

What is the calculated value of *t*? ______________

10-147
Hard
Goal: 4

What is our decision? ______________

10-148
Med
Goal: 4

This is an example of what type of test? ______________________

Questions 149-154 refer to the following:
A nationwide survey of college students was conducted and found that students spend two hours per class hour studying. A professor at your college wants to determine whether the time students spend at your college is significantly different from the two hours. A random sample of fifteen statistics students is carried out and the findings indicate an average of 1.75 hours with a standard deviation of 0.24 hours. The *t*-test is to be conducted at the 5% level of significance.

10-149
Med
Goal: 4

What is H_0? _______________________

10-150
Med
Goal: 4

What is H_1? _______________________

10-151
Med
Goal: 4

What is the critical value of *t*? ______________

10-152
Hard
Goal: 4

What is the calculated value of *t*? ______________

10-153
Hard
Goal: 4

What is our decision? ______________

10-154
Med
Goal: 4

This is an example of what type of test? ________________________

Questions 155-162 refer to the following:
One of the major U.S. tire makers wishes to review its warranty for their rainmaker tire. The warranty is for 40,000 miles. The tire company believes that the tire actually more than 40,000 miles. A sample 49 tires revealed that the mean number of miles is 45,000 miles with a standard deviation of 15,000 miles. Test the hypothesis with a 0.05 significance level.

10-155
Med
Goal: 4

What is H_0? ______________________

10-156
Med
Goal: 4

What is H_1? ______________________

10-157
Med
Goal: 4

What is the decision rule ? ______________

10-158
Hard
Goal: 4

What is the calculated value of *t*? ______________

10-159
Hard
Goal: 4

What is our decision? ______________

10-160
Med
Goal: 4

This is an example of what type of test? ______________________

10-161
Hard
Goal: 7

If the actual true tire mileage is 42,000 miles, what is the probability of a Type II error? ____________________

10-162
Hard
Goal: 7

If the actual true tire mileage is 45,000 miles, what is the probability of a Type II error? ____________________

Answers to Fill-In Questions

Chapter 10. One Sample Tests of Hypothesis

10-83 increases

10-84 state the null and alternative hypotheses

10-85 ± 2.120

10-86 +3.499

10-87 – 2.861

10-88 ± 1.533

10-89 standard normal distribution

10-90 research hypothesis

10-91 Significance level

10-92 alpha

10-93 Type I

10-94 Type II

10-95 Critical value

10-96 Reject H_0

10-97 One-tail test

10-98 Two-tail test

10-99 hypothesis

10-100 false

10-101 reject H_0

10-102 number of successes

10-103 proportion of successes

10-104 sample proportion

10-108 $\pi \geq 0.01$

10-109 $\pi < 0.01$

10-110 $z = -2.33$

10-111 $z = +2.25$

10-112 –2.06

10-113 Fail to reject

10-114 Reject

10-115 Reject

10-116 Reject

10-143 $\mu \leq 200$

10-144 $\mu > 200$

10-145 + 1.796

10-146 + 5.77

10-147 reject

10-148 One-tail hypothesis test

10-149 $\mu = 2$

10-150 $\mu \neq 2$

10-151 ± 2.145

10-152 –4.03

10-153 reject

10-154 two-tailed test

10-155 $\mu \leq 40{,}000$

10-156 $\mu > 40{,}000$

10-157 Reject if $Z > 1.65$

10-158 +2.33

10-159 Reject

10-160 One-tail test

10-161 Type II error = 0.7611

10-162 Type II error = 0.2483

Chapter 11. Tests of Hypothesis: Two samples

TRUE/FALSE QUESTIONS

11-1 F
Easy
Goal: 2

If the null hypothesis states that there is no difference between the mean income of males and the mean income of females, then the test is one-tailed.

11-2 T
Easy
Goal: 2

If we are testing for the difference between two population means, it is assumed that the sample observations from one population are independent of the sample observations from the other population.

11-3 T
Easy
Goal: 2

If we are testing for the difference between two population means, it is assumed that the two populations are approximately normal and have equal variances.

11-4 F
Easy
Goal: 2

When sample sizes are less than 30, a test for the differences between two population means has $n-1$ degrees of freedom.

11-5 T
Easy
Goal: 5

If samples taken from two populations are not independent, then a test of paired differences is applied.

11-6 F
Easy
Goal: 5

The paired difference test has $(n_1 + n_2 - 2)$ degrees of freedom.

11-7 T
Med
Goal: 4

We use the pooled estimate of the proportion in testing the difference between two population proportions.

11-8 F
Med
Goal: 4

The pooled estimate of the proportion is found by dividing the total number of samples by the total number of successes.

11-9 F
Easy
Goal: 5

The paired t test is especially appropriate for when the sample sizes of two groups are the same.

11-10 F
Hard
Goal: 4

A committee studying employer-employee relations proposed that each employee would rate his or her immediate supervisor and in turn the supervisor would rate each employee. To find reactions regarding the proposal, 120 office personnel and 160 plant personnel were selected at random. Seventy-eight of the office personnel and 90 of the plant personnel were in favor of the proposal. Computed $z = 1.48$. At the 0.05 level, it was concluded that there is sufficient evidence to support the belief that the proportion of office personnel in favor of the proposal is greater than that of the plant personnel.

11-11 F
Easy
Goal: 5

A statistic professor wants to compare grades of two different groups of students taking the same course in two different sections. This is an example of a paired sample.

MULTIPLE CHOICE QUESITONS

11-12 B
Hard
Goal: 4

If the decision is to reject the null hypothesis at the 5% level of significance, what are the acceptable alternate hypothesis and rejection region?

A. $\pi_1 \neq \pi_2$; $z > 1.65$ and $z < -1.65$
B. $\pi_1 \neq \pi_2$; $z > 1.96$ and $z < -1.96$
C. $\pi_1 > \pi_2$; $z < -1.65$
D. $\pi_1 > \pi_2$; $z < -1.96$
E. None of the above

11-13 D
Med
Goal: 4

A poll of 400 people from Dobbs Ferry showed 250 preferred chocolate raspberry coffee while 170 out of 350 in Irvington preferred the same flavor. To test the hypothesis that there is no difference in preferences in the two villages, what is the alternate hypothesis?

A. $\pi_1 < \pi_2$
B. $\pi_1 > \pi_2$
C. $\pi_1 = \pi_2$
D. $\pi_1 \neq \pi_2$
E. None of the above

11-14 C
Med
Goal: 2

If the null hypothesis that two means are equal is true, where will 97% of the computed *z*-values lie between?

A. ± 2.58
B. ± 2.33
C. ± 2.17
D. ± 2.07
E. None of the above

11-15 A
Med
Goal: 4

How is a pooled estimate represented?

A. p_c
B. z
C. π
D. $n\pi$
E. None of the above

11-16 B
Med
Goal: 4

Suppose we are testing the difference between two proportions at the 0.05 level of significance. If the computed *z* is –1.07, what is our decision?

A. Reject the null hypothesis
B. Do not reject the null hypothesis
C. Take a larger sample
D. Reserve judgment
E. None of the above

11-17 E
Hard
Goal: 3

The net weights of a sample of bottles filled by a machine manufactured by Edne, and the net weights of a sample filled by a similar machine manufactured by Orno, Inc., are (in grams):

Edne: 5, 8, 7, 6, 9 and 7

Orno: 8, 10, 7, 11, 9, 12, 14 and 9

Testing the claim at the 0.05 level the mean weight of the bottles filled by the Orno machine is greater than the mean weight of the bottles filled by the Edne machine, what is the critical value?

A. −1.96
B. −2.837
C. −6.271
D. +3.674
E. None of the above

11-18 D
Med
Goal: 2

Which of the following conditions must be met to conduct a test for the difference in two sample means?

A. Data must be at least of interval scale
B. Populations must be normal
C. Variances in the two populations must be equal
D. All the above are correct
E. None of the above are correct

11-19 D
Med
Goal: 5

When is it appropriate to use the paired difference *t*-test?

A. Four samples are compared at once
B. Any two samples are compared
C. Two independent samples are compared
D. Two dependent samples are compared
E. None of the above is correct

11-20 B
Med
Goal: 5

Using two independent samples, two population means are compared to determine if a difference exists. The number in the first sample is fifteen and the number in the second sample is twelve. How many degrees of freedom are associated with the critical value?

A. 24
B. 25
C. 26
D. 27
E. None of the above

11-21 B
Med
Goal: 2

Administering the same test to a group of 15 students and a second group of 15 students to see which group scores higher is an example of

A. a one sample test of means.
B. a two sample test of means.
C. a paired *t*-test.
D. a test of proportions.
E. none of the above.

11-22 B
Med
Goal: 3

What is the critical value for a one-tailed hypothesis test in which a null hypothesis is tested at the 5% level of significance based on two samples, both sample sizes are 13?

A. 1.708
B. 1.711
C. 2.060
D. 2.064
E. None of the above

11-23 A
Hard
Goal: 5

If two samples are used in a hypothesis test for which the combined degrees of freedom is 24, which one of the following is NOT true about the two sample sizes?

A. Sample A = 11; sample B = 13
B. Sample A = 12; sample B = 14
C. Sample A = 13; sample B = 13
D. Sample A = 10; sample B = 16
E. Cannot determine from the above information

11-24 E
Hard
Goal: 5

If two samples are used in a hypothesis test for which the combined degrees of freedom is 27, which one of the following is true about the two sample sizes?

A. Sample A = 14; sample B = 13
B. Sample A = 12; sample B = 13
C. Sample A = 15; sample B = 14
D. Sample A = 20; sample B = 9
E. Cannot determine from the above information

11-25 C
Med
Goal: 5

A random sample of 20 statistics students were given 15 multiple-choice questions and 15 open-ended questions – all on the same material. The professor was interested in determining which type of questions the students scored higher. This experiment is an example of

A. a one sample test of means.
B. a two sample test of means.
C. a paired *t*-test.
D. a test of proportions.
E. none of the above

FILL-IN QUESTIONS

11-26
Med
Goal: 3

What is the critical value of t for a two-tail test of the difference of two means, a level of significance of 0.10 and sample sizes of seven and fifteen? _________

11-27
Med
Goal: 3

What is the critical value of t for the claim that the difference of two means is less than zero with $\alpha = 0.025$ and sample sizes of nine and seven? _________

Questions 28-29 refer to the following:
Of 250 adults who tried a new multi-grain cereal, Wow!, 187 rated it excellent; of 100 children sampled, 66 rated it excellent.

11-28 C
Med
Goal: 3

Using the 0.1 significance level and the alternate hypothesis π_1 not equal to π_2, what is the null hypothesis?

A. $\pi_1 > \pi_2$
B. $\pi_1 < \pi_2$
C. $\pi_1 = \pi_2$
D. None of the above

11-29 A
Med
Goal: 4

What test statistic should we use?

A. *z*-statistic
B. Right one-tailed test
C. Left one-tailed test
D. Two-tailed test
E. None of the above

Questions 30-37 refer to the following:
A national manufacturer of ball bearings is experimenting with two different processes for producing precision ball bearings. It is important that the diameters be as close as possible to an industry standard. The output from each process is sampled and the average error from the industry standard is calculated. The results are presented below.

	Process A	*Process B*
Mean	0.002mm	0.0026mm
Standard Deviation	0.0001mm	0.00012mm
Sample Size	12	14

The researcher is interested in determining whether there is evidence that the two processes yields different average errors from the industry standard.

11-30 A
Med
Goal: 2

The researcher is interested in determining whether there is evidence that the two processes yields different average errors from the industry standard.
What is the null hypothesis?

A. $\mu_A = \mu_B$
B. $\mu_A \neq \mu_B$
C. $\mu_A \leq \mu_B$
D. $\mu_A > \mu_B$
E. None of the above

11-31 B
Med
Goal: 2

What is the alternate hypothesis?

A. $\mu_A = \mu_B$
B. $\mu_A \neq \mu_B$
C. $\mu_A \leq \mu_B$
D. $\mu_A > \mu_B$
E. None of the above

11-32 D
Med
Goal: 3

What is the degrees of freedom?

A. 10
B. 13
C. 26
D. 24
E. None of the above.

11-33 D
Med
Goal: 3

What is the critical *t* value at the 1% level of significance?

A. +2.779
B. –2.492
C. ±1.711
D. ±2.797
E. None of the above.

11-34 C
Hard
Goal: 3

What is the computed value of *t*?

A. +2.797
B. –2.797
C. –13.70
D. +13.70
E. None of the above.

11-35 A
Hard
Goal: 3

What is the decision at the 1% level of significance?

A. Reject the null hypothesis and conclude the means are different.
B. Reject the null hypothesis and conclude the means are the same.
C. Fail to reject the null hypothesis and conclude the means are the same.
D. Fail to reject the null hypothesis and conclude the means are different.
E. None of the above.

11-36 C
Hard
Goal: 3

Assume calculated *t* to be +2.70, at the 0.01 level of significance what would be the decision?

A. Reject the null hypothesis and conclude the means are different.
B. Reject the null hypothesis and conclude the means are the same.
C. Fail to reject the null hypothesis and conclude the means are the same.
D. Fail to reject the null hypothesis and conclude the means are different.
E. None of the above.

11-37 B
Med
Goal: 3

This example is what type of test?

A. One sample test of means.
B. Two sample test of means.
C. Paired *t*-test.
D. Test of proportions.
E. None of the above

Questions 38-40 refer to the following:
The results of a mathematics placement exam at Mercy College for two campuses is as follows:

Campus	*Number*	*Mean*	*Std. Deviation*
1	330	33	8
2	310	31	7

11-38 E
Med
Goal: 2

What is the null hypothesis if we want to test the hypothesis that the mean score on Campus 1 is higher than on Campus 2?

A. $\mu_1 = 0$
B. $\mu_2 = 0$
C. $\mu_1 = \mu_2$
D. $\mu_1 > \mu_2$
E. None of the above

11-39 C
Hard
Goal: 2

What is the computed value of the test statistic?

A. 9.3
B. 2.6
C. 3.4
D. 1.9
E. None of the above

11-40 B
Med
Goal: 4

What is the p-value if the computed test statistic is 4.1?

A. 1.0
B. 0.0
C. 0.05
D. 0.95
E. None of the above

Questions 41-44 refer to the following:
A study by a bank compared the average savings of customers who were depositors for three years or less, with those who had been depositors for more than three years. The results of a sample are:

	$\leq$ 3 Years	> 3 Years
Mean Savings Balance	$1,200	$1,250
Standard Deviation	$100	$250
Sample Size	100	150

11-41
Med
Goal: 4

Assuming that the financial officer wants to show that there is a difference in the average savings balance between the two classes of depositors, what is the null hypothesis? ____________________

11-42
Hard
Goal: 2

For $\alpha = 0.05$, what is the critical value of z? __________

11-43
Hard
Goal: 2

What is the computed test statistic? ______________

11-44
Hard
Goal: 2

What is the p-value if α = .05 and the test statistic is 3.15? _____

Questions 45-51 refer to the following:
Accounting procedures allow a business to evaluate their inventory at LIFO (Last In First Out) or FIFO (First In First Out). A manufacturer evaluated its finished goods inventory (in $ thousands) for five products both ways. Based on the following results, is LIFO more effective in keeping the value of his inventory lower?

Product	*FIFO (F)*	*LIFO (L)*
1	225	221
2	119	100
3	100	113
4	212	200
5	248	245

11-45 C
Med
Goal: 5

What is the null hypothesis?
A. $\mu_F = \mu_L$
B. $\mu_F \neq \mu_L$
C. $\mu_F \leq \mu_L$
D. $\mu_F > \mu_L$
E. None of the above

11-46 D
Med
Goal: 5

What is the alternate hypothesis?
A. $\mu_F = \mu_L$
B. $\mu_F \neq \mu_L$
C. $\mu_F \leq \mu_L$
D. $\mu_F > \mu_L$
E. None of the above

11-47 A
Med
Goal: 5

What is the degrees of freedom?
A. 4
B. 5
C. 15
D. 10
E. 9

11-48 E
Med
Goal: 5

If you use the 5% level of significance, what is the critical t value?
A. +2.571
B. ±2.776
C. +2.262
D. ±2.228
E. None of the above.

11-49 A
Hard
Goal: 5

What is the value of calculated *t*?

A. +1.93
B. ±2.776
C. +0.0.47
D. –2.028
E. None of the above.

11-50 D
Hard
Goal: 5

What is the decision at the 5% level of significance?

A. Fail to reject the null hypothesis and conclude LIFO is more effective.
B. Reject the null hypothesis and conclude LIFO is more effective.
C. Reject the alternate hypothesis and conclude LIFO is more effective.
D. Fail to reject the null hypothesis and conclude LIFO is not more effective.
E. None of the above.

11-51 C
Med
Goal: 5

This example is what type of test?

A. One sample test of means.
B. Two sample test of means.
C. Paired *t*-test.
D. Test of proportions.
E. None of the above

Questions 52-60 refer to the following:
To compare the effect of weather on sales of soft drinks, a soda manufacturer sampled two regions of the country with the following results. Is there a difference in sales between the 2 regions?

	Region A	*Region B*
Sample Size	1000	1500
Sales	400	500

11-52
Med
Goal: 5

What is the null hypothesis? ____________________

11-53
Med
Goal: 5

What is the alternate hypothesis? ____________________

11-54
Easy
Goal: 5

What is the proportion of sales made in Market Area 1? ______

11-55
Easy
Goal: 5

What is the proportion of sales made in Market Area 2? ______

11-56
Hard
Goal: 5

What is the pooled estimate of the population proportion? _______

11-57
Med
Goal: 5

Using the 1% level of significance, what is the critical value? _____

11-58
Hard
Goal: 5

What is the *z*-statistic? _____________

11-59
Med
Goal: 5

What is your decision?

____

11-60
Med
Goal: 5

What is your decision if $\alpha = 0.01$ and the *z*-statistic is –1.96?

____

Answers to Fill-In Questions

Chapter 11. Tests of Hypothesis: Two Samples

11-26 ± 1.734

11-27 -2.179

11-41 $\mu_{less} = \mu_{more}$

11-42 ± 1.96

11-43 11.00

11-44 Approximately 0.00

11-52 $\pi_a = \pi_b$

11-53 $\pi_a \neq \pi_b$

11-54 0.40

11-55 0.33

11-56 0.36

11-57 ± 2.58

11-58 3.57

11-59 Reject

11-60 Fail to reject

Chapter 12. Analysis of Variance

TRUE/FALSE QUESTIONS

12-1 T
Easy
Goal: 1

To employ ANOVA, the populations should have approximately equal standard deviations.

12-2 T
Easy
Goal: 2

One characteristic of the *F* distribution is that *F* cannot be negative.

12-3 F
Easy
Goal: 2

One characteristic of the *F* distribution is that computed *F* can only range between –1 and +1.

12-4 T
Easy
Goal: 2

The *F* distribution is positively skewed and its values may range from 0 to plus infinity.

12-5 T
Med
Goal: 2

The shape of the *F* distribution is determined by the degrees of freedom for the *F*-statistic, one for the numerator and one for the denominator.

12-6 F
Easy
Goal: 2

Unlike Student's *t* distribution, there is only one *F* distribution.

12-7 T
Easy
Goal: 2

Like Student's *t* distribution, a change in the degrees of freedom causes a change in the shape of the F distribution.

12-8 F
Med
Goal: 5

For the population means, the alternate hypothesis used in the analysis of variance test states that $\mu_1 = \mu_2 = \mu_3$.

12-9 T
Med
Goal: 6

The alternate hypothesis for ANOVA states that not all the means are equal.

12-10 T
Med
Goal: 6

For an ANOVA test, rejection of the null hypothesis does not identify which populations differ significantly.

12-11 T
Med
Goal: 5

A treatment is a specific source or cause of variation in a set of data.

12-12 T
Med
Goal: 2

The *F* distribution's curve is positively skewed.

12-13 T
Med
Goal: 2

There is one, unique *F* distribution for a F-statistic with 29 degrees of freedom in the numerator and 28 degrees of freedom in the denominator.

12-14 F
Med
Goal: 6

If the computed value of *F* is 4.01 and the critical value is 2.67, we would conclude that all the population means are equal.

12-15 F
Med
Goal: 6

If the computed value of *F* is 11.1 and the 0.05 level is used, we would assume that a mistake in arithmetic has been made.

12-16 T
Med
Goal: 3

If the computed value of *F* is 0.99 and the critical value is 3.89, we would not reject the null hypothesis.

12-17 F
Med
Goal: 4

In ANOVA, *k* represents the total number of sample observations and *n* represents the total number of treatments.

12-18 T
Easy
Goal: 7

If we want to determine which treatment means differ, one method is confidence intervals.

12-19 T
Med
Goal: 7

If the confidence interval includes 0, there is no difference in the pair of treatment means.

12-20 F
Med
Goal: 7

If both end points of a confidence interval are of the same sign, it indicates that the treatment means are not different.

12-21 T
Easy
Goal: 1

To employ ANOVA, the populations being studied must be approximately normally distributed.

12-22 F
Easy
Goal: 2

The test statistic used in ANOVA is *Student's t*.

MULTIPLE CHOICE QUESTIONS

12-23 C
Med
Goal: 4

A large department store examined a sample of the 18 credit card sales and recorded the amounts charged for each of three types of credit cards: MasterCard, Visa and Discover. Six MasterCard sales, seven Visa and five Discover sales were recorded. The store used ANOVA to test if the mean sales for each credit card were equal. What are the degrees of freedom for the *F* statistic?

A. 18 in the numerator, 3 in the denominator
B. 3 in the numerator, 18 in the denominator
C. 2 in the numerator, 15 in the denominator
D. 0 in the numerator, 15 in the denominator
E. None of the above

12-24 B
Med
Goal: 4

Suppose that an automobile manufacturer designed a radically new lightweight engine and wants to recommend the grade of gasoline to use. The four grades are: below regular, regular, premium, and super premium. The test car made three trial runs on the test track using each of the four grades. Assuming any grade can be used at the 0.05 level, what is the critical value of *F*?

Kilometers per liter

Below Regular	*Regular*	*Premium*	*Super Premium*
39.31	36.69	38.99	40.04
39.87	40.00	40.02	39.89
39.87	41.01	39.99	39.93

A. 1.96
B. 4.07
C. 2.33
D. 12.00
E. None of the above

12-25 C
Easy
Goal: 4

In ANOVA, a *F statistic* is used to test a null hypothesis such as:

A. H_o: $\sigma^2_1 = \sigma^2_2 = \sigma^2_3$
B. H_o: $\sigma^2_1 \neq \sigma^2_2 \neq \sigma^2_3$
C. H_o: $\mu_1 = \mu_2 = \mu_3$
D. H_o: $\mu_1 \neq \mu_2 \neq \mu_2$
E. None of the above

12-26 B
Easy
Goal: 2

A *F statistic* is:

A. a ratio of two means.
B. a ratio of two variances.
C. the difference between three means.
D. a population parameter.

12-27 B
Easy
Goal: 7

In a two-way ANOVA, a blocking variable is used to
A. increase the error sum of squares.
B. decrease the error sum of squares.
C. increase the treatment sum of squares.
D. decrease the treatment sum of squares.

12-28 D
Easy
Goal: 6

An electronics company wants to compare the quality of their cell phones to the cell phones from three competitors. They sample 10 phones from each company and count the number of defects for each phone. If ANOVA is used to compare the average number of defects, the treatments would be defined as:
A. the number of cell phones sampled.
B. the average number of defects.
C. The total number of phones
D. The four companies.

12-29 C
Med
Goal: 4

Three different fertilizers were applied to a field of celery. In computing *F*, how many degrees of freedom are there in the numerator?
A. 0
B. 1
C. 2
D. 3
E. None of the above

12-30 C
Med
Goal: 4

Suppose a package delivery company purchased 14 trucks at the same time. Five trucks were purchased from manufacturer A, four from B and five from manufacturer C. The cost of maintaining each truck was recorded. The company used ANOVA to test if the mean maintenance cost for trucks from each manufacturer were equal. To apply the *F* test, how many degrees of freedom are in the denominator?
A. 2
B. 3
C. 11
D. 14
E. None of the above

12-31 B
Med
Goal: 6

Several employees have submitted different methods of assembling a subassembly. Sample data for each method are:

Minutes Required for Assembly

Sample Number	*Lind's Method*	*Szabo's Method*	*Carl's Method*	*Manley's Method*
1	16.6	22.4	31.4	18.4
2	17.0	21.5	33.4	19.6
3	16.9	22.6	30.1	17.6

How many treatments are there?

A. 3
B. 4
C. 12
D. 0
E. None of the above

12-32 D
Med
Goal: 4

In an effort to determine the most effective way to teach safety principles to a group of employees, four different methods were tried. Some employees were given programmed instruction booklets and worked through the course at their own pace. Other employees attended lectures. A third group watched a television presentation, and a fourth group was divided into small discussion groups. A high of 10 was possible. A sample of five tests were selected from each group. The test grade results were:

Sample Number	*Programmed Instruction*	*Lecture*	*TV*	*Group Discussion*
1	6	8	7	8
2	7	5	9	5
3	6	8	6	6
4	5	6	8	6
5	6	8	5	5

At the 0.01 level, what is the critical value?

A. 1.00
B. 1.96
C. 3.24
D. 5.29
E. None of the above

12-33 B
Med
Goal: 2

What distribution does the *F* distribution approach as the sample size increases?

A. Binomial
B. Normal
C. Poisson
D. Exponential
E. None of these is correct

12-34 A
Med
Goal: 2

Which statement is correct about the *F* distribution?
A. Cannot be negative
B. Cannot be positive
C. Is the same as the *t* distribution
D. Is the same as the *z* distribution
E. None of these is correct

12-35 C
Med
Goal: 6

If an ANOVA test is conducted and the null hypothesis is rejected, what does this indicate?
A. Too many degrees of freedom
B. No difference between the population means
C. A difference between at least one pair of population means
D. None of the above

12-36 B
Med
Goal: 6

A preliminary study of hourly wages paid to unskilled employees in three metropolitan areas was conducted. Seven employees were included from Area A, 9 from Area B and 12 from Area C. The test statistic was computed to be 4.91. What can we conclude at the 0.05 level?
A. Mean hourly wages of unskilled employees all areas are equal
B. Mean hourly wages in at least 2 metropolitan areas are different
C. More degrees of freedom are needed
D. None of these is correct

12-37 A
Med
Goal: 2

In ANOVA analysis, when the null hypothesis is rejected, we can find which means are different by
A. constructing confidence intervals.
B. adding another treatment.
C. doing an additional ANOVA.
D. doing a *t* test.
E. none of the above.

12-38 D
Med
Goal: 1

Analysis of variance is used to
A. compare nominal data.
B. compute *t* test.
C. compare population proportion.
D. simultaneously compare several population means.
E. none of the above.

FILL-IN QUESITONS

12-39
Med
Goal: 1

The samples should be randomly selected to employ ANOVA and the populations should be ______________ and ________________.

12-40
Easy
Goal: 1

A technique that is efficient when simultaneously comparing more than two population means is known as ____________________.

12-41
Easy
Goal: 2

What is the test statistic used in ANOVA? ________________

12-42
Med
Goal: 1

What is the least number of sources of variation in ANOVA? _________

12-43
Med
Goal: 6

What does not rejecting the null hypothesis in ANOVA indicate about the population means? ________________

12-44
Med
Goal: 2

The calculated *F* value must be equal to or greater than? _________

12-45
Med
Goal: 4

What is the difference between the total number of observations and the number of treatments defined as? ___________

12-46
Med
Goal: 2

What is the shape of the *F* distribution?______________________

12-47
Med
Goal: 4

In ANOVA, how many degrees of freedom are associated with the numerator of the *F* ratio?

12-48
Hard
Goal: 4

What is the sum of squares divided by its corresponding degrees of freedom equal? _________________

12-49
Med
Goal: 6

What is the null hypothesis for an ANOVA? ____________________

12-50
Easy
Goal: 1

What is the statistical technique used to test the equality of three or more population means called? ______________________

12-51
Med
Goal: 2

What kind of values can the *F* distribution not have? ______________

12-52
Med
Goal: 1

The *F* distribution is a ______________ distribution.

12-53
Med
Goal: 4

In ANOVA, what is the numerator of the *F* ratio called? ____________

12-54
Med
Goal: 4

In which tail of the *F* distribution is the rejection region for analysis of variance? ________

12-55
Med
Goal: 3

When comparing two population variances we use the ___________ distribution.

12-56
Med
Goal: 5

When a second treatment is included in the ANOVA analysis, that treatment is called a _________________.

12-57
Med
Goal: 7

When doing ANOVA analysis and H_0 is rejected, the means which are different can be identified by constructing ______________________.

Questions 58-67 refer to the following:
A manufacturer of automobile transmissions uses three different processes. The management ordered a study of the production costs to see if there is a difference among the three processes. A summary of the findings is shown below.

	Process 1	*Process 2*	*Process 3*	*Total*
Process Totals ($ 100's)	137	108	107	352
Sample Size	10	10	10	30
Sum of Squares	1893	1188	1175	4256

12-58 B
Hard
Goal: 4

What is the sum of squares for the treatment?
A. 67.80
B. 58.07
C. 149.34
D. 23.47
E. None of the above

12-59 A
Hard
Goal: 4

What is the sum of squares of the error?
A. 67.80
B. 58.07
C. 149.34
D. 23.47
E. None of the above

12-60 C
Hard
Goal: 6

What is the critical value of F at the 5% level of significance?

A. 19.45
B. 3.00
C. 3.35
D. 3.39
E. None of the above

12-61 B
Hard
Goal: 6

What is the critical value of F at the 1% level of significance?

A. 99.46
B. 5.49
C. 5.39
D. 4.61
E. None of the above

12-62 A
Med
Goal: 4

What are the degrees of freedom for the numerator of the F ratio?

A. 2
B. 3
C. 10
D. 27
E. None of the above

12-63 C
Med
Goal: 4

What is the degrees of freedom for the denominator?

A. 3
B. 10
C. 27
D. 30
E. None of the above

12-64 C
Med
Goal: 4

What is the total degrees of freedom?

A. 27
B. 28
C. 29
D. 30
E. None of the above

12-65 D
Hard
Goal: 4

What is the mean square for treatments?

A. 2.511
B. 2.151
C. 33.9
D. 29.035
E. None of the above

12-66 A
Hard
Goal: 4

What is the mean square for error?

A. 2.511
B. 2.151
C. 33.9
D. 29.035
E. None of the above

12-67 C
Hard
Goal: 4

What is the calculated *F*?

A. 0.086
B. 1.168
C. 11.56
D. 13.50
E. None of the above

Questions 68-77 refer to the following:
In a study of low tar cigarettes, five cigarettes from each of three brands were tested to see if the mean amount of tar per cigarette differs among the brands.

12-68
Med
Goal: 4

What is the degrees of freedom for the numerator? ______

12-69
Med
Goal: 4

What is the degrees of freedom for the denominator? ______

12-70
Hard
Goal: 4

If the sum of squares for the brands is 0.07, what is the mean square for brands? ______

12-71
Hard
Goal: 4

If the sum of squares for the error is 0.09, what is the mean square for the error? ______

12-72
Med
Goal: 6

What is the *F* critical value for $\alpha = 0.05$? ______

12-73
Hard
Goal: 4

What is the calculated value of *F* if SS brands is 0.07 and SS error is 0.09? ______

12-74
Hard
Goal: 6

If *F* calculated is 4.75 what is the decision if $\alpha = 0.05$? __________

12-75
Med
Goal: 6

If the calculated *F* is 4.74, what would the decision be if $\alpha = 0.01$?

____

12-76
Hard
Goal: 6

If the sum of squares for the brands is 0.05 and the sum of squares for the error is 0.09, what is the decision rule if $\alpha = 0.05$?

____

12-77
Hard
Goal: 6

If the sum of squares for the brands is 0.07 and the sum of squares for the error is 0.11, what is the decision rule at $\alpha = 0.05$?

____

Questions 78-82 refer to the following:
Given the following Analysis of Variance table for three treatments each with six observations.

Source	Sum of Squares	df	Mean Square
Treatments	1116		
Error	1068		
Total	2184		

12-78 D
Med
Goal: 4

What are the degrees of freedom for the numerator and denominator?

A. 3 and 18
B. 2 and 17
C. 3 and 15
D. 2 and 15
E. None of the above

12-79 C
Med
Goal: 4

What is the critical value of *F* at the 5% level of significance?

A. 3.29
B. 3.68
C. 3.59
D. 3.20
E. None of the above

12-80 C
Hard
Goal: 4

What is the mean square for treatments?

A. 71.2
B. 71.4
C. 558
D. 534
E. None of the above

12-81 B
Hard
Goal: 4

What is the computed value of *F*?

A. 7.48
B. 7.84
C. 8.84
D. 8.48
E. None of the above

12-82 A
Hard
Goal: 6

What is the decision?

A. Reject H_0 -- there is a difference in treatments
B. Fail to reject H_0 -- there is a difference in treatments
C. Reject H_0 -- there is a difference in errors
D. Fail to reject H_0 -- there is a difference in errors
E. None of the above

Questions 83-94 refer to the following:
A bottle cap manufacture with four machines and six operators wants to see if variation in production is due to the machines and/or the operators. Each operator is assigned to each machine with the following Analysis of Variance table.

Source	Sum of Squares	df	Mean Square
Machines	114		
Operators	215		
Error	54		
Total	383		

12-83
Med
Goal: 4

What are the degrees of freedom for the machines? ______

12-84
Med
Goal: 4

What is the degrees of freedom for the operators? _____

12-85
Med
Goal: 4

What is the degrees of freedom for the errors? _____

12-86
Med
Goal: 6

What is the critical value of *F* for the machines at the 1% level of significance? ____

12-87
Med
Goal: 6

What is the critical value of *F* for the operators at the 1% level of significance? ____

12-88
Hard
Goal: 4

What is the mean square for machines? _____

12-89
Hard
Goal: 4

What is the mean square for operators? _____

12-90
Hard
Goal: 4

What is the mean square for errors? _____

12-91
Hard
Goal: 4

What is the computed value of *F* for the machines? _____

12-92
Hard
Goal: 4

What is the computed value of F for the operators? _____

12-93
Hard
Goal: 6

What is the decision for the machines? ______________________________

12-94
Hard
Goal: 6

What is the decision for the operators? ______________________________

Questions 95-103 refer to the following:
Two accounting professors decided to compare the variation of their grading procedures. To accomplish this they each graded the same 10 exams with the following results:

	Mean Grade	*Std Dev*
Professor 1	79.3	22.4
Professor 2	82.1	12.0

12-95 A
Med
Goal: 3

What is H_0?
A. $\sigma^2_1 = \sigma^2_2$
B. $\sigma^2_1 \neq \sigma^2_2$
C. $\mu_1 = \mu_2$
D. $\mu_1 \neq \mu_2$
E. None of the above

12-96 B
Med
Goal: 3

What is H_1?
A. $\sigma^2_1 = \sigma^2_2$
B. $\sigma^2_1 \neq \sigma^2_2$
C. $\mu_1 = \mu_2$
D. $\mu_1 \neq \mu_2$
E. None of the above

12-97 B
Med
Goal: 3

What are the degrees of freedom for the numerator of the F ratio?
A. 8
B. 9
C. 10
D. 18
E. 20

12-98 D
Med
Goal: 3

What are the degrees of freedom for the denominator of the F ratio?
A. 20
B. 18
C. 10
D. 9
E. 8

12-99 B
Med
Goal: 3

What is the critical value of F at the 0.01 level of significance?

A. 5.85
B. 5.35
C. 6.51
D. 4.03
E. None of the above

12-100 C
Med
Goal: 3

What is the critical value of F at the 0.05 level of significance?

A. 5.85
B. 5.35
C. 3.18
D. 4.03
E. None of the above

12-101 A
Hard
Goal: 3

The calculated F ratio is

A. 3.484
B. 1.867
C. 3.18
D. 5.35
E. None of the above

12-102 D
Hard
Goal: 3

At the 1% level of significance, what if the decision?

A. Reject the null hypothesis and conclude the variance is different.
B. Fail to reject the null hypothesis and conclude the variance is different.
C. Reject the null hypothesis and conclude the variance is the same.
D. Fail to reject the null hypothesis and conclude the variance is the same.
E. None of the above

12-103 A
Hard
Goal: 3

At the 5% level of significance, what if the decision?

A. Reject the null hypothesis and conclude the variance is different.
B. Fail to reject the null hypothesis and conclude no significant difference in the variance.
C. Reject the null hypothesis and conclude the variance is the same.
D. Fail to reject the null hypothesis and conclude the variance is the same.
E. None of the above

Questions 104-107 refer to the following:
A random sample of 30 executives from companies with assets over $1 million was selected and asked for their annual income and level of education. The ANOVA comparing the average income among three levels of education rejected the null hypothesis. The Mean Square Error (MSE) was 243.7. The following table summarized the results:

	High School or less	Undergraduate degree	Master's Degree of More
Number sampled	7	11	12
Mean salary (1,000's)	49	76.3	78.3

12-104 C
Med
Goal: 7

When comparing the mean salaries to test for differences between treatment means, the *t statistic* based on:

A. The treatment degrees of freedom.
B. The total degrees of freedom.
C. The error degrees of freedom
D. The ratio of treatment and error degrees of freedom

12-105 A
Hard
Goal: 7

When comparing the mean annual incomes for executives with Undergraduate and Master's Degree or more, the following 95% confidence interval can be constructed:

A. $2.0 \pm 2.052*6.51$
B. $2.0 \pm 3.182*6.51$
C. $2.0 \pm 2.052*42.46$
D. None of the above

12-106 A
Med
Goal: 7

Based on the comparison between the mean annual incomes for executives with Undergraduate and Master's Degree or more,

A. A confidence interval shows that the mean annual incomes are not significantly different.
B. The ANOVA results show that the mean annual incomes are significantly different.
C. A confidence interval shows that the mean annual incomes are significantly different.
D. The ANOVA results show that the mean annual incomes are not significantly different.

12-107 C
Hard
Goal: 7

When comparing the mean annual incomes for executives with a High School education or less and Undergraduate Degree, the 95% confidence interval shows an interval of 11.7 to 42.7 for the difference. This result indicates that

A. There is no significant difference between the two incomes.
B. The interval contains a difference of zero.
C. Executives with and Undergraduate Degree earn significantly more than executives with a High School education or less.
D. Executives with and Undergraduate Degree earn significantly less than executives with a High School education or less.

Answers to Fill-In Questions

Chapter 12. Analysis of Variance

12-39 normal and independent

12-40 analysis of variance (ANOVA)

12-41 *F*

12-42 two

12-43 they are equal

12-44 zero (0)

12-45 $n - k$

12-46 Positively skewed

12-47 $k - 1$

12-48 mean square

12-49 $\mu_1 = \mu_2 = \mu_3$

12-50 analysis of variance (ANOVA)

12-51 negative values

12-52 continuous

12-53 treatment mean square

12-54 upper

12-55 *F*

12-56 blocking variable

12-57 confidence intervals

12-68 2

12-69 12

12-70 0.035

12-71 0.0075

12-72 3.89

12-73 4.66

12-74 Reject H_0

12-75 Do not reject H_0

12-76 Do not reject H_0 since calculated F = 3.33 & $F(0.05) = 3.89$

12-77 Do not reject H_0 since calculated F = 3.88 & $F(0.05) = 3.89$

12-83 3

12-84 5

12-85 15

12-86 5.42

12-87 4.56

12-88 38

12-89 43

12-90 3.6

12-91 10.55

12-92 11.94

12-93 Reject H_0; there is no difference in the machines

12-94 Reject H_0; there is no difference in the operators

Chapter 13. Linear Regression and Correlation

TRUE/FALSE QUESTIONS

13-1 T
Easy
Goal: 3

Correlation analysis is a group of statistical techniques used to measure the strength of the relationship (correlation) between two variables.

13-2 T
Easy
Goal: 3

The purpose of correlation analysis is to find how strong the relationship is between two variables.

13-3 T
Easy
Goal: 1

A scatter diagram is a chart that portrays the relationship between two variables.

13-4 F
Easy
Goal: 2

There are two variables in correlation analysis referred to as the dependent and determination variables.

13-5 T
Easy
Goal: 3

Originated by Karl Pearson about 1900, the coefficient of correlation describes the strength of the relationship between two, interval or ratio-scaled variables.

13-6 F
Easy
Goal: 3

The coefficient of correlation r is often referred to as Spearman's rho.

13-7 T
Easy
Goal: 3

The coefficient of correlation r is often referred to as the Pearson product-moment correlation coefficient.

13-8 T
Easy
Goal: 3

A correlation coefficient of –1 or +1 indicates perfect correlation.

13-9 F
Easy
Goal: 3

The strength of the correlation between two variables depends on the sign of the coefficient of correlation.

13-10 T
Easy
Goal: 3

A coefficient of correlation r close to 0 (say, 0.08) shows that the relationship between two variables is quite weak.

13-11 T
Easy
Goal: 3

Coefficients of –0.91 and +0.91 have equal strength.

13-12 F
Easy
Goal: 1

If a scatter diagram shows very little scatter about a straight line drawn through the plots, it indicates a rather weak relationship.

13-13 T
Med
Goal: 4

The basic question in testing the significance of rho is to see if there is zero correlation in the population from which the sample was selected.

13-14 F
Easy
Goal: 5

One assumption underlying linear regression is that the *Y* values are statistically dependent. This means that in selecting a sample, the *Y* values chosen, for a particular *X* value, depend on the *Y* values for any other *X* value.

13-15 T
Easy
Goal: 3

The coefficient of correlation is a measure of the strength of relationship between two variables.

13-16 F
Easy
Goal: 3

A coefficient of correlation of –0.96 indicates a very weak negative correlation.

13-17 T
Easy
Goal: 3

The coefficient of determination is the proportion of the total variation in the dependent variable *Y* that is explained or accounted for by its relationship with the independent variable *X*.

13-18 F
Easy
Goal: 3

The coefficient of determination is found by taking the square root of the coefficient of correlation.

13-19 F
Med
Goal: 3

If the coefficient of correlation is –0.90, the coefficient of determination is –0.81.

13-20 T
Med
Goal: 3

If the coefficient of correlation is 0.68, the coefficient of determination is 0.4624.

13-21 F
Easy
Goal: 3

The coefficient of determination is the proportion of total variation in *Y* that is not explained by *X*.

13-22 T
Easy
Goal: 3

The coefficient of determination can only be positive.

13-23 T
Med
Goal: 4

A t - test is used to test the significance of the coefficient of correlation.

13-24 F
Med
Goal: 4

We use the *z* test for samples of 10 or more observations to test the significance of Pearson's *r*.

13-25 T
Med
Goal: 4

When testing the strength of the relationship between two variables, the null hypothesis is: H_0: $\rho = 0$.

13-26 T
Med
Goal: 4

When testing the strength of the relationship between two variables, the alternate hypothesis is: H_0: $\rho \neq 0$.

13-27 T
Easy
Goal: 3

Pearson's product-moment correlation coefficient *r* requires that the data be interval or ratio scaled, such as incomes and weights.

13-28 F
Easy
Goal: 3

Pearson's coefficient of correlation can be used if the data is nominally scaled.

13-29 F
Easy
Goal: 5

The technique used to measure the strength of the relationship between two sets of variables using the coefficient of correlation and the coefficient of determination is called regression analysis.

13-30 T
Easy
Goal: 5

In order to visualize the form of the regression equation, we can draw a scatter diagram.

13-31 T
Easy
Goal: 5

The equation for a straight line going through the plots on a scatter diagram is called a regression equation. It is alternately called an estimating equation and a predicting equation.

13-32 T
Med
Goal: 6

Trying to predict weekly sales with a standard error of estimate of $1,955, we would conclude that 68 percent of the predictions would not be off more than $1,955, 95 percent would not be off by more $3,910, and 99.7 percent would not be off by more than $5,865.

13-33 T
Easy
Goal: 5

A regression equation is a mathematical equation that defines the relationship between two variables.

13-34 T
Easy
Goal: 5

A regression equation may be determined using a mathematical method called the least squares principle.

13-35 T
Easy
Goal: 5

A line found using the least squares principle is the best-fitting line because the sum of the squares of the vertical deviations between the actual and estimated values is minimized.

13-36 T
Easy
Goal: 5

The least squares technique minimizes the sum of the squares of the vertical distances between the actual *Y* values and the predicted values of *Y*.

13-37 T
Easy
Goal: 5

The values of *a* and *b* in the regression equation are called the regression coefficients.

13-38 T
Med
Goal: 5

One assumption underlying linear regression is that for each value of *X* there is a group of *Y* values that is normally distributed.

13-39 T
Med
Goal: 6

The standard error of estimate is used to set confidence intervals when the sample size is large and the scatter about the regression line is somewhat normally distributed.

13-40 T
Med
Goal: 6

A confidence interval can be determined for the mean value of *Y* for a given value of *X*.

13-41 F
Med
Goal: 6

The smaller the sample, the smaller the possible error as measured by the standard error of estimate.

13-42 T
Med
Goal: 5

The regression equation is used to estimate a value of the dependent variable *Y* based on a selected value of the independent variable *X*.

13-43 T
Med
Goal: 3

The standard error of estimate measures the accuracy of our prediction.

13-44 T
Med
Goal: 3

In regression analysis, the predicted value of *Y'* rarely agrees exactly with the actual *Y* value, i.e., we expect some prediction error.

13-45 T
Easy
Goal: 3

Explained variation equals total variation minus unexplained variation.

13-46 T
Med
Goal: 2

An economist is interested in predicting the unemployment rate based on gross domestic product. Since the economist is interested in predicting unemployment, the independent variable is gross domestic product.

13-47 F
Med
Goal: 6

For a set of observations, there is no difference in the width of a confidence interval and the width of a predictor interval.

MULTIPLE CHOICE QUESTIONS

13-48 A
Med
Goal: 2

What is the variable used to predict the value of another called?
A. Independent
B. Dependent
C. Correlation
D. Determination
E. None of the above

13-49 D
Med
Goal: 3

Which of the following statements regarding the coefficient of correlation is true?
A. It ranges from –1.0 to +1.0 inclusive
B. It measures the strength of the relationship between two variables
C. A value of 0.00 indicates two variables are not related
D. All of the above
E. None of the above

13-50 D
Hard
Goal: 4

A hypothesis test is conducted at the .05 level of significance to test whether or not the population correlation is zero. If the sample consists of 25 observations and the correlation coefficient is 0.60, then what is the computed value of the test statistic?
A. 1.96
B. 2.07
C. 2.94
D. 3.60
E. None of the above

13-51 C
Med
Goal: 3

What does a coefficient of correlation of 0.70 infer?
A. Almost no correlation because 0.70 is close to 1.0
B. 70% of the variation in one variable is explained by the other
C. Coefficient of determination is 0.49
D. Coefficient of nondetermination is 0.30
E. None of the above

13-52 C
Easy
Goal: 3

What is the range of values for a coefficient of correlation?
A. 0 to +1.0
B. –3 to +3 inclusive
C. –1.0 to +1.0 inclusive
D. Unlimited range
E. None of the above

13-53 E
Med
Goal: 3

The Pearson product-moment correlation coefficient r requires that variables are measured with:
A. An interval scale
B. A ratio scale
C. An ordinal scale
D. A nominal
E. Either A or B, or both.

13-54 B
Med
Goal: 8

The difference between formulas for constructing a confidence interval and a prediction interval is

A. the prediction interval is the square root of the confidence interval.
B. the addition of "1" to the quantity under the radical sign.
C. the prediction interval uses r^2 and the confidence interval uses r.
D. no difference.
E. none of the above.

13-55 A
Easy
Goal: 3

If the correlation between two variables is close to one, the association is

A. strong.
B. moderate.
C. weak.
D. none.

13-56 A
Easy
Goal: 3

If the correlation coefficient between two variables equals zero, what can be said of the variables X and Y?

A. Not related
B. Dependent on each other
C. Highly related
D. All of the above are correct
E. None of the above is correct

13-57 C
Easy
Goal: 3

What can we conclude if the coefficient of determination is 0.94?

A. Strength of relationship is 0.94
B. Direction of relationship is positive
C. 94% of total variation in one variable is explained by variation in the other variable
D. All of the above are correct
E. None of the above is correct

13-58 E
Med
Goal: 3

What does it indicate if $r = -1.00$?

A. Dependent variable can be perfectly predicted by the independent variable
B. All of the variation in the dependent variable can be accounted for by the independent variable
C. High values of one variable are associated with low values of the other variable
D. Coefficient of determination is 100%.
E. All of the above are correct

13-59 B
Easy
Goal: 3

If $r = 0.65$, what does the coefficient of determination equal?

A. 0.194
B. 0.423
C. 0.577
D. 0.806
E. None of the above

13-60 C
Med
Goal: 3

What does the coefficient of determination equal if $r = 0.89$?

A. 0.94
B. 0.89
C. 0.79
D. 0.06
E. None of the above

13-61 B
Easy
Goal: 3

Which value of r indicates a stronger correlation than 0.40?

A. –0.30
B. –0.50
C. +0.38
D. 0
E. None of the above

13-62 D
Easy
Goal: 3

What is the range of values for the coefficient of determination?

A. –1 to +1 inclusive
B. –100% to +100% inclusive
C. –100% to 0% inclusive
D. 0% to 100% inclusive
E. None of the above

13-63 C
Easy
Goal: 4

If the decision in the hypothesis test of the population correlation coefficient is to reject the null hypothesis, what can we conclude about the correlation in the population?

A. Is zero
B. Could be zero
C. Is not zero
D. Equals the computed sample correlation
E. None of the above is correct

13-64 A
Med
Goal: 5

In the regression equation, what does the letter "*a*" represent?

A. *Y* intercept
B. Slope of the line
C. Any value of the independent variable that is selected
D. None of the above

13-65 B
Med
Goal: 5

In the regression equation, what does the letter "*b*" represent?

A. *Y* intercept
B. Slope of the line
C. Any value of the independent variable that is selected
D. Value of Y when X=0
E. None of the above

13-66 C
Med
Goal: 5

Suppose the least squares regression equation is $Y' = 1202 + 1{,}133X$. When $X = 3$, what does Y' equal?

A. 5,734
B. 8,000
C. 4,601
D. 4,050
E. None of the above

13-67 B
Med
Goal: 5

What is the general form of the regression equation?

A. $Y' = ab$
B. $Y' = a + bX$
C. $Y' = a - bX$
D. $Y' = abX$
E. None of the above

13-68 C
Med
Goal: 3

What is the measure that indicates how precise a prediction of Y is based on X or, conversely, how inaccurate the prediction might be?

A. Regression equation
B. Slope of the line
C. Standard error of estimate
D. Least squares principle
E. None of the above

13-69 D
Hard
Goal: 5

Which of the following are true assumptions underlying linear regression: 1) for each value of X, there is a group of Y values which are normally distributed; 2) the means of these normal distributions of Y values all lie on the straight line of regression; and/or 3) the standard deviations of these normal distributions are equal?

A. Only (1) and (2)
B. Only (1) and (3)
C. Only (2) and (3)
D. All of them
E. None of them

13-70 A
Med
Goal: 5

Based on the regression equation, we can

A. predict the value of the dependent variable given a value of the independent variable.
B. predict the value of the independent variable given a value of the dependent variable.
C. measure the association between two variables.
D. all of the above.
E. none of the above.

13-71 A
Med
Goal: 3

What is the chart called when the paired data (the dependent and independent variables) are plotted?

A. Scatter diagram
B. Bar
C. Pie
D. Linear regression
E. None of the above

13-72 C
Med
Goal: 3

If all the plots on a scatter diagram lie on a straight line, what is the standard error of estimate?

A. −1
B. +1
C. 0
D. Infinity
E. None of the above

13-73 C
Med
Goal: 5

In the equation $Y' = a + bX$, what is Y'?

A. Slope of the line
B. Y intercept
C. Predicted value of Y, given a specific X value
D. Value of Y when X=0
E. None of the above

13-74 A
Med
Goal: 5

What is the variable used to predict another variable called?

A. Independent
B. Dependent
C. Important
D. Causal
E. None of the above

13-75 B
Med
Goal: 6

Which of the following is NOT a difference between a confidence interval and a prediction interval?

A. Addition of "1" under the radical for the prediction interval.
B. Confidence interval uses the standard error of estimate and the prediction interval does not.
C. Prediction interval refers to a specific case.
D. Confidence interval is narrower than the prediction interval.

13-76 B
Easy
Goal: 6

When comparing the 95% confidence and prediction intervals for a given regression analysis,

A. the confidence interval is wider than a prediction interval
B. the confidence interval is narrower than a prediction interval
C. there is no difference between confidence and prediction intervals
D. None of the above

13-77 A
Med
Goal: 5

Assume the least squares equation is $Y' = 10 + 20X$. What does the value of 10 in the equation indicate?

A. Y intercept
B. For each unit increased in Y, X increases by 10
C. For each unit increased in X, Y increases by 10
D. None of the above

13-78 D
Med
Goal: 3

Which of the following is true about the standard error of estimate?

A. Measure of the accuracy of the prediction
B. Based on squared vertical deviations between Y and Y'
C. Cannot be negative
D. All of the above
E. None of the above

13-79 B
Med
Goal: 5

In the least squares equation, $Y' = 10 + 20X$ the value of 20 indicates

A. the Y intercept.
B. each unit increased in X, Y increases by 20.
C. each unit increased in Y, X increases by 20.
D. none of the above.

FILL-IN QUESTOINS

13-80
Easy
Goal: 1

In plotting the paired data on a scatter diagram, on which axis is the dependent variable scaled? ____________________

13-81
Easy
Goal: 2

If we are studying the relationship between high school performance and college performance, and want to predict college performance, what kind of variable is high school performance? ________________

13-82
Easy
Goal: 3

How do we designate the coefficient of correlation? _____

13-83
Easy
Goal: 3

If there is absolutely no relationship between two variables, what will Pearson's r equal? _____

13-84
Easy
Goal: 3

If the coefficient of correlation is 0.80, what is the coefficient of determination? ______

13-85
Med
Goal: 3

If the coefficient of determination is 0.81, what is the coefficient of correlation? ______

13-86
Med
Goal: 3

If the coefficient of correlation is –0.81, what is the coefficient of determination? _______

13-87
Hard
Goal: 3

How is the coefficient of determination computed? ________

13-88
Easy
Goal: 3

What is the range of values that the coefficient of determination can assume? _____ and ______

13-89
Med
Goal: 2

A financial advisor is interested in predicting bond yield based on bond term, i.e., one year, two years, etc. What is the dependent variable?
____

13-90
Med
Goal: 4

Suppose a sample of 15 homes recently sold in your area is obtained. The correlation between the area of the home, in square feet, and the selling price is 0.40. We want to test the hypothesis that the correlation in the population is zero versus the alternate that it is greater than zero. What tail will the rejection region fall if this is a one-tailed test and we use a 0.01 significance level? _____

13-91
Easy
Goal: 3

If the value of r is –0.96, what does this indicate about the dependent variable as the independent variable increases? ___________

13-92
Easy
Goal: 4

Perfect correlation means that the scatter diagram will appear as a ________________________.

13-93
Easy
Goal: 3

What is the relationship between the coefficient of determination and the correlation coefficient? _______________________

13-94
Easy
Goal: 3

What is the proportion of explained variation called? _________________

13-95
Med
Goal: 3

What is the value of the correlation coefficient if there is perfect correlation? ___________

13-96
Med
Goal: 3

If the correlation between sales and advertising is +0.6, what percent of the variation in sales can be attributed to advertising? ______

13-97
Easy
Goal: 1

What is a chart designed to portray the relationship between two variables called? ________________________

13-98
Med
Goal: 3

What is the correlation coefficient developed by Karl Pearson formally known as? ______________________________________

13-99 Easy Goal: 3

What type of correlation designates an inverse relationship between two variables? ____________________

13-100 Easy Goal: 5

What is the technique used to predict or estimate the value of the dependent variable *Y* based on a selected value of the independent variable *X* called? ____________________________

13-101 Easy Goal: 5

What is the equation used to estimate *Y* based on *X*? ______________

13-102 Easy Goal: 5

What principle minimizes the sum of the squares of the vertical deviations about the line? ________________

13-103 Med Goal: 3

The standard error of the estimate measures the scatter or dispersion of the observed values around a _____________________

13-104 Med Goal: 5

The technique that minimizes the sum of the squared vertical deviations about the ________________________ is called "least squares."

13-105 Med Goal: 5

What do the coefficient of correlation and the slope of the regression line always have in common? ___________________

13-106 Med Goal: 3

If the dependent variable is in dollars, the standard error of estimate is in? _______________

13-107 Med Goal: 5

What is the best model to best describe a linear relationship between two variables? __________________________

13-108 Med Goal: 5

What is another name for the regression or estimating equation?
____

13-109 Med Goal: 5

How is the best fitting regression line determined? __________________

13-110 Med Goal: 5

What is the general form of the regression equation? ______________

13-111
Med
Goal: 3

What is a measure of the scatter of observed values around the regression line called? ____________________

13-112
Med
Goal: 3

An assumption of linear regression states that for each value of *X*, there is a group of *Y* values that are statistically ____________________ and normally distributed about the regression line.

13-113
Med
Goal: 6

Approximately what percent of the values lie within two standard errors of the regression line? ________

13-114
Easy
Goal: 5

What is the direction of a regression line if its slope equals zero, indicating a lack of a relationship? ____________________ between *X* and *Y*.

13-115
Med
Goal: 3

What variation does the coefficient of determination measure? _______

13-116
Med
Goal: 6

How does the prediction interval for an individual value of *Y* compare to the confidence interval for the mean value of *Y*? _______________

13-117
Med
Goal: 5

The *Y*-intercept is the point on the vertical axis where the regression line does what to the *Y*-axis? _______________

Questions 118-123 refer to the following:
Given the following five points: (–2,0), (–1,0), (0,1), (1,1), and (2,3).

13-118 D
Med
Goal: 5

What is the slope of the line?
A. 0.0
B. 0.5
C. 0.6
D. 0.7
E. None of the above

13-119 C
Med
Goal: 5

What is the *Y* intercept?
A. 0.0
B. 0.7
C. 1.0
D. 1.5
E. None of the above

13-120 D
Med
Goal: 3

What is the standard error of the estimate?

A. 0
B. 0.135
C. 0.367
D. 0.606
E. None of the above

13-121 D
Med
Goal: 6

What is the critical value necessary to determine a confidence interval for a 95% level of confidence?

A. 2.132
B. 2.353
C. 2.776
D. 3.182
E. None of the above

13-122 D
Med
Goal: 6

What is the critical value necessary to determine a confidence interval for a 90% level of confidence?

A. 1.533
B. 1.638
C. 2.132
D. 2.353
E. None of the above

13-123 B
Med
Goal: 5

If the regression equation is $Y' = 2 - 0.4X$, what is the value of Y' when $X = -3$?

A. 0.8
B. 3.2
C. –10.0
D. 14.0
E. None of the above

Questions 124-130 refer to the following:
The following table shows the number of workdays absent based on the length of employment in years.

Number of Workdays Absent	2	3	3	5	7	7	8
Length of Employment (in yrs)	5	6	9	4	2	2	0

13-124
Med
Goal: 5

What is the independent variable (X)? ________________

13-125
Med
Goal: 5

What is the dependent variable (Y)? ____________________

13-126
Med
Goal: 5

What is the slope of the linear equation? _______________

13-127
Med
Goal: 5

What is the Y intercept of the linear equation? ______________

13-128
Med
Goal: 5

What is the least squares equation for the data? ___________________

13-129
Easy
Goal: 5

What is the meaning of a negative slope?
____

13-130
Hard
Goal: 3

What is the standard error of estimate? _____________

Questions 131-135 refer to the following:
The relationship between interest rates as a percent (X) and housing starts (Y) is given by the linear equation $Y' = 4094 - 269X$.

13-131
Med
Goal: 5

What will be the number of housing starts if the interest rate is 8.25%?
____

13-132
Med
Goal: 5

What will be the number of housing starts if the interest rate rose to 16%? __________

13-133
Med
Goal: 5

At what interest rate will there be no permits for housing starts?
____

13-134
Med
Goal: 5

What happens to housing starts as interest rates fall? ________

13-135
Med
Goal: 5

For what interest rate will the maximum number of housing starts be achieved? _______

Questions 136-147 refer to the following:
A sales manager for an advertising agency believes there is a relationship between the number of contacts and the amount of the sales. To verify this believe, the following data was collected:

Salesperson	*Number of Contacts*	*Sales (in thousands)*
1	14	24
2	12	14
3	20	28
4	16	30
5	46	80
6	23	30
7	48	90
8	50	85
9	55	120
10	50	110

13-136 C
Med
Goal: 2

What is the dependent variable?
A. Salesperson
B. Number of contacts
C. Amount of sales
D. All the above
E. None of the above

13-137 B
Med
Goal: 2

What is the independent variable?
A. Salesperson
B. Number of contacts
C. Amount of sales
D. All the above
E. None of the above

13-138 A
Hard
Goal: 5

What is the *Y*-intercept of the linear equation?
A. –12.201
B. 2.1946
C. –2.1946
D. 12.201
E. None of the above

13-139 C
Hard
Goal: 5

What is the slope of the linear equation?
A. –12.201
B. 12.201
C. 2.1946
D. –2.1946
E. None of the above

13-140 A
Hard
Goal: 3

What is the value of the standard error of estimate?
A. 9.3104
B. 8.778
C. 8.328
D. 86.68
E. None of the above

13-141 B
Hard
Goal: 3

What is the value of the coefficient of correlation?
A. 0.6317
B. 0.9754
C. 0.9513
D. 9.3104
E. None of the above

13-142 D
Hard
Goal: 3

What is the value of the coefficient of determination?
A. 9.3104
B. 0.9754
C. 0.6319
D. 0.9513
E. None of the above

13-143 C
Hard
Goal: 6

The 95% confidence interval for 30 calls is
A. 55.8, 51.5
B. 51.4, 55.9
C. 46.7, 60.6
D. 31.1, 76.2
E. None of the above

13-144 D
Hard
Goal: 8

The 95% prediction interval for a particular person making 30 calls is
A. 55.8, 51.5
B. 51.4, 55.9
C. 46.7, 60.6
D. 31.1, 76.2
E. None of the above

13-145 B
Hard
Goal: 5

What is the regression equation?
A. $Y' = 2.1946 - 12.201X$
B. $Y' = -12.201X + 2.1946X$
C. $Y' = 12.201 + 2.1946X$
D. $Y' = 2.1946 + 12.201X$
E. None of the above

13-146 A
Hard
Goal: 7

The SS total is
A. 14249.
B. 13555.
C. 693.48.
D. 156.37.
E. none of the above.

13-147 A
Hard
Goal: 7

The calculated F value is
A. 156.37.
B. 02.64.
C. 86.68.
D. 9.31.
E. none of the above.

Questions 148-154 refer to the following ANOVA table from a regression analysis:

	Coefficients
Constant	-12.8094
Independent Variable	2.179463

ANOVA

	df	*SS*	*MS*	*F*
SSR	1	12323.56	12323.56	90.04814
SSE	8	1094.842	136.8552	
SS Total	9	13418.4		

13-148 C
Medium
Goal: 7

What is the standard error of the estimate?
A. 136.8552
B. 12323.56
C. 11.6985
D. Cannot be computed

13-149 A
Medium
Goal:7

What is the coefficient of determination?
A. 91.8%
B. 8.2%
C. 90.0%
D. Cannot be computed

13-150 B
Medium
Goal: 7

What is the correlation coefficient?
A. 0.81
B. 0.958
C. –0.84
D. 0.006

13-151 A
Medium
Goal:7

Using a 95% significance level, what is the critical value for the F-statistic?
A. 5.32
B. 239
C. 3.23
D. 241

13-152 B
Medium
Goal: 7

The regression equation is:

A. Y' = 2.179463 – 12.8094 X
B. Y' = -12.80894 + 2.179463
C. 12.8094 X = 2.179463 Y'
D. None of the above

13-153 C
Medium
Goal: 7

The regression analysis can be summarized as follows:

A. No significant relationship between the variables
B. A significant negative relationship exists between the variables
C. A significant positive relationship exists between the variables
D. For every unit increase in X, Y decreases by 12.8094

13-154 A
Medium
Goal:7

If testing the hypothesis: H_O: $\rho = 0$, the computed t – statistic is:

A. 9.45
B. 8.84
C. 8.18
D. Cannot be computed

Questions 155-156 are based on the following information:
A regression analysis yields the following information:
Y' = 2.24 + 1.49 X
$S_{y \cdot x} = 1.66$; $\Sigma x = 32$; $\Sigma x^2 = 134$; n = 10

13-155 C
Medium
Goal: 6

Estimate the value of Y' when X = 4.

A. 10.45
B. 3.73
C. 8.20
D. Cannot be computed

13-156 D
Hard
Goal: 6

Compute the 95% confidence interval when X = 4.

A. 0.0, 4.05
B. 4.15, 12.25
C. 2.67, 5.33
D. 6.87, 9.53

Answers to Fill-In Questions

Chapter 13. Linear Regression and Correlation

13-80 Y

13-81 independent

13-82 r

13-83 zero (0)

13-84 0.64

13-85 0.9 or –0.9

13-86 0.6561

13-87 r^2

13-88 0% and 100%

13-89 bond yield

13-90 upper

13-91 decreases

13-92 straight line

13-93 Coefficient of determination = r^2

13-94 coefficient of determination

13-95 ±1.00

13-96 36%

13-97 scatter diagram

13-98 Pearson product moment

13-99 negative

13-100 regression analysis

13-101 regression

13-102 least squares

13-103 regression line

13-104 regression line

13-105 their sign

13-106 dollars ($)

13-107 straight line

13-108 predicting equation

13-109 principle of least squares

13-110 $Y' = a + bX$

13-111 standard error of estimate

13-112 independent

13-113 95%

13-114 horizontal

13-115 explained relative to total variation

13-116 wider or larger

13-117 intersects

13-124 Number of years employed

13-125 Number of work days absent

13-126 –0.6852

13-127 7.7407

13-128 $Y' = 7.7107 - 0.6852X$

13-129 inverse relationship between variables

13-130 1.31

13-131 1875 (1874.75)

13-132 zero (0) since you can't have negative housing starts

13-133 15.22

13-134 rise

13-135 0

Chapter 14. Multiple Regression and Correlation Analysis

TRUE/FALSE QUESTIONS

14-1 T
Easy
Goal: 1

Multiple regression is used when two or more independent variables are used to predict a value of a single dependent variable.

14-2 T
Easy
Goal: 1

The values of b_1, b_2 and b_3 in a multiple regression equation are called the net regression coefficients. They indicate the change in the predicted value for a unit change in one *X* when the other *X* variables are held constant.

14-3 F
Med
Goal: 2

Multiple regression analysis examines the relationship of several dependent variables on the independent variable.

14-4 F
Med
Goal: 2

The multiple coefficient of determination, R^2, reports the proportion of the variation in *Y* that is not explained by the variation in the set of independent variables.

14-5 T
Easy
Goal: 2

The coefficient of multiple determination reports the strength of the association between the dependent variable and the set of independent variables.

14-6 T
Easy
Goal: 1

A multiple regression equation defines the relationship between the dependent variable and the independent variables in the form of an equation.

14-7 T
Easy
Goal: 2

The multiple standard error of estimate for two independent variables measures the variation about a regression plane.

14-8 F
Easy
Goal: 2

A multiple correlation determination equaling –0.76 is definitely possible.

14-9 T
Easy
Goal: 2

Multiple R^2 measures the proportion of explained variation relative to total variation.

14-10 F
Easy
Goal: 5

The validity of the regression relationship in multiple regression analysis is tested using the t-statistic.

14-11 F
Easy
Goal: 2

A dummy variable is added to the regression equation to control for error.

14-12 T
Easy
Goal: 1

Autocorrelation often happens when data has been collected over periods of time.

14-13 T
Easy
Goal: 1

The multiple standard error of estimate measures the variation about the regression plane when two independent variables are considered.

14-14 F
Easy
Goal: 1

Homoscedasticity occurs when the variance of the residuals (Y – Y') is different for different values of Y'.

MULTIPLE CHOICE QUESTIONS

14-15 C
Med
Goal: 2

How is the degree of association between the set of independent variables and the dependent variable is measured?

A. Confidence intervals.
B. Autocorrelation
C. Coefficient of multiple determination
D. Standard error of estimate
E. None of the above

14-16 A
Med
Goal: 2

What is the measurement of explained variation?

A. Coefficient of multiple determination
B. Coefficient of multiple nondetermination
C. Regression coefficient
D. Correlation matrix
E. None of the above

14-17 A
Easy
Goal: 2

If the coefficient of multiple determination is 0.81, what percent of variation is not explained?

A. 19%
B. 90%
C. 66%
D. 81%
E. None of the above

14-18 C
Easy
Goal: 5

Which test statistic do we apply to test the null hypothesis that the multiple regression coefficients are all zero?

A. z
B. t
C. F
D. SPSS-X
E. None of the above

14-19 C
Med
Goal: 2

What is the range of values for multiple *R*?

A. –100% to –100% inclusive
B. –100% to 0% inclusive
C. 0% to +100% inclusive
D. Unlimited range
E. None of the above

14-20 C
Med
Goal: 3

When does multicollinearity occur in a multiple regression analysis?

A. Dependent variables are highly correlated
B. Independent variables are minimally correlated
C. Independent variables are highly correlated
D. Independent variables have no correlation
E. None of the above

14-21 B
Hard
Goal: 3

What is it called when the independent variables are highly correlated?

A. Autocorrelation
B. Multicollinearity
C. Homoscedasticity
D. Zero correlation
E. None of the above

14-22 C
Hard
Goal: 5

What test investigates whether all the independent variables have zero net regression coefficients?

A. Multicollinearity
B. Autocorrelation
C. Global
D. Pearson
E. None of the above

14-23 E
Easy
Goal: 1

How is the *Y* intercept in the multiple regression equation represented?

A. b_1
B. x_1
C. b_2
D. x_2
E. None of the above

14-24 B
Easy
Goal: 1

If there are four independent variables in a multiple regression equation, there are also four

A. *Y*-intercepts.
B. regression coefficients.
C. dependent variables.
D. constant terms.
E. None of the above.

14-25 B
Med
Goal: 2

What does the multiple standard error of estimate measure?

A. Change in Y' for a change in X_1
B. Variation of the data points between Y and Y'.
C. Variation due to the relationship between the dependent and independent variables
D. Amount of explained variation
E. None of the above

14-26 C
Med
Goal: 2

If a multiple regression analysis is based on ten independent variables collected from a sample of 125 observations, what will be the value of the denominator in the calculation of the multiple standard error of estimate?

A. 125
B. 10
C. 114
D. 115
E. None of the above

14-27 D
Easy
Goal: 3

If the correlation between the two independent variables of a regression analysis is 0.11 and each independent variable is highly correlated to the dependent variable, what does this indicate?

A. Multicollinearity between these two independent variables
B. Negative relationship is not possible
C. Only one of the two independent variables will explain a high percent of the variation
D. An effective regression equation
E. None of the above

14-28 B
Easy
Goal: 3

What does the correlation matrix for a multiple regression analysis contain?

A. Multiple correlation coefficients
B. Simple correlation coefficients
C. Multiple coefficients of determination
D. Multiple standard errors of estimate
E. None of the above

14-29 B
Easy
Goal: 6

What can we conclude if the net regression coefficients in the population are not significantly different from zero?

A. Strong relationship exists among the variables
B. No relationship exists between the dependent variable and the independent variables
C. Independent variables are good predictors
D. Good forecasts are possible
E. None of the above

14-30 A
Med
Goal: 4

What is the degrees of freedom associated with the regression sum of squares?

A. Number of independent variables
B. 1
C. F-ratio
D. (n – 2)
E. None of the above

14-31 B
Med
Goal: 5

Which of the following is a characteristic of the *F*-distribution?

A. Normally distributed
B. Skewed positive
C. Skewed both negative and positive
D. Equal to the t-distribution
E. None of the above

14-32 C
Med
Goal: 4

In a regression analysis, three independent variables are used in the equation based on a sample of forty observations. What are the degrees of freedom associated with the *F*-statistic?

A. 3 and 39
B. 4 and 40
C. 3 and 36
D. 2 and 39
E. None of the above

14-33 A
Easy
Goal: 5

Hypotheses concerning individual regression coefficients are tested using which statistic?

A. *t-statistic*
B. *z-statistic*
C. χ^2 (chi-square statistic)
D. *H*
E. None of the above

14-34 A
Med
Goal: 2

The coefficient of determination measures the proportion of

A. explained variation.
B. variation due to the relationship among variables.
C. error variation.
D. variation due to regression.
E. none of the above.

14-35 E
Med
Goal: 2

What happens as the scatter of data values about the regression plane increases?

A. Standard error of estimate increases
B. R^2 decreases
C. $(1 - R^2)$ increases
D. Residual sum of squares increases
E. All of the above are correct

14-36 B
Easy
Goal: 1

For a unit change in the first independent variable with other things being held constant, what change can be expected in the dependent variable in the multiple regression equation $Y' = 5.2 + 6.3X_1 - 7.1X_2$?

A. -7.1
B. $+6.3$
C. $+5.2$
D. $+4.4$
E. None of the above

14-37 B
Med
Goal: 1

If the correlation between two variables, X and Y, is +0.67, what is the regression coefficient for these two variables?

A. $+0.67$
B. > 0
C. < 0
D. $= 0$
E. None of the above

14-38 A
Easy
Goal: 5

The best example of a null hypothesis for a global test of a multiple regression model is:

A. H_O: $\beta_1 = \beta_2 = \beta_3 = \beta_4$
B. H_O: $\mu_1 = \mu_2 = \mu_3 = \mu_4$
C. H_O: $\beta_1 = 0$
D. If F is greater than 20.00 then reject

14-39 C
Easy
Goal: 5

The best example of an alternate hypothesis for a global test of a multiple regression model is:

A. H_1: $\beta_1 = \beta_2 = \beta_3 = \beta_4$
B. H_1: $\beta_1 \neq \beta_2 \neq \beta_3 \neq \beta_4$
C. H_1: Not all the β's are 0
D. If F is less than 20.00 then fail to reject

14-40 C
Easy
Goal: 6

The best example of a null hypothesis for testing an individual regression coefficient is:

A. H_O: $\beta_1 = \beta_2 = \beta_3 = \beta_4$
B. H_O: $\mu_1 = \mu_2 = \mu_3 = \mu_4$
C. H_O: $\beta_1 = 0$
D. If F is greater than 20.00 then reject

14-41 C
Easy
Goal: 1

In multiple regression analysis, residuals $(Y - Y')$ are used to:

A. Provide a global test of a multiple regression model.
B. Evaluate multicollinearity
C. Evaluate homoscedasticity
D. Compare two regression coefficients

14-42 C
Easy
Goal: 1

In multiple regression, a dummy variable can be included in a multiple regression model as

A. An additional quantitative variable
B. A nominal variable with three or more values
C. A nominal variable with only two values
D. A new regression coefficient

14-43 B
Easy
Goal: 1

Multiple regression analysis is applied when analyzing the relationship between

A. An independent variable and several dependent variables
B. A dependent variable and several independent variables
C. Several dependent variables and several independent variables
D. Several regression equations and a single sample
E. None of the above

FILL-IN QUESTIONS

14-44
Med
Goal: 1

Violating the need for successive observations of the dependent variable to be uncorrelated is called ______________________.

14-45
Med
Goal: 2

Multiple R^2 measures the proportion of ______________________.

14-46
Easy
Goal: 2

A variable whose possible outcomes are coded as a "1" or a "0" is called a(n) ______________________ .

14-47
Easy
Goal: 1

If the relationship between the dependent variable and independent variables is inverse, what are the regression coefficients for the independent variables? ____________

14-48
Easy
Goal: 3

A frequent use of a correlation matrix is to check for ____________.

14-49
Med
Goal: 2

What does the number of degrees of freedom associated with the regression sum of squares in the regression equation model equal?
______________________ .

14-50
Easy
Goal: 6

If the null hypothesis $\beta_4 = 0$ is not rejected, then the independent variable X_4 has what effect in predicting the dependent variable? ______

14-51
Easy
Goal: 2

What is the proportion of total variation in the dependent variable that is explained by the independent variable for a multiple $R^2 = 0.90$? _______

14-52
Easy
Goal: 1

Given a multiple linear equation $Y' = 5.1 + 2.2X_1 - 3.5X_2$, what will a unit increase ~~change~~ in the second independent variable, assuming other things are held constant, mean in the change of Y? ________

14-53
Med
Goal: 1

When the differences between the actual and the predicted values of the dependent variable are approximately the same, the variables are said to exhibit ______________________________ .

Questions 54-57 refer to the following computer output:
The following correlations were computed as part of a multiple regression analysis that used education, job, and age to predict income.

	Income	*Education*	*Job*	*Age*
Income	1.000			
Education	0.677	1.000		
Job	0.173	– 0.181	1.000	
Age	0.369	0.073	0.689	1.000

14-54 D
Med
Goal: 3

What is this table called?
A. Net regression coefficients
B. Coefficients of nondetermination
C. Analysis of variance
D. Correlation matrix
E. None of the above

14-55 A
Med
Goal: 1

Which is the dependent variable?
A. Income
B. Age
C. Education
D. Job
E. None of the above

14-56 C
Med
Goal: 3

Which independent variable has the strongest association with the dependent variable?
A. Income
B. Age
C. Education
D. Job
E. None of the above

14-57 D
Med
Goal: 3

Which independent variable has the weakest association with the dependent variable?
A. Income
B. Age
C. Education
D. Job
E. None of the above

Questions 58-64 refer to the following:
It has been hypothesized that overall academic success for freshmen at college as measured by grade point average (GPA) is a function of IQ scores (X_1), hours spent studying each week (X_2), and one's high school average (X_3). Suppose the regression equation is:

$$Y' = -6.9 + 0.055X_1 + 0.107X_2 + 0.0083X_3.$$

The multiple standard error is 6.313 and $R^2 = 0.826$.

14-58
Med
Goal: 1

What is the predicted GPA for a student with an IQ of 108, 32 hours spent studying per week and a high school average of 82? _____

14-59
Med
Goal: 1

What will the GPA be if the number of hours spent studying is 30 if the IQ is 108 and the high school average is 82? ______

14-60
Med
Goal: 1

Assuming other independent variables are held constant, what effect on the GPA will there be if the numbers of hours spent studying per week increases from 32 to 36? ________

14-61
Med
Goal: 1

For which independent variable does a unit change have the least effect on GPA? ____________________

14-62
Med
Goal: 1

For which independent variable does a unit change have the greatest effect on the GPA? _________________

14-63
Med
Goal: 2

How many dependent variables are in the regression equation? ___

14-64
Med
Goal: 2

How will a student's GPA be affected if an additional hour is spent studying each weeknight? ________

Questions 65-71 refer to the following:

Twenty-one executives in a large corporation were randomly selected for a study in which several factors were examined to determine their effect on annual salary (expressed in $000's). The factors selected were age, seniority, years of college, number of company divisions they had been exposed to and the level of their responsibility. A regression analysis was performed using a popular spreadsheet program with the following regression output:

Constant	23.00371
Std Error of *Y* estimate	2.91933
R^2	0.91404
No. of Observations	21
Degrees of Freedom	15

	Age	*Sen*	*Educ*	*# of Div*	*Level*
X Coefficients	– 0.031	0.381	1.452	– 0.089	3.554
Std Err of Coef.	0.183	0.158	0.387	0.541	0.833

14-65 D
Med
Goal: 1

Which one of the following is the dependent variable?

A. Age
B. Seniority
C. Level of responsibility
D. Annual salary
E. Experience in number of company divisions

14-66
Med
Goal: 1

Write out the multiple regression equation? ____________________

14-67
Med
Goal: 2

Which of the following has the most influence on salary -- 20 years of seniority, 5 years of college or attaining 55 years of age? _______

14-68
Med
Goal: 1

What is the effect on salary for an increase of one level of responsibility if the other variables are held constant? ___________

14-69
Med
Goal: 1

What is the effect on salary of an increase in age of two years if other variables are held constant? ________________

14-70
Med
Goal: 2

What is the proportion of the variation in salary accounted for by the set of independent variables? ___________

14-71
Hard
Goal: 2

What is the value of the denominator in the calculation of the multiple standard error of estimate? ___________

Questions 72-77 refer to the following:
The production of automobile tires in any given year is related to the number of automobiles produced this year and in prior years. Suppose our econometric model resulted in the following data.

	Coef	*t*-ratio
X_1 = Automobiles produced this year	5.00	10.4
X_2 = Automobiles produced last year	0.25	0.6
X_3 = Automobiles produced 2 years ago	0.67	1.4
X_4 = Automobiles produced 3 years ago	2.12	2.7
X_5 = Automobiles produced 4 years ago	3.44	6.5
Constant	– 50,000	
Multiple R	0.83	

14-72
Med
Goal: 3

Which variable in the model is the most significant predictor of tire production? __________

14-73
Med
Goal: 2

What is the proportion of variation in tires produced by our predictor variables in the model? ________

14-74
Med
Goal: 2

Which variable in the model is the least significant in predicting tire production? _________

14-75
Med
Goal: 1

What is the equation for our model? ____________________________

14-76
Med
Goal: 2

How much does tire production increase for every thousand cars produced two years ago? _____

14-77
Med
Goal: 2

How much does tire production change for every thousand cars produced three years ago? _____

Questions 78-85 refer to the following:
A real estate agent developed a model to relate a house's selling price (Y) to the area of floor space (X) and the area of floor space squared (X^2). The multiple regression equation for this model is:

$$Y = 125 - 3X + X^2$$

where: Y = selling price (times \$1000)
X = square feet of floor space (times 100)

14-78
Med
Goal 1

What is the intercept (a)? _____________

14-79
Med
Goal: 1

What is the selling price of a house with 1000 square feet? ______

14-80
Hard
Goal: 1

What is the selling price of a house with 1500 square feet? ______

14-81
Med
Goal: 1

What is the selling price of a house with 2000 square feet? ______

14-82
Med
Goal: 1

What is the lowest selling price of a house using this model? ______

14-83
Hard
Goal: 1

What is the difference in selling prices of a house with 1600 square feet and one with 1700 square feet? ______

14-84
Hard
Goal: 1

What is the difference in selling prices of a house with 1700 square feet and one with 1800 square feet? ______

14-85
Hard
Goal: 1

What is the difference in selling prices of a house with 1650 square feet and one with 1750 square feet? ______

Questions 86-90 refer to the following:
A manager at a local bank analyzed the relationship between monthly salary and three independent variables: length of service (measured in months), gender (0 = female, 1 = male) and job type (0 = clerical, 1 = technical). The following ANOVA summarizes the regression results:

ANOVA

	df	*SS*	*MS*	*F*
Regression	3	1004346.771	334782.257	5.96
Residual	26	1461134.596	56197.48445	
Total	29	2465481.367		

	Coefficients	*Standard Error*	*t Stat*	*P-value*
Intercept	784.92	322.25	2.44	0.02
Service	9.19	3.20	2.87	0.01
Gender	222.78	89.00	2.50	0.02
Job	-28.21	89.61	-0.31	0.76

14-86 B
Medium
Goal: 5

Based on the ANOVA and a 0.05 significance level, the global null hypothesis test of the multiple regression model

A. Will be rejected and conclude that monthly salary is related to all of the independent variables
B. Will be rejected and conclude that monthly salary is related to at least one of the independent variables.
C. Will not be rejected.
D. Will show a high multiple coefficient of determination

14-87 C
Medium
Goal: 2

Based on the ANOVA, the multiple coefficient of determination is

A. 5.957%
B. 59.3%
C. 40.7%
D. cannot be computed

14-88 C
Medium
Goal: 6

Based on the hypothesis tests for the individual regression coefficients,

A. All the regression coefficients are not equal to zero.
B. "job" is the only significant variable in the model
C. Only months of service and gender are significantly related to monthly salary.
D. "service" is the only significant variable in the model

14-89 D
Easy
Goal: 1

In the regression model, which of the following are dummy variables?

A. Intercept
B. Service
C. Service and gender
D. Gender and job
E. Service, gender, and job

14-90 A
Medium
Goal: 6

The results for the variable gender show that

A. males average $222.78 more than females in monthly salary
B. females average $222.78 more than males in monthly salary
C. gender is not related to monthly salary
D. Gender and months of service are correlated.

Answers to Fill-In Questions

Chapter 14. Multiple Regression and Correlation Analysis

14-44 autocorrelation

14-45 explained variation

14-46 dummy variable

14-47 negative

14-48 multicollinearity

14-49 number of independent variables

14-50 none

14-51 90% or 0.90

14-52 - 3.5

14-53 homoscedasticity

14-58 3.1446

14-59 2.9306

14-60 + 0.428

14-61 High school average (X_3)

14-62 Hours spent studying per week (X_2)

14-63 one

14-64 Increases by 0.535

14-66 $Y' = 23.004 - 0.031X_1 + 0.381X_2 + 1.452X_3 - 0.089X_4 + 0.554X_5$

14-67 20 years of seniority

14-68 + $3,554

14-69 - $62

14-70 91.4%

14-71 15

14-72 X_1

14-73 0.69

14-74 X_2

14-75 $Y' = -50{,}000 + 5.00X_1 + 0.25X_2 + 0.67X_3 + 2.12X_4 + 3.44X_5$

14-76 670

14-77 2,120

14-78 $125 (in thousands)

14-79 $195,000

14-80 $305,000

14-81 $465,000

14-82 $122,750 (based on 150 square feet)

14-83 $30,000 ($363,000 – $333,000)

14-84 $32,000 ($395,000 – $363,000)

14-85 $31,000 ($378,750 – $347,750)

Chapter 15. Nonparametric Methods: Chi-Square Applications

TRUE/FALSE QUESTIONS

15-1 T
Easy
Goal: 1

Nonparametric tests require no assumptions about the shape of the population distribution.

15-2 F
Easy
Goal: 2

The claim that "male and female University of Toledo students prefer different parking lots on campus" is an example of a chi-square null hypothesis.

15-3 F
Easy
Goal: 3

The goodness-of-fit test cannot be used when determining if sample observations come from a continuous distribution.

15-4 T
Easy
Goal: 1

Tests of hypotheses for nominal or ordinal levels of measurement are called nonparametric or distribution-free tests.

15-5 T
Easy
Goal: 1

The chi-square goodness-of-fit test is appropriate for nominal and ordinal levels of data.

15-6 T
Easy
Goal: 2

The chi-square test statistic used in a goodness-of-fit test has k–1 degrees of freedom.

15-7 T
Easy
Goal: 2

The chi-square goodness-of-fit test can be applied if there are equal or unequal expected frequencies.

15-8 T
Easy
Goal: 1

There is not one, but a family of chi-square distributions. There is a chi-square distribution for 1 degree of freedom, another for 2 degrees of freedom, another for 3 degrees of freedom, and so on.

15-9 F
Easy
Goal: 2

For a goodness-of-fit test, the number of degrees of freedom is determined by k–2, where k is the number of categories.

15-10 F
Med
Goal: 1

The shape of the chi-square distribution depends on the size of the sample.

15-11 T
Easy
Goal: 1

The chi-square distribution is positively skewed.

15-12 F
Med
Goal: 2

The sum of the expected frequencies in a goodness-of-fit test need not equal the sum of the observed frequencies.

15-13 F
Med
Goal: 1

Nonparametric tests of hypotheses, which are also called distribution free tests, require the population to be normally distributed.

15-14 T
Med
Goal: 2

A goodness-of-fit test is a nonparametric test involving a set of observed frequencies and a corresponding set of expected frequencies.

15-15 T
Easy
Goal: 2

For a goodness-of-fit test, the following are possible null and alternate hypotheses.

Null: Sales are uniformly distributed among the five locations.
Alternate: Sales are not uniformly distributed among the five locations.

15-16 F
Med
Goal: 2

For the goodness-of-fit test, the use of chi-square would be permissible in the following problem.

Individual	*Observed Frequency*	*Expected Frequency*
Literate	639	642
Illiterate	6	3

15-17 T
Med
Goal: 2

A small number of expected frequencies (less than 5) in a cell, might result in an erroneous conclusion for the application of chi-square since the number of expected frequencies appears in the denominator, and dividing by a very small number makes the quotient quite large.

15-18 F
Med
Goal: 2

If there are more than two cells, chi-square should not be applied if more than 50 percent of the expected frequency cells have expected frequencies of less than ten.

15-19 T
Med
Goal: 2

In the goodness-of-fit test, the chi-square distribution is used to determine how well an observed set of observations "fits" an "expected" set of observations.

15-20 T
Med
Goal: 2

The sum of the expected frequencies and the sum of the observed frequencies must be equal.

15-21 F
Med
Goal: 4

For a contingency table, the expected frequency for a cell is found by dividing the row total by the grand total.

15-22 T
Med
Goal: 1

The shape of the chi-square distribution changes for each number of degrees of freedom.

15-23 F
Med
Goal: 2

If the computed value of chi-square is less than the critical value, reject the null hypothesis at a predetermined level of significance.

MULTIPLE CHOICE QUESTIONS

15-24 C
Easy
Goal: 2

A question has these possible choices—excellent, very good, good, fair and unsatisfactory. How many degrees of freedom are there using the goodness-of-fit test to the sample results?
A. 0
B. 2
C. 4
D. 5
E. None of the above

15-25 D
Med
Goal: 2

What is the critical value at the 0.05 level of significance for a goodness-of-fit test if there are six categories?
A. 3.841
B. 5.991
C. 7.815
D. 11.070
E. None of the above

15-26 A
Med
Goal: 2

What is our decision regarding the differences between the observed and expected frequencies if the critical value of chi-square is 9.488 and the computed value is 6.079?
A. Due to chance; do not reject the null hypothesis
B. Not due to chance; reject the null hypothesis
C. Not due to chance; do not reject the alternate hypothesis
D. Too close; reserve judgment
E. None of the above

15-27 A
Med
Goal: 1

The chi-square distribution can assume
A. only positive values.
B. only negative values.
C. negative and positive values or zero.
D. only zero.
E. none of the above.

15-28 A
Med
Goal: 1

The chi-square distribution is
A. positively skewed.
B. negatively skewed.
C. normally distributed.
D. negatively or positively skewed.
E. none of the above.

15-29 B
Med
Goal: 1

Two chi-square distributions were plotted on the same chart. One distribution was for 3 degrees of freedom and the other was for 12 degrees of freedom. Which distribution would tend to approach a normal distribution?

A. 3 degrees
B. 12 degrees
C. 15 degrees
D. All would
E. None of the above

15-30 C
Med
Goal: 2

A distributor of personal computers has five locations in the city. The sales in units for the first quarter of the year were as follows:

Location	*Observed Sales (Units)*
North Side	70
Pleasant Township	75
Southwyck	70
I–90	50
Venice Avenue	35
	300

What is the critical value at the 0.01 level of risk?

A. 7.779
B. 15.033
C. 13.277
D. 5.412
E. None of the above

15-31 A
Med
Goal: 2

What is our decision for a goodness-of-fit test with a computed value of chi-square of 1.273 and a critical value of 13.388?

A. Do not reject the null hypothesis
B. Reject the null hypothesis
C. Unable to reject or not reject the null hypothesis based on data
D. Should take a larger sample
E. None of the above

15-32 D
Easy
Goal: 4

The following table classifies an individual in two ways—by gender and by educational choice.

		College Attended		
Gender	*None*	*Two-Year*	*Four-Year*	*Total*
Male	7	13	30	50
Female	13	17	20	50
Total	20	30	50	100

What is this two way classification called?

A. Goodness-of-fit test
B. Frequency table
C. No-load table
D. Contingency table
E. None of the above

15-33 D
Med
Goal: 4

To analyze data cross-classified in a contingency table, how are the degrees of freedom found?

A. N–1
B. Rows – Columns
C. (Rows) x (Columns)
D. (Rows – 1) x (Columns – 1)
E. None of the above

15-34 C
Med
Goal: 4

The following table shows the adjustment to civilian life and place of residence.

Residence After	*Adjustment to Civilian Life*			
Release From Prison	*Outstanding*	*Good*	*Fair*	*Unsatisfactory*
Hometown	27	35	33	25
Not hometown	13	15	27	25
Total	40	50	60	50

What is the critical value for this contingency table at the 0.01 level of significance?

A. 9.488
B. 2.070
C. 11.345
D. 13.277
E. None of the above

15-35 C
Med
Goal: 4

The educational level and the social activity of a sample of executives follow.

	Social Activity		
Education	*Above Average*	*Average*	*Below Average*
College	30	20	10
High School	20	40	90
Grade School	10	50	130

What does the expected frequency for the "above average" social activity and "high school" education equal?

A. 9.50
B. 60.00
C. 22.50
D. 28.50
E. None of the above

15-36 E
Med
Goal: 1

Which of the following assumptions is necessary to apply a nonparametric test of hypothesis using chi-square?

A. Normal population is required
B. Interval scale of measurement is required
C. Population variance must be known
D. Both "a" and "c"
E. None of the above

15-37 C
Med
Goal: 1

Which of the following are correct statements regarding the chi-square distribution?

A. Distribution is negatively skewed
B. Chi-square is based on two sets of degrees of freedom, one for the numerator and one for the denominator
C. Its shape is based on the degrees of freedom
D. All of the above are true
E. None of the above are true

15-38 A
Med
Goal: 2

Which of the following are correct statements regarding the goodness-of-fit test?

A. Data may be of nominal scale
B. Population must be normal
C. All the expected frequencies must be equal
D. All of the above are true
E. None of the above are true

15-39 B
Easy
Goal: 4

A sample of 100 production workers is obtained. The workers are classified by gender (male, female) and by age (under 20, 20–29, 30–39 and 40 or over). How many degrees of freedom are there?

A. 0
B. 3
C. 6
D. 5
E. None of the above

15-40 D
Med
Goal: 1

The chi-square distribution becomes more symmetrical as

A. number of variables increase.
B. the chi-square value increases.
C. degrees of freedom decrease.
D. degrees of freedom increase.
E. none of the above.

15-41 B
Med
Goal: 2

For any chi-square goodness-of-fit problem, the number of degrees of freedom is found by

A. $n - k - 1$.
B. $k - 1$.
C. $n + 1$.
D. $n + k$.
E. none of the above.

15-42 C
Easy
Goal: 1

The chi-square has

A. one distribution.
B. two distributions.
C. a family of distribution.
D. a uniform distribution.
E. none of the above.

15-43 B
Med
Goal: 2

Three new colors have been proposed for the Jeep Grand Cherokee vehicle. They are silvered-blue, almond, and willow green. The null hypothesis for a goodness-of-fit test would be

A. willow green preferred over the other colors.
B. no preference between the colors.
C. any one color preferred over the other colors.
D. impossible to determine.
E. none of the above.

15-44 D
Med
Goal: 4

For a chi-square test involving a contingency table, suppose the null hypothesis is rejected. We conclude that the two variables are

A. linear.
B. curvilinear.
C. not related.
D. related.
E. none of the above.

15-45 A
Med
Goal: 4

Which of the following can be used to test if two nominal variables or characteristics are related?

A. a contingency table.
B. a chi-square table.
C. an ANOVA table.
D. a scatter diagram.
E. none of the above.

15-46 C
Med
Goal: 2

When determining how well an observed set of frequencies fit an expected set of frequencies the test is the

A. *F* test.
B. *t* test.
C. goodness-of-fit test
D. test for association.
E. none of the above.

15-47 B
Med
Goal: 2

In the chi-square test, the null hypothesis (no difference between sets of observed and expected frequencies) is rejected when the

A. computed chi-square is less then the critical value.
B. difference between the observed and expected frequencies is significant.
C. difference between the observed and expected frequencies is small.
D. difference between the observed and expected frequencies occurs by chance.
E. none of the above.

15-48 A
Med
Goal: 2

The computed chi-square value is positive because the difference between the observed and expected frequencies is

A. squared.
B. linear.
C. uniform.
D. always positive.
E. none of the above.

FILL-IN QUESTIONS

15-49
Med
Goal: 1

The computed value of chi-square is always positive because the difference between the observed frequencies and the expected frequencies are? ______________

15-50
Med
Goal: 2

What should the expected frequencies be for a goodness-of-fit test if there are only two cells? __________

15-51
Med
Goal: 2

What statistical test is used to determine how well an observed set of data fits an expected set of data?
____

15-52
Med
Goal: 1

What are small differences between observed and expected frequencies are due to? ____________

15-53
Med
Goal: 1

What does the chi-square distribution approach with large degrees of freedom? ______________________

15-54
Med
Goal: 2

What is the null hypothesis in the goodness-of-fit test? __________

15-55
Med
Goal: 1

What is the lowest level of data for which the chi-square goodness-of-fit test is appropriate? ____________

15-56
Med
Goal: 2

What hypothesis states that there is a difference between the observed frequencies and the expected frequencies? ____________

15-57
Med
Goal: 2

What is the number of degrees of freedom appropriate for the chi-square goodness-of-fit test? ________________________

15-58
Med
Goal: 2

What is the decision if there are extremely large differences between observed and expected frequencies? __________

15-59
Med
Goal: 1

What is the minimum computed value of chi-square? _______

15-60
Med
Goal: 1

What is the shape of the chi-square distribution?_________________

15-61
Med
Goal: 2

What is the degrees of freedom for a contingency table classifying three levels of income with each gender? ______

15-62
Med
Goal: 2

Taking the row total times the column total and dividing by the ___________ computes the expected frequency for a cell.

15-63
Med
Goal: 4

For contingency table analysis using the chi-square test, multiplying the number of rows minus 1 by the number of columns minus 1 will give you what? _________________________________

Questions 64-69 refer to the following

The personnel manager is concerned about absenteeism. She decides to sample the records to determine if absenteeism is distributed evenly throughout the six-day workweek. The null hypothesis to be tested is: Absenteeism is distributed evenly throughout the week. The 0.01 level is to be used. The sample results are:

Day of Week	*Number Absent*
Monday	12
Tuesday	9
Wednesday	11
Thursday	10
Friday	9
Saturday	9

15-64 D
Easy
Goal: 2

What kind of frequencies are the numbers 12, 9, 11, 10, and 9 called?

A. Acceptance
B. Critical value
C. Expected
D. Observed
E. None of the above

15-65 D
Med
Goal: 2

How many degrees of freedom are there?

A. 0
B. 3
C. 4
D. 5
E. None of the above

15-66 B
Med
Goal: 2

What is the expected frequency?
A. 9
B. 10
C. 11
D. 12
E. None of the above

15-67 C
Med
Goal: 2

What is the calculated value of chi-square?
A. 1.0
B. 0.5
C. 0.8
D. 8.0
E. None of the above

15-68
Med
Goal: 2

If the computed value of chi-square is less than the critical value, what is our decision? ______________________________

15-69
Med
Goal: 2

If the computed value of chi-square is greater than the critical value, what is our decision? ______________________________

Questions 70-76 refer to the following:
Six people have declared their intentions to run for a trustee seat in the next local election. A political poll is conducted during the campaign among 1,020 voters to determine if there is any clear preference among the voters. The responses are shown below.

Candidate	*A*	*B*	*C*	*D*	*E*	*F*
Responses	180	240	200	130	125	145

15-70
Med
Goal: 2

What is the null hypothesis? ______________________________________

15-71
Med
Goal: 2

What is the alternative hypothesis?
____

15-72
Med
Goal: 2

How many degrees of freedom are there? ______

15-73
Med
Goal: 2

What is the critical value at the 5% level of significance? ________

15-74
Med
Goal: 2

What is the critical value at the 1% level of significance? ________

15-75
Med
Goal: 2

What is the expected frequency for each candidate? ______

15-76
Med
Goal: 2

If the computed chi-square is 30, what is your decision at the 1% level of significance? ______________________________

Questions 77-88 refer to the following:
A survey of the opinions of property owners about a street widening project was taken to determine whether the resulting opinion was related to the distance of front footage. A randomly selected sample of 100 property owners was contacted and the results are shown below.

	Opinion		
Front-Footage	*For*	*Undecided*	*Against*
Under 45 feet	12	4	4
45 – 120 feet	35	5	30
Over 120 feet	3	2	5

15-77 C
Med
Goal: 4

How many degrees of freedom are there?
A. 2
B. 3
C. 4
D. 5
E. None of the above

15-78 B
Med
Goal: 4

What is the critical value at the 5% level of significance?
A. 7.779
B. 9.488
C. 9.236
D. 11.070
E. None of the above

15-79 A
Med
Goal: 4

What is the critical value at the 10% level of significance?
A. 7.779
B. 9.236
C. 9.488
D. 11.070
E. None of the above

15-80 D
Med
Goal: 4

What is the expected frequency for people who are undecided about the project and have property front-footage between 45 and 120 feet?
A. 2.2
B. 3.9
C. 5.0
D. 7.7
E. None of the above

15-81 A
Med
Goal: 4

What is the expected frequency for people who are in favor of the project and have less than 45 feet of property foot-frontage?

A. 10
B. 12
C. 35
D. 50
E. None of the above

15-82 B
Med
Goal: 4

What is the expected frequency for people against the project and who have over 120 feet of property foot-frontage?

A. 1.1
B. 3.9
C. 5.0
D. 5.5
E. None of the above

15-83
Med
Goal: 4

What kind of table is this classification? ________________

15-84
Med
Goal: 4

What is the null hypothesis?
____

15-85
Med
Goal: 4

What is the alternative hypothesis?
____

15-86
Hard
Goal: 4

What is the computed value of chi-square? _________

15-87
Med
Goal: 4

If the computed chi-square is 8.5, what is your decision at the 5% level of significance? __________________________

15-88
Med
Goal: 4

If the computed chi-square is 8.5, what is your decision at the 10% level of significance? _____________________________

Questions 89-97 refer to the following:
A student asked the statistics professor if grades were marked "on the curve." The professor decided to give the student a project to determine if last year's statistics grades were normally distributed. The professor told the student to assume a mean of 75 and a standard deviation of 10 and to use the following results.

Letter Grade	*Grade Average*	*Observed*	*Expected*
	Over 100	0	0.70
A	90 up to 100	15	
B	80 up to 90	20	
C	70 up to 80	40	
D	60 up to 70	30	
F	50 up to 60	10	7.00
	Under 50	0	0.00

15-89
Med
Goal: 3

What is the null hypothesis? ______________________

15-90
Med
Goal: 3

What is the alternative hypothesis?______________________

15-91
Med
Goal: 3

What is the expected number of B's?__________

15-92
Med
Goal: 3

What is the expected number of C's? __________

15-93
Med
Goal: 3

What is the expected number of D's? __________

15-94
Med
Goal: 3

What is the critical value of chi-square at the .05 level? __________

15-95
Hard
Goal: 3

What is the calculated value of chi-square? __________

15-96
Hard
Goal: 3

What is your decision if $\alpha = 0.05$? ______________________

15-97
Hard
Goal: 3

What is your decision if $\alpha = 0.01$? ______________________

Questions 98-104 refer to the following:
Recently, students in a marketing research class were interested the driving behavior of students driving to school. Specifically, the marketing students were interested if exceeding the speed limit was related to gender. They collected the following responses from 100 randomly selected students:

	Speeds	Does not Speed
Males	40	25
Females	10	25

15-98 C
Easy
Goal: 4

The appropriate test to analyze the relationship between gender and speeding is:
A. regression analysis
B. Analysis of variance
C. Contingency table analysis
D. Goodness-of-fit

15-99 C
Easy
Goal: 4

The appropriate test statistic for the analysis is:
A. F-statistic
B. T-statistic
C. Chi-square statistic
D. Z-statistic

15-100 A
Easy
Goal: 4

The null hypothesis for the analysis is:
A. There is no relationship between gender and speeding.
B. The correlation between gender and speeding is zero.
C. As gender increases, speeding increases.
D. The mean of gender equals the mean of speeding.

15-101 A
Easy
Goal: 4

The degrees of freedom for the analysis is:
A. 1
B. 2
C. 3
D. 4

15-102 A
Easy
Goal: 4

Using 0.05 as the significance level, what is the critical value for the test statistic?
A. 3.841
B. 5.991
C. 7.815
D. 9.488

15-103 B
Medium
Goal: 4

What is the value of the test statistic?

A. 100
B. 9.89
C. 50
D. 4.94

15-104 C
Medium
Goal: 4

Based on the analysis, what can be concluded?

A. Gender and speeding are correlated.
B. Gender and speeding are not related.
C. Gender and speeding are related.
D. No conclusion is possible.

Answers to Fill-In Questions

Chapter 15. Nonparametric Methods: Chi-square Applications

15-49 Squared

15-50 five or more

15-51 Chi-square goodness-of-fit test

15-52 chance

15-53 normality or a normal distribution

15-54 There is no difference

15-55 nominal

15-56 alternative

15-57 number of categories minus 1

15-58 Reject H_0

15-59 Zero

15-60 positively skewed

15-61 2

15-62 grand total

15-63 degrees of freedom

15-68 Do not reject H_0; absenteeism is distributed evenly

15-69 Reject H_0; absenteeism is not distributed evenly

15-70 No preference among candidates exists

15-71 Preference among candidates exists

15-72 5

15-73 11.070

15-74 15.086

15-75 170

15-76 Reject H_0; preferences among the candidates exist

15-83 Contingency

15-84 Opinions and property front-footage are independent

15-85 Opinion and property front-footage are related

15-86 6.79

15-87 Reject H_0; opinion and property front-footage are related

15-88 Do not reject H_0; opinion and property frontage are independent

15-89 Observed grades are normally distributed with μ = 75 and σ = 10

15-90 Observed grades are not normally distributed

15-91 27.8

15-92 44.0

15-93 27.8

15-94 12.592

15-95 14.555

15-96 Reject H_0

15-97 Do not reject H_0

Chapter 16. Nonparametric Methods: Analysis of Ranked Data

TRUE/FALSE QUESTIONS

16-1 T
Easy
Goal: 1

Three tests—rank correlation, Kruskal-Wallis and Wilcoxon signed rank test—require that the data be at least ordinal (ranked) level of measurement.

16-2 T
Med
Goal: 1

We can apply non-parametric tests that require ordinal level of measurement to problems involving interval or ratio data.

16-3 F
Easy
Goal: 1

We can apply parametric tests, such as the *t* test, to ordinal or ranked level of measurement.

16-4 T
Med
Goal: 1

If we have interval or ratio level of measurement and if certain specified assumptions are met, such as normality of the population, a parametric test should be performed.

16-5 T
Med
Goal: 1

If we have interval or ratio level of measurement and if the assumptions of normality and other assumptions cannot be met, a distribution free test should be used.

16-6 T
Med
Goal: 4

The Kruskal-Wallis one-way analysis of variance by ranks is especially appropriate to test whether three or more population means are equal if the data is ordinal scaled and/or the populations are not normal.

16-7 F
Med
Goal: 4

To apply the Kruskal-Wallis test, the samples selected from the populations must be dependent.

16-8 T
Med
Goal: 4

For the Kruskal-Wallis test, all the sample values are combined, combined values are ordered from low to high and ordered values are replaced by ranks starting with 1 for the smallest value.

16-9 T
Med
Goal: 4

Samples selected from the populations must be independent to apply the Kruskal-Wallis test.

16-10 T
Med
Goal: 4

The test statistic for the Kruskal-Wallis test is designated H and the distribution of the sample H statistic is very close to the chi-square distribution with $k - 1$ degrees of freedom if every sample size is at least five.

16-11 T
Easy
Goal: 4

The Kruskal-Wallis test is a distribution-free test.

16-12 T
Med
Goal: 4

If we cannot assume equal standard deviations, the Kruskal-Wallis test is substituted for ANOVA.

16-13 T
Easy
Goal: 2

The Wilcoxon signed rank test can replace the paired *t* test when the assumptions for *t* cannot be met.

16-14 T
Easy
Goal: 2

The Wilcoxon signed rank test of differences requires that the data be at least ordinal scaled and that the two samples are related.

16-15 T
Med
Goal: 2

The paired *t* test is used if we assume that the differences between two sets of paired observations approximate a normal distribution.

16-16 T
Easy
Goal: 1

The sign test is an appropriate nonparametric test for dependent experiments.

16-17 T
Easy
Goal: 1

The null hypothesis for the sign test is $\pi \geq 0.50$ if the alternate hypothesis is $\pi < 0.50$.

16-18 F
Med
Goal: 1

For small samples, the test statistic for the sign test is the normal distribution.

16-19 T
Med
Goal: 1

For small samples, the test statistic for the sign test is the binomial distribution.

16-20 F
Easy
Goal: 1

To apply the sign test, at least an interval level of measurement is required.

16-21 F
Easy
Goal: 2

The sign test is more efficient than the Wilcoxon signed-rank test.

16-22 T
Easy
Goal: 1

The sign test ignores the amount of the difference between two numbers.

16-23 T
Easy
Goal: 1

The sign test is based on the sign of the difference between two numbers.

16-24 T
Med
Goal: 2

The Wilcoxon signed rank test requires that the two samples be at least at the ordinal level of measurement and that the data be paired.

16-25 T
Easy
Goal: 1

If we want to find out if the median income of senior citizens is $17,680, the null hypothesis (H_0) is: Median = $17,680.

16-26 F
Easy
Goal: 1

The rank correlation test should be applied to test a hypothesis about a median.

16-27 F
Easy
Goal: 1

Nonparametric tests require that the populations of interest are normally distributed and that the observations be at least interval scale.

16-28 T
Easy
Goal: 5

Spearman's rank-order correlation coefficient may assume a value from –1 to +1.

16-29 F
Easy
Goal: 5

A Spearman's rank-order correlation coefficient of 0.91 indicates a very weak relationship.

16-30 T
Med
Goal: 6

The alternate hypothesis states that rho in the population is greater than zero. Since the words "greater than "predict a direction, the test of significance is one-tailed.

MULTPLE CHOICE QUESTIONS

16-31 B
Med
Goal: 4

To determine whether four populations are equal, a sample from each population was selected at random and using the Kruskal-Wallis test, H was computed to be 2.09. What is our decision at the 0.05 level of risk?

A. Fail to reject the null hypothesis because 0.05 < 2.09
B. Fail to reject the null hypothesis because 2.09 < 7.815
C. Reject the null hypothesis because 7.815 is > 2.09
D. Reject the null hypothesis because 2.09 > critical value of 1.96
E. None of the above

16-32 A
Med
Goal: 1

A one-tailed sign test is applied to a set of paired data. There were 14 pairs and the 0.10 level of significance was selected. There were 9 pluses and 5 minuses. What is the decision regarding the null hypothesis?

A. Fail to reject it
B. Reject it
C. Neither reject it nor fail to reject it based on information given
D. None of the above

16-33 A
Med
Goal: 1

If a sign test is applied, what is the null hypothesis for a two-tailed test?

A. $H_0:\pi = 0.50$
B. $H_0:\pi$ not equal to 0.50
C. $H_0:\pi > 0.50$
D. $H_0:\pi < 0.50$
E. None of the above

16-34 B
Med
Goal: 1

What is the test statistic for the sign test if the sample size is large?

A. Chi-square
B. Standard normal z
C. Binomial
D. Wilcoxon signed-rank
E. None of the above

16-35 D
Med
Goal: 1

For the sign test large-sample procedure, the sample size is at least

A. 2
B. 8
C. 100
D. 10
E. None of the above

16-36 A
Med
Goal: 1

To use the sign test with paired data, successive trials must be:

A. Independent
B. Dependent
C. Both dependent and independent at the same time
D. Equal to an a of 0.05
E. None of the above

16-37 D
Med
Goal: 1

What is a null hypothesis for a one-tail sign test?

A. $\pi = 0$
B. $\pi < 0.5$
C. $\pi = 0.50$
D. $\pi \leq 0.50$
E. None of the above

16-38 C
Med
Goal: 1

What is the first step in applying the sign test?

A. Rank the paired data from high to low or vice versa
B. Apply a correction factor to each observation
C. Determine sign of difference between each observed pair of data
D. Determine the number of degrees of freedom
E. None of the above

16-39 E
Med
Goal: 1

What is the decision rule for small sample sign test?

A. Fail to reject H_0 if computed $\pi = 0.50$
B. Reject Ho if computed π does not equal 0.50
C. Fail to reject H_0 if the computed value of chi-square > 11.070
D. Fail to reject H_0 if $z = 0.50$
E. None of the above

16-40 B
Med
Goal: 1

Which statement is true when using the sign test and a large sample?

A. Chi-square value is applied to arrive at the degrees of freedom
B. A normal distribution should be used to approximate a binomial distribution by including a continuity correction factor
C. Wilcoxon Z is used as the test statistic
D. All of the above are correct
E. None of the above

16-41 B
Med
Goal: 1

If a test is to be used to test H_0: Median equals $12.40 and the alternate hypothesis: Median does not equal $12.40, what is the critical value of z at the 10% level of significance?

A. + 1.96
B. + 1.65
C. + 2.33
D. + 0.10
E. None of the above

16-42 B
Med
Goal: 1

A two-tailed test of hypothesis was conducted and 60 values were above the median. Computed $z = 1.61$. At the 0.05 level, what is the decision regarding the null hypothesis?

A. Reject it
B. Fail to reject it
C. Neither reject it nor fail to reject it
D. None of the above

16-43 D
Med
Goal: 4

If there are three or more populations with ordinal data and we wish to test whether the distributions are equal, what is the appropriate test?

A. z
B. *t*
C. ANOVA
D. Kruskal-Wallis
E. None of the above

16-44 D
Med
Goal: 2

What test is an appropriate substitute for the ANOVA procedure if the assumptions for ANOVA cannot be met?

A. *z*
B. *t*
C. Rank correlation
D. Kruskal-Wallis
E. None of the above

16-45 C
Med
Goal: 2

If the assumptions for the paired *t* test cannot be met, what is the nonparametric alternative test?

A. Rank correlation
B. Kruskal-Wallis
C. Wilcoxon signed rank
D. Median
E. None of the above

16-46 B
Med
Goal: 1

Which of the following tests is not a distribution-free test?
A. Rank correlation
B. Student's t
C. Kruskal-Wallis
D. Wilcoxon
E. None of the above

16-47 B
Med
Goal: 4

This test is used when the assumptions for the parametric analysis of variance (ANOVA) cannot be met. Its purpose is to test whether three or more populations are equal. The data must be at least ordinal scaled. What nonparametric test is this?
A. Students' *t*
B. Kruskal-Wallis
C. Mann-Whitney
D. ANOVA
E. None of the above

16-48 E
Med
Goal: 3

This nonparametric test requires at least ordinal level data. Its purpose is to find out if there is any difference between two sets of related observations and it is used if the assumptions required for the paired *t* test cannot be met. Which test is it?
A. Students' *t*
B. ANOVA
C. Rank correlation
D. Kruskal-Wallis
E. None of the above

16-49 D
Med
Goal: 1

Which of the following statements is true regarding the sign test?
A. It is based on the sign of the difference
B. It is used in "before" and "after" experiments
C. The binomial distribution is used as the test statistic.
D. All of the above
E. None of the above

16-50 A
Med
Goal: 5

What is the distribution for Spearman's rank correlation?
A. t
B. z
C. F
D. Chi-square
E. None of the above

16-51 B
Med
Goal: 4

What is a requirement that must be met before the Kruskal-Wallis one-way analysis of variance by ranks test can be applied?
A. Populations must be normal or near normal
B. Samples must be independent
C. Population standard deviations must be equal
D. Data must be at least interval level
E. None of the above

16-52 C
Med
Goal: 4

The distribution of the sample statistic (H) for the Kruskal-Wallis test is approximately equal to

A. *F.*
B. *t.*
C. chi-square.
D. standard normal.
E. none of the above.

16-53 A
Med
Goal: 2

Under what conditions would the Kruskal-Wallis test be chosen over ANOVA when the sample data is at least interval level?

A. Assumption concerning the population being normal cannot be made
B. ANOVA is too difficult to calculate
C. ANOVA formulas are overly precise
D. ANOVA is not helpful for unequal sample sizes
E. None of the above

16-54 B
Med
Goal: 5

The scale of measurement for the coefficient of rank correlation is the

A. nominal.
B. ordinal.
C. interval.
D. ratio.
E. none of the above.

16-55 A
Med
Goal: 5

Which of the following values of Spearman's (rho) indicates the strongest relationship between two variables?

A. –0.91
B. –0.05
C. +0.64
D. +0.89
E. 0

16-56 C
Med
Goal: 5

Suppose ranks are assigned to a set of data from low to high with $10 being ranked 1, $12 being ranked 2 and $21 being ranked 3. What ranks would be assigned to $26, $26 and $26?

A. 4, 5, 6
B. 4, 4, 4
C. 5, 5, 5
D. 5.5, 5.5, 5.5
E. None of the above

16-57 A
Med
Goal: 5

For a given set of twelve ranked data values, the sum of the squared differences is 63.18. What is Spearman's coefficient of rank correlation for the data?

A. +.7791
B. –.7791
C. +.2209
D. –.2209
E. None of the above is correct

16-58 B
Med
Goal: 5

A hypothesis test is to be conducted at the 5% level of significance to determine whether the population rho is zero. If Spearman's (rho) is 0.86 for a sample of 15 observations, what is the computed value of the *t* statistic?

A. 0.456
B. 6.08
C. 0.425
D. 2.16
E. None of the above

FILL-IN QUESTIONS

16-59
Med
Goal: 1

What kind of sign test should be applied if H_0: $\pi \leq 0.50$, H_1: $\pi > 0.50$ and the level of significance is 0.05?__________________

16-60
Med
Goal: 2

Which test requires that the observations be paired?
____

16-61
Med
Goal: 2

Which test do we apply to test whether three or more population means are equal and the data nonparametric?____________________

16-62
Med
Goal: 2

In which test must the samples be dependent? __________________

16-63
Med
Goal: 5

If two movie critics ranked the current week's releases in opposite orders, what would Spearman's rank correlation be? _____________

16-64
Med
Goal: 4

Which test statistic follows the chi-square distribution? __________

16-65
Med
Goal: 2

Which test is used for before and after situations? _______________

16-66
Med
Goal: 2

Which test pairs the data? ______________

16-67
Med
Goal: 5

In testing the significance of Spearman's rank-order coefficient, what is the null hypothesis? _______________

16-68
Med
Goal: 5

In testing the significance of Spearman's rank-order coefficient, what is the alternate hypothesis? ____________________

16-69
Med
Goal: 5

What is the value of the Spearman rank-order correlation coefficient that indicates no association between the two variables? _____

Questions 70-72 refer to the following:
A study was conducted on the percent of total advertising dollars spent by ten local firms for advertising in the press and on cable television. Results were ranked with a resulting sum of squared differences equal to 128.

16-70 B
Med
Goal: 5

What is Spearman's coefficient of rank correlation?
A. –0.871
B. +0.224
C. +0.234
D. –0.234
E. None of the above

16-71 D
Med
Goal: 5

If $r_s = 0.345$, then the computed value of t is
A. 0.655.
B. 0.968.
C. 1.206.
D. 1.0396.
E. none of the above.

16-72 C
Med
Goal: 5

What is the sum of the differences in ranks?
A. 128
B. 100
C. 0
D. 1
E. None of the above

Questions 73-80 refer to the following:
A soap manufacturer is experimenting with several formulas of soap powder and three of the formulas were selected for further testing by a panel of homemakers. The ratings for the three formulas are as follows:

A	35	36	44	42	37	40
B	43	44	42	32	39	41
C	46	47	40	36	45	49

16-73
Med
Goal: 4

The soap manufacturer decided to use the Kruskal-Wallis test. What is the null hypothesis? ______________________________

16-74
Med
Goal: 4

What is the number of degrees of freedom? _______

16-75
Med
Goal: 4

What is the value of chi-square at the 5% level of significance?
____

16-76
Med
Goal: 4

What is the sum of the ranks for Formula A? _______

16-77
Med
Goal: 4

What is the sum of the ranks for Formula B? _______

16-78
Med
Goal: 4

What is the sum of the ranks for Formula C? _______

16-79
Med
Goal: 4

What is the value of H? _______

16-80
Med
Goal: 4

If H is less than the critical value, what is our decision rule?
____

Questions 81-83 refer to the following:
In a market research study involving eleven people, seven preferred Product X, three preferred Product Y and one expressed no preference. A sign test is selected using the 0.05 level of significance.

16-81
Med
Goal: 1

What is the null hypothesis? ____________________

16-82
Med
Goal: 1

What is the alternate hypothesis? __________________

16-83
Med
Goal: 1

What is the decision rule if the test statistic is the number of people preferring Product X? ________________________________

Questions 84-89 refer to the following:
Two movie reviewers gave their ratings (0 to 4 stars) to seven movies released this past month as follows:

Movie	*A*	*B*	*C*	*D*	*E*	*F*	*G*
S's Rating	4	2	3½	1	0	3	2½
T's Rating	3	3	3	2½	1½	3½	4

The Wilcoxon signed-rank test of difference is to be used.

16-84
Med
Goal: 2

What is the null hypothesis? ______________________

16-85
Med
Goal: 2

What is the alternate hypothesis?
____

16-86
Med
Goal: 2

What is the sum of the ranks? _______

16-87
Med
Goal: 2

What is the critical value at the 5% level of significance? ______

16-88
Med
Goal: 2

What is the test statistic? ______

16-89
Med
Goal: 2

What is your decision at the 5% level of significance? __________

Questions 90-93 refer to the following:
Two movie reviewers gave their ratings (0 to 4 stars) to seven movies released this past month as follows:

Movie	*A*	*B*	*C*	*D*	*E*	*F*	*G*
S's Rating	4	2	3½	1	0	3	2½
T's Rating	3	3	3	2½	1½	3½	4

The Wilcoxon rank-sum test is to be used. Assume 4 is ranked first.

16-90
Med
Goal: 2

What is the sum of the ranks for S? ______________________

16-91
Med
Goal: 2

What is the sum of the ranks for T? ______________________

16-92
Med
Goal: 2

What is W if S is identified as population #1? ________________

16-93
Hard
Goal: 2

What is the value of calculated z? __________________

Questions 94-102 refer to the following:
Two movie reviewers gave their ratings (0 to 4 stars) to ten movies released this past month as follows:

Movie	*A*	*B*	*C*	*D*	*E*	*F*	*G*	*H*	*I*	*J*
S's Rating	4	2	3½	1	0	3	2½	4	2	0
T's Rating	3	3	3	2½	1½	3½	4	3	2	1

The rank order correlation is to be used.

16-94
Med
Goal: 5

What is the value of d? __________

16-95
Med
Goal: 5

What is the value of d^2? __________

16-96
Hard
Goal: 5

What is the rank order correlation? __________

16-97
Med
Goal: 5

What is the null hypothesis for rank order correlation? __________

16-98
Med
Goal: 5

What is the alternate hypothesis for rank order correlation? ________

16-99
Med
Goal: 5

What are the degrees of freedom? ________

16-100
Hard
Goal: 5

What is the critical value at $\alpha = 0.05$? ________

16-101
Hard
Goal: 5

What is the computed value of t? ________

16-102
Hard
Goal: 5

What is your decision? ________

Questions 103-107 refer to the following:
The following are the ratings (0 to 4) given by 12 individuals for two possible new flavors of soft drinks.

Flavor	*A*	*B*	*C*	*D*	*E*	*F*	*G*	*H*	*I*	*J*	*K*	*L*
#1	4	2	3½	1	0	3	2½	4	2	0	3	2
#2	3	3	3	2½	1½	3½	4	3	2	1	2	2

Wilcoxon rank-sum is to be used. Assume that the "0" is ranked first.

16-103 A
Hard
Goal: 2

What is the sum of the ranks for flavor #1?
A. 144
B. 139
C. 156
D. 153
E. None of the above

16-104 D
Hard
Goal: 2

What is the sum of the ranks for flavor #2?
A. 153
B. 139
C. 144
D. 156
E. None of the above

16-105 C
Hard
Goal: 2

What is W if flavor #1 is identified as population 1?
A. 153
B. 156
C. 144
D. 139
E. None of the above

16-106 A
Hard
Goal: 2

What is the absolute value of calculated z?
A. 0.3464
B. 0.1732
C. 0.0165
D. 0.2807
E. None of the above

16-107 B
Hard
Goal: 2

At the 0.05 level of significance, what is the decision?
A. Fail to reject null hypothesis; critical value is ± 1.65
B. Fail to reject null hypothesis; critical value is ± 1.96
C. Reject null hypothesis; critical value is 0.1732
D. Reject null hypothesis; critical value is 0.3464
E. None of the above

Questions 108-111 refer to the following:

20 economists were sampled and asked to predict if the national economy would improve during the next twelve months. Eleven of the economists predicted an increase, two economists predicted no change, and seven economists predicted a decrease in the economy. Conduct a hypothesis test at the 0.10 significance level to determine if the majority of economists predict an increase.

16-108 C
Easy
Goal: 1

The null hypothesis is:

A. $H_O: \pi = 0.5$
B. $H_O: \pi \neq 0.5$
C. $H_O: \pi \leq 0.5$
D. $H_O: \pi \geq 0.5$

16-109 B
Easy
Goal: 1

The correct analysis would be:

A. A sign test based on the binomial distribution
B. A sign test based on the standard normal distribution
C. A chi square test
D. A Wilcoxon signed rank test

16-110 A
Medium
Goal: 1

The test statistic is:

A. 0.707
B. 1.179
C. 1.707
D. 0.179

16-111 C
Medium
Goal: 1

Based on the analysis, we would conclude that:

A. The economists favor an increase in the economy
B. The economists favor a decrease in the economy
C. The economists favor no change in the economy
D. No conclusion can be reached.

Answers to Fill-In Questions

Chapter 16. Nonparametric Methods: Analysis of Ranked Data

16-59 one-tailed
16-60 Wilcoxon sign rank or sign test
16-61 Kruskal-Wallis
16-62 Wilcoxon signed-rank or sign test
16-63 –1
16-64 Kruskal-Wallis H statistic
16-65 Sign test
16-66 Wilcoxon or sign test
16-67 = zero
16-68 ≠ zero
16-69 zero
16-73 No difference in the ratings
16-74 2
16-75 5.991
16-76 42
16-77 52
16-78 77
16-79 3.801
16-80 Do not reject H_0 -- no difference in mean rating scores
16-81 $H_0 : \pi = .50$
16-82 $H_1 : \pi \neq .50$
16-83 Do not reject H_0 if 2–8 people prefer *X*; else, reject H_0
16-84 No difference in the movie ratings
16-85 There is a difference in the movie ratings
16-86 23
16-87 3
16-88 5
16-89 Do not reject H_0
16-90 46
16-91 59
16-92 46
16-93 –0.83
16-94 0
16-95 48
16-96 0.7091
16-97 = 0
16-98 ≠ 0
16-99 8
16-100 2.306
16-101 2.844
16-102 Reject H_o

Chapter 17. Statistical Quality Control

TRUE/FALSE QUESTIONS

17-1 F
Easy
Goal: 5

Mean charts are designed to determine whether the range is in or out of control.

17-2 T
Easy
Goal: 1

Dr. Walter A. Shewhart introduced the concepts of "controlling" the quality rather than inspecting it into the part.

17-3 T
Easy
Goal: 2

There are two general types of causes of variations in a manufacturing process—chance and assignable.

17-4 F
Easy
Goal: 2

Assignable causes are usually large in number and random in nature, and they cannot be entirely eliminated.

17-5 F
Easy
Goal: 2

Chance causes of variation are usually few in number and not random in nature, and they can readily be reduced or eliminated.

17-6 T
Easy
Goal: 2

Assignable causes can generally be corrected easily, while chance causes cannot usually be corrected or stabilized economically.

17-7 T
Easy
Goal: 2

The purpose of a statistical quality control chart is to identify when assignable causes of variation or changes in process level have entered the production system so that the cause may be identified and corrected.

17-8 T
Easy
Goal: 2

Quality control charts indicate whether the production of a part or parts is in control or out of control.

17-9 T
Easy
Goal: 2

Control charts have been developed for both variables and attributes.

17-10 T
Easy
Goal: 5

Mean charts are designed to determine whether the arithmetic mean is in or out of control.

17-11 T
Easy
Goal: 5

Summing the means of the samples and dividing that sum by the number of sample means can compute the mean of an X bar chart.

17-12 T
Easy
Goal: 5

The purpose of a mean chart is to portray the fluctuations in the sample means.

17-13 T
Med
Goal: 5

The upper control limit (UCL) and the lower control limit (LCL) of a chart report the limits of the variation expected by chance.

17-14 T
Med
Goal: 5

For a range chart, about 997 sample ranges out of 1,000 will fall between the upper and lower control limits.

17-15 T
Easy
Goal: 5

A range chart shows variation in the ranges of the samples.

17-16 T
Easy
Goal: 5

If a range should fall outside the control limits, it is very likely that some assignable cause affected the production.

17-17 T
Easy
Goal: 6

Percent defective charts, which are also known as P charts or p bar charts, show the percent of the production that is or is not acceptable.

17-18 F
Easy
Goal: 6

A *c* bar chart shows the percent of the production that is defective.

17-19 T
Easy
Goal: 6

The following are examples of attributes: A weld has a crack in it or it doesn't; a relay works or it doesn't; a radiator leaks or it doesn't; the lock on a car door works or it doesn't; a tire fits on the rim or it doesn't.

17-20 T
Easy
Goal: 6

The purpose of a *c* bar chart is to show how many defects appear in a unit of production.

17-21 F
Easy
Goal: 6

A value of 4.0 is recorded on the centerline of a *c* bar chart. This indicates that the lowest number of defects per unit is 4.0.

17-22 T
Easy
Goal: 2

Chance causes of variation cannot be entirely eliminated.

17-23 F
Easy
Goal: 7

In acceptance sampling, usually 100% of the incoming lot is checked.

17-24 T
Easy
Goal: 7

In acceptance sampling, if the number of defects in a sample is less or equal to the acceptance number, then the incoming lot is accepted.

MULTIPLE CHOICE QUESTIONS

17-25 D
Hard
Goal: 6

Samples of 200 parts were taken every day and the number of defectives were counted. What are the upper and lower limits for the percent defective chart?

Day	1	2	3	4
Number Defective	4	3	5	4

A. 0.02 and 0
B. 0.2970 and 0
C. 0.0297 and 0
D. 0.0497 and 0
E. None of the above

17-26 E
Hard
Goal: 6

A subassembly is inspected and number of defects recorded. A new group of assemblers began work Monday morning. The number of defects per subassembly for the first 10 they produced was: 3, 2, 0, 5, 4, 6, 0, 7, 7, and 6. What are the upper and lower limits for the *c* bar chart?

A. 15 and 0
B. 4 and 0
C. 1.12 and 0
D. 6 and –2
E. None of the above

17-27 C
Med
Goal: 7

What is usually developed to evaluate a sampling plan?

A. Frequency polygon
B. Scatter diagram
C. Operating characteristic curve
D. Simple bar chart
E. None of the above

17-28 D
Med
Goal: 8

Which probability distribution is used to develop an operating characteristic curve?

A. Normal distribution
B. Chi-square distribution
C. Mann-Whitney test
D. Binomial distribution
E. None of the above

17-29 A
Med
Goal: 2

Of what type of variation would rain be an example?

A. Chance
B. External
C. Assignable
D. Standard variation
E. None of the above

17-30 D
Hard
Goal: 8

A sampling plan states that if 20 incoming transistors are checked and 2 or less defects are found that the lot is accepted. If an incoming lot is 10 percent defective, what is the probability of accepting the lot of transistors?

A. 0
B. 1
C. 0.037
D. 0.667
E. 0.323

17-31 C
Hard
Goal: 8

A sampling plan states that if 20 incoming bolts are checked and 2 or less defective bolts are discovered the lot will be rejected. If an incoming lot is 10 percent defective, what is the probability of rejecting the lot?

A. 0
B. 1
C. 0.323
D. 0.667
E. None of the above

17-32 C
Hard
Goal: 8

Cappelli Inc., designs and manufactures women's apparel using material from various mills. Their acceptance sampling plan states that 20 two inch squares of the incoming material must be carefully checked. If 3 or less squares reveal imperfections, the lot is accepted. What is the probability that an incoming lot from Blufton Mills that contains 40 percent imperfect cloth will be accepted?

A. 0
B. 0.239
C. 0.015
D. 0.0024
E. None of the above

17-33 A
Easy
Goal: 1

What is the process by which a company can insure that a quality product or service is being produced?

A. SPC
B. Pareto
C. Fishbone
D. Diagnostic chart
E. None of the above

17-34 C
Med
Goal: 2

What type of variation can be reduced, or even eliminated, and is usually nonrandom in nature?

A. Chance
B. External
C. Assignable
D. Co-variation
E. None of the above

17-35 C
Med
Goal: 2

Equipment failure would be an example of ____________ variation.

A. chance
B. external
C. assignable
D. standard variation
E. above of the above

17-36 B
Med
Goal: 3

The technique that tallies numbers and types of defects is called

A. range charts.
B. Pareto charts.
C. control charts.
D. fishbone diagram.
E. none of the above.

17-37 D
Med
Goal: 4

The cause-and-effect chart is an example of

A. range charts.
B. Pareto charts.
C. control charts.
D. fishbone diagram.
E. none of the above.

17-38 D
Med
Goal: 5

In a control chart, expected variation is defined by

A. standard deviation.
B. standard error of the distribution.
C. only upper control limits.
D. upper and lower control limits.
E. none of the above.

17-39 A
Med
Goal: 5

Control charts are used to determine if a process is

A. in or out of control.
B. measurable.
C. fixable.
D. testable.
E. none of the above.

17-40 D
Easy
Goal: 6

The Quality Assurance Department selected a sample of 12 printed circuit boards and tested them. The number of defects in each circuit board were 3, 3, 0, 5, 1, 1, 5, 6, 6, 2, 0, and1. What kind of control chart should be constructed to monitor the process?

A. Mean chart
B. Range chart
C. Percent defective chart
D. C-bar chart

17-41 C
Easy
Goal: 6

The Quality Assurance Department selected 12 samples of 100 printed circuit boards and tested them. The number of defective printed circuit boards in each sample was 3, 3, 0, 5, 1, 1, 5, 6, 6, 2, 0, and1. What kind of control chart should be constructed to monitor the process?

A. Mean chart
B. Range chart
C. Percent defective chart
D. C-bar chart

17-42 C
Med
Goal: 5

The upper and lower control limits are usually set at

A. the mean.
B. above the mean.
C. ±3 standard deviations from the mean.
D. ±2 standard deviations from the mean.
E. none of the above.

FILL-IN QUESTIONS

17-43
Med
Goal: 6

Which chart portrays the number of defects per unit of production? ____________

17-44
Med
Goal: 6

In an acceptance sampling plan, what happens to the incoming lot if the number of defective items in the sample is less or equal to the acceptance number? ________________

17-45
Med
Goal: 7

What error has been committed if an incoming lot of computer chips contains more defective chips than it should, but is accepted? _______

17-46
Med
Goal: 7

If the binomial distribution is used to develop an operating characteristic curve for an acceptance sampling plan, then it is imperative that the trials be ________________

17-47
Med
Goal: 1

If the binomial distribution is used to develop an operating characteristic curve for an acceptance sampling plan, how many possible outcomes can there be? _______

17-48
Med
Goal: 1

In what decade were the concepts of statistical quality control developed?________

17-49
Med
Goal: 1

One of the most important concepts on the production line is that no two products are ________________

17-50
Med
Goal: 2

What does a statistical quality control chart identify? ___________

17-51
Med
Goal: 1

Control charts may portray measurement or _____________, or control charts may portray a product description, i.e., acceptable or defective, or an ___________________.

17-52
Med
Goal: 5

What is the purpose of the mean chart?
____

17-53
Med
Goal: 5

How is the mean of the sample means designated? _______

17-54
Med
Goal: 5

A range chart shows variation in the ranges of? ____________

17-55
Med
Goal: 5

If the ranges of the sample fall within the upper and lower control limits, then it can be assumed that production is? ___________

17-56
Med
Goal: 6

A p bar chart shows graphically the portion of production that is not acceptable. What is another name for the p bar chart?
____

17-57
Med
Goal: 6

What chart portrays the number of defects per unit? ___________

17-58
Med
Goal: 1

What is the "in control" region of a control chart called?
____

17-59
Med
Goal: 1

What causes of variation cannot be entirely eliminated? ____________

17-60
Med
Goal: 2

What variation is due to slight changes in materials or process conditions and is random in nature? _______________

Questions 61-67 refer to the following:
A new machine fills tubes of toothpaste at precisely 6.75 ounces. Sample of 6 tubes are taken every three hours and weighed with the following results:

Time	*Weight of Toothpaste*					
7 am	6.69	6.68	6.79	6.77	6.74	6.76
10 am	6.71	6.72	6.71	6.76	6.75	6.74
1 pm	6.66	6.68	6.67	6.71	6.76	6.78
4 pm	6.73	6.74	6.72	6.76	6.78	6.75
7 pm	6.75	6.73	6.75	6.77	6.79	6.75

17-61 C
Med
Goal: 5

If the mean of the ranges is 0.08, what is the value of the upper control limit (UCL) for the range?
A. 0.00
B. 0.08
C. 0.16
D. 2.00
E. None of the above

17-62 A
Med
Goal: 5

If the mean of the ranges is 0.08, what is the value for the lower control limit (LCL) of the range?
A. 0.00
B. 0.08
C. 0.16
D. 2.00
E. None of the above

17-63 B
Med
Goal: 5

What is X bar for 7 am?
A. 6.73
B. 6.74
C. 6.75
D. 6.76
E. None of the above

17-64 A
Med
Goal: 5

What is X bar for 10 am?
A. 6.73
B. 6.74
C. 6.75
D. 6.76
E. None of the above

17-65 E
Med
Goal: 5

What is X bar for 1 pm?
A. 6.73
B. 6.74
C. 6.75
D. 6.76
E. None of the above

17-66 C
Med
Goal: 5

What is X bar for 4 pm?

A. 6.73
B. 6.74
C. 6.75
D. 6.76
E. None of the above

17-67 D
Med
Goal: 5

What is X bar for 7 pm?

A. 6.73
B. 6.74
C. 6.75
D. 6.76
E. None of the above

17-68 D
Med
Goal: 5

What is the value of A_2, the control limit factor for averages?

A. 0
B. 1
C. 0.577
D. 0.483
E. None of the above

17-69 C
Med
Goal: 5

What is the range of the samples at 7 am?

A. 0.05
B. 0.06
C. 0.11
D. 0.12
E. None of the above

17-70 A
Med
Goal: 5

What is the range of the samples at 10 am?

A. 0.05
B. 0.06
C. 0.11
D. 0.12
E. None of the above

17-71 D
Med
Goal: 5

What is the range of the samples at 1 pm?

A. 0.05
B. 0.06
C. 0.11
D. 0.12
E. None of the above

17-72 B
Med
Goal: 5

What is the range of the samples at 4 pm?

A. 0.05
B. 0.06
C. 0.11
D. 0.12
E. None of the above

17-73 B
Med
Goal: 5

What is the range of the samples at 7 pm?
A. 0.05
B. 0.06
C. 0.11
D. 0.12
E. None of the above

17-74 C
Med
Goal: 5

What is the value of the upper control factor of the range?
A. 0
B. 2.115
C. 2.004
D. 3.0
E. None of the above

17-75 A
Med
Goal: 5

What is the value of the lower control factor of the range?
A. 0
B. 2.115
C. 2.004
D. 3.0
E. None of the above

17-76 C
Med
Goal: 5

If the mean of the sample means is 6.738 and R bar is 0.08, what is the upper control limit (UCL)?
A. 6.738
B. 6.999
C. 6.777
D. 7.221
E. None of the above

17-77 C
Med
Goal: 5

If the mean of the sample means is 6.738 and R bar is 0.08, what is the lower control limit?
A. 6.738
B. 6.669
C. 6.699
D. 6.255
E. None of the above

Questions 78-79 refer to the following:
Every half hour, the quality control inspector checks four pieces and records the outside diameters of each of them, as shown below.

	Sample Piece			
Time	1	2	3	4
9:00 A.M.	1	4	5	2
9:30 A.M.	2	3	2	1
10:00 A.M.	1	7	3	5

17-78 B
Med
Goal: 5

What are the upper and lower control limits of the mean chart?
A. 5.916. and 0
B. 5.916 and 0.084
C. 0.729 and 0
D. 4 and 0
E. None of the above

17-79 A
Med
Goal: 5

What are the upper and lower limits of the range chart?
A. 9.128 and 0
B. 2.282 and 4
C. 2.282 and 0
D. 100 and 0
E. None of the above

Questions 80-82 refer to the following:
A new machine used in the production of motor mount bolts was put into operation. Five samples of size 100 were randomly selected and the number of defectives in each sample was noted.

Sample	*1*	2	3	*4*	5
Defectives	3	1	3	4	2

17-80 C
Med
Goal: 6

What is the average percent defective?
A. 2.0%
B. 2.3%
C. 2.6%
D. 2.9%
E. None of the above

17-81 B
Med
Goal: 6

What is the upper control limit (UCL)?
A. 0.067
B. 0.074
C. 0.081
D. 1.000
E. None of the above

17-82 A
Med
Goal: 6

What is the lower control limit (LCL)?
A. 0
B. –0.022
C. 0.048
D. 0.160
E. None of the above

Questions 83-86 refer to the following:
Subgroups of 4 items each are taken from a manufacturing process at regular intervals and a certain quality characteristic is measured. After 25 subgroups, $\Sigma\overline{X}$ = 15,350 and ΣR = 411.4.

17-83 B
Med
Goal: 5

What is the value for the mean of the means?

A. 15,350
B. 614
C. 411.4
D. 3837.5
E. None of the above

17-84 C
Med
Goal: 5

What is the value for R bar?

A. 411.4
B. 614
C. 16.46
D. 102.88
E. None of the above

17-85
Med
Goal: 5

What is the upper control limit (UCL) for the mean? _____

17-86
Med
Goal: 5

What is the lower control limit (LCL) for the mean? _______

Questions 87-89 refer to the following:
A contact lens manufacturer requires that each lens is clear and is not scratched. To guard against scratched lenses, the manufacturer sampled 100 lenses over the last nine days. They found the following number of scratched lenses: 5, 3, 2, 7, 0, 1, 2, 3, 4. With this data, the manufacturer wants to construct a statistical process control chart.

17-87 B
Easy
Goal: 6

What is the center line for the chart?

A. 27
B. 0.03
C. 3
D. Cannot be computed

17-88 C
Medium
Goal: 6

What is the upper control limit?

A. 0.017
B. 0.051
C. 0.081
D. 0.03

17-89 C
Medium
Goal: 6

What is the lower control limit?

A. 0.017
B. –0.021
C. 0.000
D. 0.03

Answers to Fill-In Questions

Chapter 17. Statistical Quality Control

17-43 c bar

17-44 lot is accepted

17-45 consumers risk

17-46 independent

17-47 two

17-48 1920's

17-49 identical

17-50 assignable causes

17-51 variables and attributes

17-52 portrays fluctuations or variations in sample means

17-53 X double bar

17-54 samples

17-55 in control

17-56 defective chart

17-57 c bar

17-58 acceptance region

17-59 chance

17-60 chance

17-85 625.996

17-86 602.004

Chapter 18. Index Numbers

TRUE/FALSE QUESTIONS

18-1 T
Easy
Goal: 1

An index number is a percent that measures the change in price, quantity, value, or some other item of interest from one time to another.

18-2 T
Easy
Goal: 1

An index of 239.2 and an index of 86.4 are actually percents.

18-3 F
Easy
Goal: 1

All indexes have the same base, namely 1982-84, written 1982-84=100.

18-4 T
Easy
Goal: 1

The base period for one index might be 1982-84, while the base period for another index might be 1977.

18-5 F
Easy
Goal: 1

The base number for most indexes is 1.

18-6 T
Easy
Goal: 6

No systematic approach to collecting and reporting data in index form was evident in the United States until about 1900.

18-7 T
Easy
Goal: 1

An Italian, G.R. Carli, has been credited with originating the first index numbers in 1764.

18-8 T
Easy
Goal: 6

An index is a convenient way of comparing changes for different variables, i.e., average income and food prices.

18-9 T
Easy
Goal: 1

Most business and economic indexes are carried either to the nearest whole percent, such as 312 or 96, or to the nearest 10th of a percent, such as 97.5 and 178.6.

18-10 T
Easy
Goal: 1

Converting data to indexes makes it easier to compare the trend in a series composed of exceptionally large numbers.

18-11 F
Easy
Goal: 2

The base-period price is designated as p_n and the price for the given period is designated p_0.

18-12 T
Easy
Goal: 3

Etienne Laspeyres developed a method in the latter part of the 18th century to determine a weighted index using base-period weights.

18-13 T
Easy
Goal: 4

Two methods of computing a weighted price index are the Laspeyres' method and Paasche's method.

18-14 T
Easy
Goal: 2

The Laspeyres' method uses the amounts consumed in the base period, q_0 , as weights to determine a price index.

18-15 T
Easy
Goal: 3

If we are constructing a weighted index of the price of food for 2000 using the Laspeyres' method and 1982-84 = 100, we use the amounts consumed in the base period, q_0, as weights.

18-16 F
Med
Goal: 6

The CPI serves only one major function: as an economic indicator of the rate of inflation in the United States.

18-17 T
Easy
Goal: 6

To construct a special-purpose index designed to measure general business activity, the weights are based on the judgments of the statistician and assigned to each series.

18-18 T
Easy
Goal: 6

The Consumer Price Index measures the change in prices of a fixed market basket of goods and services from one period to another.

18-19 T
Easy
Goal: 6

One function of CPI is to allow consumers to determine the degree to which their purchasing power is being eroded by price increases and as such, it is a yardstick for revising wages, pensions and other income payments to keep pace with changes in prices.

18-20 T
Easy
Goal: 6

The Consumer Price Index originated in 1913 and has been published regularly since 1921.

18-21 T
Easy
Goal: 6

The CPI is not just one index, but includes a large number of groups, subgroups and selected items, such as a food index, a medical care index and an entertainment index.

18-22 T
Easy
Goal: 6

The Consumer Price Index is based on about 400 items, and about 250 part-time and full-time agents collect price data monthly. Prices are collected from more than 18,000 tenants, 24,000 retail establishments and 18,000 housing units in 85 urban areas across the country. The prices of baby cribs, bread, beer, cigars and operating-room charges are just a few of the items included in what is often termed a typical "market basket" of goods and services.

18-23 T
Easy
Goal: 6

The first of two Consumer Price Indexes is for all urban consumers and covers about 80 percent of the total noninstitutional population, while the second one is for urban wage earners and clerical workers and covers about half the population.

18-24 T
Easy
Goal: 6

Besides measuring change in the prices of goods and services, the consumer price indexes have a number of other applications. The CPI is used to determine real disposable personal income, deflate sales or other series, find the purchasing power of the dollar and establish cost of living increases.

18-25 T
Easy
Goal: 6

The concept of real income is sometimes called deflated income or income expressed in constant dollars and the CPI is called the deflator.

18-26 F
Easy
Goal: 6

To deflate sales, the actual sales are multiplied by the wholesale price index and the result multiplied by 100.

18-27 T
Easy
Goal: 6

Social security, old-age pensions, many apartment leases and many labor contracts are tied to the change in the CPI.

18-28 T
Easy
Goal: 6

Millions of employees in automobile, steel, and other industries have their wages adjusted upward when the CPI increases. The specifics are in the management-union contracts. These clauses in the contracts are referred to as "escalator clauses."

18-29 T
Easy
Goal 6

If two or more series of index numbers have the same year as the base period, then they can be compared directly.

18-30 T
Easy
Goal: 6

When two or more series of index numbers to be compared do not have the same base period, we select a common base period for all series. Then we use the respective base numbers as the denominators and convert each base to the new base.

MULTIPLE CHOICE QUESTIONS

18-31 D
Med
Goal: 2

If the average hourly earnings in mining in 1978 was $7.67 and for the most recent month it was $14.90, what is the index of hourly earnings for the most recent month based on 1978?

A. 100.0
B. 186.9
C. 151.5
D. 194.3
E. None of the above

18-32 C
Med
Goal: 2

The Bureau of the Census reported that the farm population dropped from 30.5 million in 1940 to 6.5 million in 1999. What is the index for 1999 based on 1940?

A. 469.7
B. 100.0
C. 21.3
D. 78.7
E. None of the above

18-33 E
Med
Goal: 2

Sean McCarthy earns $20,000 a year; John Nowak, $35,000. What is John's income as an index using Sean's income as the base?

A. 1.75
B. 75.0
C. 100.0
D. 57.1
E. None of the above

18-34 A
Med
Goal: 2

The wholesale price of a straight back desk chair in 1998 was $20; in 1999, $23; and in 2000, $18. What were the indexes for 1999 and 2000 using 1998 = 100?

A. 115.0 and 90.0
B. 1.15 and 0.9
C. 1150.0 and 900.0
D. 87.0 and 111.1
E. None of the above

18-35 B
Med
Goal: 3

An index of clothing prices for 2000 based on 1983 is to be constructed. The prices for 1983 and 2000 and the quantity consumed in 1983 are shown below.

Item	*1983 Price*	*1983 Amount Sold*	*2000 Price*
Dress (each)	$35	500	$65
Shoes (pair)	40	1,200	90

Assuming that the number sold remained constant, i.e., the same number were sold in 2000 as in 1983, what is the weighted index of price for 2000 using 1983 as the base?

A. 206.7
B. 214.5
C. 48.4
D. 46.6
E. None of the above

18-36 A
Med
Goal: 6

Real income is computed by

A. dividing money income by the CPI and multiplying by 100.
B. dividing the CPI by money income and multiplying by 100.
C. multiplying money income by the CPI.
D. subtracting the CPI from money income.
E. none of the above.

18-37 C
Med
Goal: 3

Prices and the number produced for selected agricultural items are:

	Price		Production	
Item	*1980*	*2000*	*1980*	*2000*
Wheat (bushel)	$ 2.00	$ 4.00	100	700
Eggs (dozen)	0.30	0.20	1,000	800
Pork (cwt.)	60.00	70.00	50	110

Using the Laspeyres method, what price index of agricultural production for 2000 (1980 = 100)?

A. 42.5
B. 257.5
C. 117.1
D. 85.3
E. None of the above

18-38 D
Hard
Goal: 5

The number of items produced and the price per item for the Duffy Manufacturing Company are:

	Price		Production	
Item Produced	*1990*	*2000*	*1990*	*2000*
Shear pins (box)	$ 3	$ 4	10,000	9,000
Cutting compound (lb.)	1	5	600	200
Tie rods (each)	10	8	3,000	5,000

What is the value index of production for 2000 using 1990 as the base period?

A. 115.2
B. 72.9
C. 110.6
D. 127.1
E. None of the above

18-39 A
Med
Goal: 6

As chief statistician for the county, you want to compute and publish every year a special-purpose index, which you plan to call Index of County Business Activity. Three series seem to hold promise as the basis for the index; namely, the price of cotton, the number of new automobiles sold and the rate of money turnover for the county (published by a local bank). Arbitrarily you decide that money turnover should have a weight of 60 percent; number of new automobiles sold, 30 percent; and the price of cotton, 10 percent.

Year	*Price of Cotton (per pound)*	*Number of Automobiles Sold*	*Rate of Money Turnover (an index)*
1981	$0.20	100,000	80
2000	0.50	80,000	120

What is the Index of County Business Activity for 1981 (the base year) and for 2000?

A. 100 for 1981, 139 for 2000
B. 139 for 1981, 100 for 2000
C. 100 for 1981, 61 for 2000
D. 100 for 1981, 100 for 2000
E. None of the above

18-40 C
Med
Goal 6

The Consumer Price Index in June 1998 was 248.4 (1982-84 = 100). What does this indicate about prices from 1982-84 to June 1998?

A. Rose 248.4%
B. Rose 548.4%
C. Rose 148.4%
D. Declined 148.4%
E. None of the above

18-41 D
Med
Goal: 6

Below is Jim Walker's income for 1985 and 2000.

Year	Income	CPI (1982-84 = 100)
1985	$ 17,000	107.6
2000	37,000	172.2

What was Jim's real income for 2000?

A. $17,000
B. $27,000
C. $15,799
D. $21,487
E. None of the above

18-42 D
Med
Goal: 6

The take home pay of an employee working in an urban area for 1973 and 2000 are:

Year	*Take Home Pay*
1970	$ 5,000
2000	13,200

If the CPI rose from 70 in 1973 to 172.2 in 2000 (1982-84 = 100), what was the "real" take home pay of the employee in 2000?

A. $5,000
B. $7,143
C. $11,200
D. $7,666
E. None of the above

18-43 A
Med
Goal: 6

How is the purchasing power of the dollar computed?

A. ($1/CPI) (100)
B. ($1 - CPI) (100)
C. ($1 x CPI) (100)
D. (CPI/$1) (100)
E. None of the above

18-44 C
Med
Goal: 6

If the Consumer Price Index is about 172.2 (1982-84 = 100), what is the purchasing power of the dollar?

A. $1.00
B. $0.33
C. $0.58
D. $0.50
E. None of the above

18-45 D
Med
Goal: 1

An index number is a percent that measures the change from one period of time to another in terms of?

A. Value
B. Price
C. Quantity
D. All of the above
E. None of the above

18-46 E
Med
Goal: 3

How can indexes be classified?

A. Price
B. Quantity
C. Value
D. Special purpose
E. All of the above

18-47 C
Medium
Goal: 6

The CPI for "personal computers and peripheral equipment" in July of 2001 was 29.3 (1982-1984=100). Interpret this index.

A. There was no significant increase in the price of "personal computers and peripheral equipment"
B. The price of "personal computers and peripheral equipment" increased 29.3%.
C. The price of "personal computers and peripheral equipment" decreased 70.7%.
D. If the average price of a computer in 1982-1984 was $3000.00, the CPI for "personal computers and peripheral equipment" would predict that the price of a computer in July 2001 would be $879.

18-48 D
Medium
Goal: 6

The CPI for "educational books and supplies" in July of 2001 was 295.1 (1982-1984=100). Interpret this index.

A. There was no significant increase in the price of "educational books and supplies".
B. The price of "educational books and supplies" increased 295.1%.
C. If the average price of a textbook in 1982-1984 was $25.00, the CPI for "educational books and supplies" would predict that the price of the textbook in July 2001 would be $73.75.
D. If the average price of a textbook in 1982-1984 was $25.00, the CPI for "educational books and supplies" would predict that the price of the textbook in July 2001 would be $48.75.

18-49 D
Med
Goal: 6

What does a typical market basket of goods and services include?

A. Bread
B. Beer
C. Milk
D. All of the above
E. None of the above

FILL-IN QUESTIONS

18-50
Med
Goal: 1

There are several indexes that reflect the overall economic activity in the United States. The federal government puts out an index of leading economic indicators. It includes such diverse economic indicators as stock prices, new orders for plants and equipment, and building permits issued. What are these indexes usually referred to as?

____

18-51
Med
Goal: 6

What is the base year for the Consumer Price Index currently? _______

18-52
Med
Goal: 1

What is the index that measures the average changes in prices received in the primary markets of the United States by producers of commodities? ______________________________

18-53 Med Goal: 1	What is a price index for a single commodity called? __________
18-54 Med Goal: 2	What is the symbol used to designate a base period price? _______
18-55 Med Goal: 2	What is the usual index number associated with the base period for the CPI? ______
18-56 Med Goal: 2	What is a major disadvantage of the unweighted price index? ______________________________
18-57 Med Goal: 4	Which method for computing a weighted price index uses current year weights? _____________
18-58 Med Goal: 2	What is another name for the unweighted method of computing an index? _____________________
18-59 Med Goal: 4	Which method of computing index numbers has the advantage that the consumption pattern is always up-to-date? _____________________
18-60 Med Goal: 5	Which index is computed using base year prices and quantities and current year prices and quantities together? _____________
18-61 Med Goal: 6	Which index measures the change in the prices of a fixed market basket of goods and services from one time period to another? ___________
18-62 Med Goal: 6	What is another term for real income? _______________
18-63 Med Goal: 6	What is the CPI called when it determines real income? ___________
18-64 Med Goal: 6	If we divide one dollar by the CPI and multiply it this result by 100, what is the result called? _________________________

18-65
Med
Goal: 1

What do we call a percent that measures the change in price, quantity, value or some other item of interest from one time period to another?

____

Questions 66-76 refer to the following:
Data for selected vegetables purchased at wholesale prices for 1995 and 2000 are shown below.

	1995		*2000*	
	Price	*Qty*	*Price*	*Qty*
Cabbage (pound)	$0.06	2,000	$0.05	1,500
Carrots (bunch)	0.10	200	0.12	200
Peas (quart)	0.20	400	0.18	500
Broccoli (bunch)	0.30	100	0.50	200

18-66 D
Med
Goal: 3

What is the unweighted aggregate price index?
A. 98.4
B. 107.0
C. 117.5
D. 128.8
E. None of the above

18-67 A
Med
Goal: 3

What is Laspeyres' price index?
A. 98.4
B. 107.0
C. 108.0
D. 117.5
E. None of the above

18-68 B
Med
Goal: 3

What is Paasche's price index?
A. 98.4
B. 107.0
C. 108.0
D. 117.5
E. None of the above

18-69 B
Med
Goal: 3

What is the value index?
A. 110.3
B. 115.6
C. 108.0
D. 118.5
E. None of the above

18-70 B
Med
Goal: 3

What is the average of Laspeyres' and Paasche's price indexes (Fisher Index)?
A. 107.5
B. 102.7
C. 112.8
D. 103.2
E. None of the above

18-71 B
Med
Goal: 3

What is the interpretation of the value index?

A. Value rose 28.8%
B. Value rose 15.6%
C. Value rose 17.5%
D. Value rose 20.0%
E. None of the above

18-72 B
Med
Goal: 3

What is your interpretation of Laspeyres' price index?

A. Prices rose 98.4%
B. Prices declined 1.6%
C. Prices rose 7.0%
D. Prices rose 8.0%
E. None of the above

18-73
Med
Goal: 2

What is the simple price relative for peas? _______

18-74
Med
Goal: 2

What is the simple price relative for broccoli? _______

18-75
Med
Goal: 2

What is the simple price relative for cabbage? _______

18-76
Med
Goal: 2

What is the simple price relative for carrots? _______

Questions 77-81 refer to the following:
Suppose your annual 1994 salary was $40,000 and your 2000 salary was $52,000. Assume the annual CPI rose from 130.7 to 172.2 during this period of time.

18-77
Med
Goal: 6

What was your real income in 1994? _______

18-78
Med
Goal: 6

What was you real income in 2000? _______

18-79
Med
Goal: 6

What was the purchasing power of the dollar in 2000? _______

18-80
Med
Goal: 6

What was the purchasing power of the dollar in 1994? _______

18-81
Med
Goal: 6

In which year was your "real" income larger? ________

Answers to Fill-In Questions

Chapter 18. Index Numbers

18-50 special purpose

18-51 1993-95

18-52 producers price index

18-53 relative

18-54 p_0

18-55 100

18-56 extremely large or small values overly influence the index

18-57 Paasche

18-58 simple aggregate

18-59 Paasche

18-60 value

18-61 Consumer Price (CPI)

18-62 deflated

18-63 deflator

18-64 purchasing power of the dollar

18-65 index number

18-73 90.0

18-74 166.7

18-75 83.3

18-76 120.0

18-77 $30,605

18-78 $30,197

18-79 $0.674

18-80 $0.581

18-81 1994

Chapter 19. Time Series and Forecasting

TRUE/FALSE QUESTIONS

19-1 T
Easy
Goal: 1

A time series is a collection of data recorded over a period of time, usually monthly, quarterly, or yearly.

19-2 T
Easy
Goal: 1

Long-term forecasts are usually from one year to more than 10 years into the future.

19-3 T
Easy
Goal: 1

A forecast is considered necessary in order to have the raw materials, production facilities, and staff available to meet estimated future demands.

19-4 F
Easy
Goal: 1

One component of a time series is the secular trend that is the smooth movement of a series over a short period of time, such as a few months or quarters.

19-5 T
Easy
Goal: 1

Many business and economic time series have a recurring seasonal pattern.

19-6 T
Easy
Goal: 1

One component of a time series is cyclical variation. An example of cyclical variation is the business cycle that consists of periods of prosperity followed by periods of recession, depression, and recovery.

19-7 F
Easy
Goal: 1

Episodic and residual variations can be projected into the future.

19-8 T
Easy
Goal: 2

In a time series analysis, the letter "a" in the linear trend equation, is the value of Y' when t = 0.

19-9 F
Easy
Goal: 2

In the linear trend equation, the letter "b" is the average change in t for each change of one unit (either increase or decrease) in Y.

19-10 T
Easy
Goal: 2

In the linear trend equation, t is any value that corresponds with a time period, i.e., month or quarter.

19-11 T
Easy
Goal: 2

The least squares method of computing the equation for a straight line going through the data of interest gives the "best fitting" line.

19-12 F Easy Goal: 2	If the sales, production or other data over a period of time tend to approximate a straight-line trend, the equation developed by the least squares method cannot be used to forecast sales for a future period.
19-13 T Easy Goal: 3	The moving average method merely smoothes out the fluctuations in the data.
19-14 T Med Goal: 3	The moving average method averages out cyclical (*C*) and irregular (*I*) components.
19-15 T Med Goal: 3	To apply the moving average method to a time series, the data should follow a linear trend and have a definite rhythmic pattern of fluctuations that repeat (say, every three years).
19-16 F Med Goal: 3	Sales, production and other economic and business series usually have periods of oscillation that are of equal length or identical amplitudes.
19-17 T Easy Goal: 2	A straight-line trend equation is used to represent the time series when it is believed that the data is increasing (or decreasing) by equal amounts, on the average, from one period to another.
19-18 T Med Goal: 4	Data that increases by increasing amounts over a period of time appear curvilinear when plotted on paper having an arithmetic scale.
19-19 T Easy Goal: 2	If the past data approximates a straight line, the equation used is $Y' = a + bt$, where a is the Y-intercept and b is the slope of the line.
19-20 F Easy Goal: 6	A typical monthly seasonal index of 107.0 indicates that sales (or whatever the variable is) are 107 percent above the annual average.
19-21 T Easy Goal: 6	Each typical seasonal index is a percent with the average for the year equal to 100.
19-22 T Easy Goal: 6	The ratio-to-moving-average method eliminates the seasonal, cyclical and irregular components from the original data (*Y*).
19-23 T Easy Goal: 6	The trend component of a time series is obtained my minimizing the sum of the squares of the errors.

19-24 F Easy Goal: 6	The cyclical component of a time series is described in terms relative to the seasonal index.
19-25 F Easy Goal: 6	The irregular component of a time series is the easiest to measure.
19-26 F Easy Goal: 6	The ratio-to-moving average method removes the time series trend component, resulting in 12 numbers that are called specific seasonals.
19-27 F Easy Goal: 6	For a monthly time series, the initial step, using the ratio-to-moving average method, is to remove the seasonal and irregular components from the time series using a 12-month moving average.
19-28 F Med Goal: 6	In the ratio-to-moving-average procedure, using the median or modified mean eliminates trend.
19-29 T Med Goal: 6	In the final step, using the ratio-to-moving-average method, the total of the 12 modified means should theoretically be equal to 1,200 because the average of the 12 months is designated as 100.
19-30 F Easy Goal: 7	The reason for deseasonalizing a sales series is to remove trend and cyclical fluctuations so that we can study seasonal fluctuations.
19-31 T Easy Goal: 7	Using the ratio-to-moving-average method, dividing the actual sales for a month by the typical seasonal for that month results in a figure that includes only trend, cycle and irregular fluctuations. This procedure is called deseasonalizing the sales.
19-32 T Easy Goal: 6	Seasonal variation is quite common in many industries, especially in the retail and wholesale trades.
19-33 T Easy Goal: 5	An analysis of past seasonal fluctuations can be helpful in planning production and in buying such items as toys, dolls, Easter eggs, and other holiday-oriented goods.
19-34 T Easy Goal: 7	Knowing the seasonal pattern in the form of indexes allows the retailer to deseasonalize sales. This is accomplished by dividing the actual sales for a month by the typical index for that month.
19-35 F Easy Goal: 5	A typical seasonal index of 103.7 for January indicates that sales for January are below the annual average.

19-36 F
Med
Goal: 7

The total of the four typical quarterly indexes should equal 100.0.

MULTIPLE CHOICE QUESTIONS

19-37 C
Easy
Goal: 1

Economic periods of prosperity followed by recession are described as:
A. Secular trend
B. Seasonal variation
C. Cyclical variation
D. Erratic variation
E. None of the above

19-38 B
Easy
Goal: 1

What is variation within a year, such as high sales at Christmas and Easter and low sales in January, called?
A. Secular trend
B. Seasonal variation
C. Cyclical variation
D. Variation
E. None of the above

19-39 D
Easy
Goal: 1

The merchants in Dallas, Texas, suffered flood damage in May 1995. Stores were closed for remodeling nearly two months. What is this type of variation in sales called?
A. Secular trend
B. Seasonal variation
C. Cyclical variation
D. Episodic variation
E. None of the above

19-40 B
Easy
Goal: 1

Since a ski resort does most of its business in the winter, what is the major source of variation in income due to?
A. Secular trend
B. Seasonal variation
C. Cyclical effect
D. None of the above

19-41 D
Med
Goal: 2

The following linear trend equation was developed for annual sales from 1995 to 2001 with 1995 the base or zero year. $Y' = 500 + 60t$ (in $ thousands). What are the estimated sales for 2005 (in $ thousands)?
A. $ 500
B. $ 560
C. $1,040
D. $1,100
E. None of the above

19-42 A
Med
Goal: 2

The following linear trend equation was developed for the annual sales of the Jordan Manufacturing Company. $Y' = 500 + 60t$ (in $ thousands). How much are sales increasing by?

A. $ 60,000 per year
B. $ 6,000 per month
C. $ 500,000 per year
D. $ 6,000 per year
E. None of the above

19-43 C
Med
Goal: 2

If the least squares equation for sales data going from 1996 to 2001 is $Y' = 10 + 1.3t$ (in $ millions), what is the value of t and the forecast for 2002?

A. $t = 6, y = 17.8$
B. $t = 0, y = 10.0$
C. $t = 7, y = 19.1$
D. $t = 10, y = 0.0$
E. None of the above

19-44 A
Med
Goal: 2

What is the formula for "*a*" in the least squares trend equation using the coded method?

A. $(\Sigma Y - b\Sigma t) \div n$
B. $\Sigma X \div n$
C. $\Sigma XY \div n$
D. X times *Y*
E. None of the above

19-45 A
Med
Goal: 4

What is the general equation for the logarithmic trend equation is log Y' = :

A. log *a* + log *b* (t)
B. log *a* t log *b* (*t*)
C. *a* t *b*(*t*)
D. *ab*(*t*)
E. None of the above

19-46 D
Med
Goal: 1

If the exports (in $ millions) for the period 1997 through 2001 were $878, $892, $864, $870 and $912 respectively, what are these values called?

A. Moving average
B. Linear trend equation
C. Logarithmic trend equation
D. Time series
E. None of the above

19-47 A
Med
Goal: 1

What is the long-term behavior of a variable over an extended period of time called?

A. Secular trend
B. Seasonal variation
C. Cyclical variation
D. Irregular or erratic variation
E. None of the above

19-48 A
Med
Goal: 1

A time series is a collection of data that:

A. Records past performance
B. Records future performance
C. is limited to yearly data
D. is limited to quarterly data
E. None of the above

19-49 E
Med
Goal: 1

Why are long range predictions considered essential to managing a firm?

A. To develop plans for possible new plants
B. To have raw materials available for future demand
C. To develop plans for future financing
D. To have enough staff for future needs
E. All of the above

19-50 B
Med
Goal: 1

Which one of the following is not a component of a time series?

A. Secular trend
B. Moving average
C. Seasonal variation
D. Irregular variation
E. All of the above are components

19-51 A
Med
Goal: 1

What is the correct order of events in a typical business cycle?

A. Prosperity, recession, depression and recovery
B. Depression, recovery, recession and prosperity
C. Recovery, depression, prosperity and recession
D. Recession, recovery, prosperity and depression
E. None of the above is correct

19-52 B
Med
Goal: 1

The crash of the telecommunications industry in 2000 exerted an impact on the economy that could be classified as:

A. Secular trend
B. Episodic variation
C. Residual variation
D. Seasonal variation
E. None of the above

19-53 B
Med
Goal: 2

In the linear trend equation, how is the average change in the dependent variable represented for every unit change in time?

A. a
B. b
C. t
D. Y'
E. None of the above

19-54 B
Med
Goal: 2

For a time series beginning with 1988 and extending up to 2001, which year would be coded with a one when using the coded method?

A. 1986
B. 1988
C. 1989
D. 1998
E. None of the above

19-55 B
Med
Goal: 3

For an annual time series extending from 1993 through 2001, how many years would be lost in a three year moving average?

A. 2 at the start and 1 at the end
B. 1 at the start and 1 at the end
C. 2 at the start and 0 at the end
D. 0 at the start and 2 at the end
E. None of the above

19-56 B
Med
Goal: 5

Given the trend equation $Y' = 25 + 0.6t$ (base year = 1996), what would be the forecast value for 2000?

A. 25
B. 28
C. 30
D. 32
E. None of the above

19-57 E
Med
Goal: 3

How can you describe the moving average method?

A. Useful in smoothing out a time series
B. Used in measuring seasonal fluctuations
C. A technique which does not result in an trend line equation
D. A method for identifying a trend
E. All of the above

19-58 C
Med
Goal: 3

For a five-year moving average, how many values will be lost at the beginning and end of the time series?

A. 0 at the start and 4 at the end
B. 3 at the start and 3 at the end
C. 2 at the start and 2 at the end
D. 0 at the start and 5 at the end
E. None of the above

19-59 C
Med
Goal: 2

A linear trend equation is used to represent time series values when the data are changing by equal?

A. Percents
B. Proportions
C. Amounts
D. Both "A" and "B" are correct
E. None of the above

19-60 C
Med
Goal: 4

How will data appear which increases or decreases by equal percents when plotted on graph paper having an arithmetic scale?

A. Straight line
B. Linear
C. Curvilinear
D. Both "A" and "B" are correct
E. None of the above

19-61 E
Med
Goal: 4

Which of the following is true for the linear equation, $Y' = a + bt$?

A. $\log a = S \log Y' / n$
B. $\log Y' = \log a + \log b(t)$
C. $\log b = S(X \log Y') / t^2$
D. All of the above are true
E. None of the above are true

19-62 C
Med
Goal: 5

Given a linear time series trend, $Y' = 5.2 + 3.1t$, what is the forecast for 2002 if the time series started in 1995?

A. 23.8
B. 26.9
C. 30.0
D. 21.7
E. None of the above

19-63 B
Med
Goal: 1

What time series component was exemplified during the 1980's when the American economy enjoyed a period of prosperity?

A. Irregular
B. Cyclical
C. Trend
D. Seasonal
E. None of the above

19-64 B
Med
Goal: 2

What is a disadvantage of the estimated method of determining a trend line equation?

A. Provides quick approximations
B. Is subject to human error
C. Provides accurate forecasts
D. Is too difficult to calculate
E. None of the above

19-65 C
Med
Goal: 4

A logarithmic straight-line trend equation should be used for forecasts when the time series is increasing by?

A. Equal amounts
B. Increasing percents
C. Increasing amounts
D. Increasing or decreasing percents
E. None of the above

19-66 D
Med
Goal: 6

If a quarterly seasonal index is 0.56, it implies that
A. the quarter's sales are 56% above the yearly average.
B. the quarter's sales are 56% of the year total sales.
C. the other three quarter percentages will total 44%.
D. the quarter's sales are 56% of the yearly average.
E. none of the above correct.

19-67 A
Med
Goal: 6

In a seasonal index (4 seasons) the total of the quarterly means will be
A. 4.0.
B. 1.0.
C. 100%
D. a variable.
E. none of the above.

FILL-IN QUESTIONS

19-68
Med
Goal: 1

What kind of fluctuations are irregular variations that are unpredictable?
____________________ and ____________________

19-69
Med
Goal: 3

What method is useful in smoothing out a time series? ______________

19-70
Med
Goal: 4

How does data that increases by equal percents over a period of time appear on arithmetic paper? ___________________

19-71
Med
Goal: 4

The trend equation for a time series that approximates a linear trend when plotted on ratio paper can be computed by using what transformed data with the least squares method? _________________

19-72
Med
Goal: 2

For a straight line trend, what represents the amount of change in Y for each increase of one in t? ________________________

19-73
Med
Goal: 1

What area is concerned with describing past trends and with predicting the future on the basis of past data?
____

19-74
Med
Goal: 2

In the linear trend equation, what is the Y-intercept? ______

19-75
Med
Goal: 2

What method is used to determine the linear equation when the best fitting straight line is required? ____________________

19-76
Med
Goal: 6

What method is most commonly used to compute the typical seasonal pattern? ________________

19-77
Med
Goal: 6

If we eliminate trend, cyclical and irregular variation from a monthly sales series, what are the 12 numbers that result called?

____

19-78
Easy
Goal: 7

A set of typical seasonal indexes is very useful in adjusting a sales series for seasonal fluctuations. What is the resulting sales series called? ________________

19-79
Med
Goal: 6

Logically, there are four typical seasonal indexes for data reported how often? ____________

19-80
Med
Goal: 5

What does a typical sales index of 96 for January indicate about sales?

____

19-81
Med
Goal: 1

Which component is it not possible for a time series to exist without?

____

Questions 82- 85 refer to the following:
Product sales since 1993 are:

Year	1993	1994	1995	1996	1997	1998	1999	2000	2001
Sales	266	264	145	205	139	98	94	94	128

The least squares trend equation using the coded method is given as $Y' = 265.12 - 21.18t$, where t is set equal to one for 1993.

19-82
Med
Goal: 2

What were the predicted sales in 2000? ________

19-83
Med
Goal: 5

What are the predicted sales for 2003? ______

19-84
Med
Goal: 2

On average, how much did sales change per year from 1993 to 2001?

____

19-85
Med
Goal: 3

What is the 3 year moving average for 1993-1995? ______

Questions 86-88 refer to the following:
Quarterly sales ($ thousands):

	1	*2*	*3*	*4*
2000	15	11	8	5
2001	13	12	9	6

19-86
Med
Goal: 5

What is the four-quarter moving average for 2000?
____

19-87
Med
Goal: 5

What is the four-quarter moving average for the period ending with the second quarter in 2001?____________________

19-88
Med
Goal: 5

The quarterly indexes for the year 2001 will total approximately
________.

Questions 89-92 refer to the following:
A plastics manufacturing performed a quarterly time series analysis for demands over the last five years (periods 1 through 20). The analysis resulted in the following trend equation and seasonal indexes:

$Y' = 920.0 + 22.6\,t$

Quarter	Index
1	0.75
2	1.04
3	1.21
4	1.00

19-89 C
Easy
Goal: 6

Based on the seasonal indexes, which quarter is expect to have 21% more demand than predicted by the trend line?
A. 1
B. 2
C. 3
D. 4

19-90 A
Easy
Goal: 6

Based on the seasonal indexes, which quarter is expect to have 25% less demand than predicted by the trend line?
A. 1
B. 2
C. 3
D. 4

19-91 C
Medium
Goal: 6

Using the trend line question and the seasonal indexes, predict demand for the third period of the next year, i.e., period 23.

A. 1439.8
B. 987.8
C. 1742.16
D. 1195.24

19-92 B
Easy
Goal: 6

The seasonal indexes have:

A. not been corrected.
B. Have been corrected.
C. Are incorrect.
D. Cannot be interpreted.

Questions 93-95 refer to the following:
The table below shows the sales for a plastics manufacturer recorded over the past year. The seasonal indexes for each quarter are also provided. To track the trend for these four quarters, use the indexes to deseasonalize the sales data

Quarter	Sales	Index	Deseasonalized Sales
1	738	0.75	
2	1012	1.04	
3	1196	1.21	
4	962	1.00	

19-93 B
Medium
Goal: 7

What is the deseasonalized sales value for quarter 1?

A. 553.5
B. 984
C. 588
D. 184.5

19-94 C
Medium
Goal: 7

What is the deseasonlized sales value for quarter 3?

A. 251.16
B. 944.84
C. 988.43
D. 1147.16

19-95 B
Hard
Goal: 7

Overall, sales are

A. increasing.
B. Decreasing.
C. show no trend.
D. cannot be determined.

Answers to Fill-In Questions

Chapter 19. Time Series and Forecasting

19-68 episodic and residual

19-69 moving average

19-70 curvilinear

19-71 logarithmic

19-72 slope of line or b

19-73 time series analysis

19-74 a

19-75 least squares

19-76 ratio-to-moving-average

19-77 seasonal index

19-78 deseasonalized sales

19-79 quarterly

19-80 4% below the average for the year

19-81 trend

19-82 95.68

19-83 32.14

19-84 –21.18

19-85 225

19-86 9.75

19-87 9.5

19-88 4

Chapter 20. An Introduction to Decision Making

TRUE/FALSE QUESTIONS

20-1 T
Easy
Goal: 1

Statistical decision theory, is defined as the collection of techniques the decision maker can apply to choose the best alternative action.

20-2 T
Easy
Goal: 1

If there are no unknown factors, a decision is made with certainty.

20-3 T
Easy
Goal: 1

In decision making, if there are one or more unknown factors, then the decision is made under conditions of uncertainty.

20-4 F
Easy
Goal: 1

The decision-maker usually has a choice among several possible alternative acts. For each of these alternative acts, there are many possible results called events.

20-5 T
Easy
Goal: 1

The decision-maker usually has no control over the states of nature.

20-6 F
Easy
Goal: 1

A decision-maker selects a course of action called a consequence or payoff.

20-7 T
Easy
Goal: 2

An analysis of the expected payoffs for the three stocks in the following table indicates that purchasing Unique Chemicals would yield the greatest expected profit.

Purchase	*Expected Payoff*
Unique Chemicals	$1,840
HBX Homes	1,760
SOS Electronics	1,600

20-8 T
Easy
Goal: 4

Another way of deciding which common stock to purchase is to determine the profit that might be lost because the exact state of nature (the market behavior) was not known at the time the investor bought the stock. This potential loss is called opportunity loss or regret.

20-9 F
Easy
Goal: 4

The maximin strategy maximizes the maximum gain.

20-10 F
Easy
Goal: 4

Maximizers advocate a maximin strategy.

20-11 F
Easy
Goal: 5

If the expected value of stock purchases under conditions of certainty is $1,900 and the expected value of stock purchases under conditions of uncertainty is $1,840, then the $60 difference is called a payoff.

20-12 T
Easy
Goal: 5

A decision tree is a picture of all the possible courses of action and the consequent possible outcomes.

20-13 T
Easy
Goal: 5

Sensitivity analysis examines the effects of various probabilities for the states of nature on the expected values of the alternatives or acts.

20-14 F
Easy
Goal: 1

Statistical decision theory had its beginning in the latter part of the 19th century.

20-15 F
Easy
Goal: 1

Statistical decision making is referred to as the traditional approach to decision making.

20-16 T
Easy
Goal: 1

In decision making, an act refers to the alternative choices open to a decision-maker.

20-17 T
Easy
Goal: 1

In decision making, another name for an event is a payoff.

20-18 F
Easy
Goal: 1

A decision-maker has no control over an act.

20-19 F
Easy
Goal: 3

Another name for expected payoff is expected opportunity loss.

20-20 F
Easy
Goal: 4

Another name for a payoff table is an opportunity loss table.

20-21 F
Easy
Goal: 4

The maximin strategy is regarded as an optimistic strategy for decision making.

20-22 T
Easy
Goal: 4

The difference between maximum payoff under certain conditions and maximum payoff under uncertain conditions equals the minimum expected opportunity loss.

20-23 F
Easy
Goal: 5

A decision tree shows the plausible range within which probability values do not cause a change in expected payoffs.

20-24 T
Easy
Goal: 3

The consequence of a decision-maker's action may be a profit, a loss or neither a profit nor a loss.

MULTIPLE CHOICE QUESTIONS

20-25 B
Med
Goal: 4

What is the most optimistic of all possible strategies?
A. Minimax
B. Maximax
C. Maximin
D. Minimax regret
E. None of the above

20-26 D
Med
Goal: 1

Which of the following is NOT a component of the decision-making process?
A. Alternatives
B. Payoff
C. States of nature
D. Seasonal indexes
E. None of the above

20-27 C
Med
Goal: 1

Of the three components in any decision-making situation, which of the following cannot be controlled?
A. Alternatives
B. Payoff
C. States of nature
D. Seasonal indexes
E. None of the above

20-28 A
Med
Goal: 2

Besides a payoff table, information can be organized using a
A. decision tree.
B. scatter diagram.
C. fishbone.
D. Pareto chart.
E. seasonal index.

20-29 B
Med
Goal: 3

Applying probabilities to a payoff table results in:
A. expected opportunity loss.
B. expected monetary value.
C. expected value of perfect information.
D. decision tree.
E. none of the above.

20-30 C
Med
Goal: 4

The decision approach of lowest expected opportunity loss and the highest expected payoff will give

A. different possible actions to follow.
B. the state of nature.
C. the same decision regarding action to follow.
D. the result in a decision tree.
E. none of the above.

20-31 D
Medium
Goal: 3

A maximin strategy will always choose the act or alternative that

A. maximizes the expected monetary value.
B. minimizes the maximum regret or opportunity loss.
C. Maximizes the potential payoff regardless of uncertainty.
D. Guarantees a payoff for any state of nature

20-32 B
Medium
Goal: 3

A minimax regret strategy will always choose the act or alternative that

A. maximizes the expected monetary value.
B. minimizes the maximum regret or opportunity loss.
C. Maximizes the potential payoff regardless of uncertainty.
D. Guarantees a payoff for any state of nature

20-33 C
Medium
Goal: 3

A maximax strategy will always choose the act or alternative that

A. maximizes the expected monetary value.
B. minimizes the maximum regret or opportunity loss.
C. Maximizes the potential payoff regardless of uncertainty.
D. Guarantees a payoff for any state of nature

20-34 A
Med
Goal: 5

Optimal decision (under conditions of uncertainty) subtracted from the expected value (under conditions of certainty) will yield

A. expected value of perfect information.
B. expected opportunity loss.
C. expected monetary value.
D. a decision tree.
E. none of the above.

FILL-IN QUESTIONS

20-35
Med
Goal: 1

In a payoff table, what are the alternatives called? _______

20-36
Med
Goal: 1

What is another term for payoff or consequence? _________________

20-37
Med
Goal: 1

What might be a profit, loss or neither a profit nor loss? _________

20-38 Med Goal: 3	Expected monetary value requires that _____________ are estimated for each state of nature.
20-39 Med Goal: 5	What is the difference between the maximum payoff under conditions of certainty and the maximum payoff under uncertainty called? ___________
20-40 Med Goal: 1	When all the facts are known in a decision-making situation, it can be said that the decision was made under conditions of _____________
20-41 Med Goal: 1	An uncertain condition in decision making referred to as: ____________________
20-42 Med Goal: 3	What is the average return to be realized for a particular act or decision alternative? ____________________
20-43 Med Goal: 4	What is the potential loss that is realized when an unexpected state of nature becomes reality called? ________________________
20-44 Med Goal: 4	In statistical decision making, the act or decision alternative yielding the maximum expected payoff also yields the minimum? __________________
20-45 Med Goal: 4	Which strategy maximizes the minimum gain? _____________
20-46 Med Goal: 5	What is a graphical sketch of all the possible courses of action and the consequent possible outcomes called? ________________
20-47 Med Goal: 1	What is a profit lost because the exact state of nature was not known called? ____________
20-48 Med Goal: 4	Which strategy maximizes the maximum gain?
20-49 Easy Goal: 2	A table to organize decision-making data, including various acts and possible profits or losses, is called a(n) ________________________.

20-50 Easy Goal: 2

A branching diagram that is useful for studying all possible decisions and consequences is the ________________________.

Questions 51-70 refer to the following:
The manager of Paul's fruit and vegetable store is considering the purchase of a new seedless watermelon from a wholesale distributor. Since this seedless watermelon costs $4, will sell for $7, and is highly perishable, he only expects to sell between 6 and 9 of them.

20-51 A Med Goal: 2

What is the payoff value for the purchase of 6 watermelons when the demand is for 6 watermelons?
A. 18
B. 21
C. 24
D. 42

20-52 A Med Goal: 2

What is the payoff value for the purchase of 6 watermelons when the demand is for 7 or more watermelons?
A. 18
B. 21
C. 28
D. 49
E. None of the above

20-53 A Med Goal: 2

What is the payoff value for the purchase of 7 watermelons when the demand is for 6 watermelons?
A. 14
B. 18
C. 21
D. 24
E. None of the above

20-54 B Med Goal: 2

What is the payoff value for the purchase of 7 watermelons when the demand is for 7 or more watermelons?
A. 18
B. 21
C. 24
D. 42
E. None of the above

20-55 D Med Goal: 2

What is the payoff value for the purchase of 8 watermelons when the demand is for 6 watermelons?
A. 17
B. 21
C. 24
D. 10
E. None of the above

20-56 A
Med
Goal: 2

What is the payoff value for the purchase of 8 watermelons when the demand is for 7 watermelons?

A. 17
B. 10
C. 24
D. 21
E. None of the above

20-57 C
Med
Goal: 2

What is the payoff value for the purchase of 8 watermelons when the demand is for 8 or more watermelons?

A. 17
B. 21
C. 24
D. 10
E. None of the above

20-58 A
Med
Goal: 2

What is the payoff value for the purchase of 9 watermelons when the demand is for 6 watermelons?

A. 6
B. 13
C. 20
D. 27
E. None of the above

20-59 B
Med
Goal: 2

What is the payoff value for the purchase of 9 watermelons when the demand is for 7 watermelons?

A. 6
B. 13
C. 20
D. 27
E. None of the above

20-60 C
Med
Goal: 2

What is the payoff value for the purchase of 9 watermelons when the demand is for 8 watermelons?

A. 6
B. 13
C. 20
D. 27
E. None of the above

20-61 D
Med
Goal: 2

What is the payoff value for the purchase of 9 watermelons when the demand is for 9 watermelons?

A. 6
B. 13
C. 20
D. 27
E. None of the above

20-62 A
Med
Goal: 4

What is the opportunity loss for purchasing 6 watermelons when the demand is for 6 watermelons?

A. 0
B. 3
C. 4
D. 6
E. None of the above

20-63 A
Med
Goal: 4

What is the opportunity loss for purchasing 8 watermelons when the demand is for 8 watermelons?

A. 0
B. 3
C. 4
D. 6
E. None of the above

20-64 D
Med
Goal: 4

What is the opportunity loss for purchasing 6 watermelons when the demand is for 8 watermelons?

A. 0
B. 3
C. 4
D. 6
E. None of the above

20-65 C
Med
Goal: 4

What is the opportunity loss for purchasing 7 watermelons when the demand is for 6 watermelons?

A. 0
B. 3
C. 4
D. 6
E. None of the above

20-66 D
Med
Goal: 4

What is the opportunity loss for purchasing 7 watermelons when the demand is for 9 watermelons?

A. 0
B. 3
C. 4
D. 6
E. None of the above

20-67 B
Med
Goal: 4

What is the opportunity loss for purchasing 8 watermelons when the demand is for 9 watermelons?

A. 0
B. 3
C. 4
D. 6
E. None of the above

20-68 C
Med
Goal: 4

What is the opportunity loss for purchasing 9 watermelons when the demand is for 7 watermelons?

A. 0
B. 4
C. 8
D. 12
E. None of the above

20-69 D
Med
Goal: 4

If the merchant purchases 7 watermelons, the maximum opportunity loss occurs when the demand is how many units?

A. 6
B. 7
C. 8
D. 9
E. None of the above

20-70 C
Med
Goal: 4

If the merchant purchases 8 watermelons, the minimum opportunity loss occurs when the demand is how many units?

A. 6
B. 7
C. 8
D. 9
E. None of the above

Questions 71-84 refer to the following:
The national sales manager for "I colored this" (ICT) T-shirts supplies all salespersons with the payoff table shown below, giving the potential profit generated when a retailer purchases from 1 to 4 dozen, as well as an opportunity loss table showing the potential lost profit for each purchase act. The probability of demand for each state of nature is also shown.

	PAYOFF				*OPPORTUNITY LOSS*			
	Demand				*Demand*			
Purchase	*1*	*2*	*3*	*4*	*1*	*2*	*3*	*4*
Probabilities	0.2	0.4	0.3	0.1	0.2	0.4	0.3	0.1
1	120	120	120	120	0	120	240	360
2	0	240	240	240	120	0	120	240
3	− 120	120	360	360	240	120	0	120
4	− 240	0	240	480	360	240	120	0

20-71 C
Med
Goal: 3

What is the expected payoff for purchasing 1 dozen T-shirts?

A. 0
B. 72
C. 120
D. 168
E. None of the above

20-72 C
Med
Goal: 3

What is the expected payoff for purchasing 2 dozen T-shirts?

A. 72
B. 120
C. 168
D. 192
E. None of the above

20-73 C
Med
Goal: 3

What is the expected payoff for purchasing 3 dozen T-shirts?

A. 72
B. 120
C. 168
D. 192
E. None of the above

20-74 A
Med
Goal: 3

What is the expected payoff for purchasing 4 dozen T-shirts?

A. 72
B. 120
C. 168
D. 192
E. None of the above

20-75 C
Med
Goal: 3

How many dozen "I colored this" T-shirts should be purchased to yield the highest payoff?

A. 0
B. 1
C. 2
D. 3
E. 4

20-76 C
Med
Goal: 4

What is the expected opportunity loss of purchasing 1 dozen T-shirts?

A. 84
B. 108
C. 156
D. 204
E. None of the above

20-77 A
Med
Goal: 4

What is the expected opportunity loss of purchasing 2 dozen T-shirts?

A. 84
B. 108
C. 156
D. 204
E. None of the above

20-78 B
Med
Goal: 4

What is the expected opportunity loss of purchasing 3 dozen T-shirts?

A. 84
B. 108
C. 156
D. 204
E. None of the above

20-79 D
Med
Goal: 4

What is the expected opportunity loss of purchasing 4 dozen T-shirts?
A. 84
B. 108
C. 156
D. 204
E. None of the above

20-80 C
Med
Goal: 4

How many dozen T-shirts should you purchase based on minimizing the expected opportunity loss?
A. 0
B. 1
C. 2
D. 3
E. 4

20-81 D
Med
Goal: 4

What is the maximum payoff under conditions of certainty?
A. 120
B. 240
C. 360
D. 480
E. None of the above

20-82 B
Med
Goal: 5

What is the value of perfect information if the expected payoff is $180?
A. 0
B. 96
C. 120
D. 150
E. None of the above

20-83 B
Med
Goal: 4

What would be the best decision if the maximin strategy is used?
A. 0
B. 1
C. 2
D. 3
E. 4

20-84 4
Med
Goal: 4

What would be the best decision if the maximax strategy is used?
A. 0
B. 1
C. 2
D. 3
E. 4

Questions 85-89 refer to the following:
You have four strategic business plans you can implement against your competitors depending on their awareness of your strategies. For each strategy (S1 – S4), the payoffs (in $ million) are as follows:

Strategy	*S1*	*S2*	*S3*	*S4*
Aware	– 4	2	3	– 1
Unaware	10	2	0	6

20-85
Med
Goal: 2

What strategy should you choose if the competitor is aware? _____

20-86
Med
Goal: 2

What strategy should you choose if the competitor is unaware? _____

20-87
Med
Goal: 4

What is the maximin choice? ______

20-88
Med
Goal: 4

What is the maximax choice? _____

20-89
Med
Goal: 4

What is the minimax choice? _____

Questions 90-95 refer to the following:
A person is trying to decide if they should buy a lottery ticket. The ticket costs $2.00. If the ticket is a winner, the prize would be $1,000. Knowing that winning $1,000 is not a certain outcome (state of nature), the person finds that the probability of winning is 0.001. Based on this information, the following payoff table can be constructed:

	Lose	Win
Buy	($2.00)	$1,000
Don't buy	$0	$0

20-90 B
Easy
Goal: 2

What is the probability of losing?
A. 0.001
B. 0.999
C. 1.00
D. Cannot be computed

20-91 A
Easy
Goal: 2

What is the decision using a maximax or optimistic approach?

A. Buy
B. Don't buy
C. Lose
D. Win

20-92 B
Easy:
Goal: 2

What is the decision using a maximin approach?

A. Buy
B. Don't buy
C. Lose
D. Win

20-93 B
Medium
Goal: B

What is the expected monetary value of buying the ticket?

A. +1
B. –0.998
C. +0.998
D. –1.998

20-94 B
Hard
Goal: 3

Based on the expected monetary value of buying a ticket, what is the best decision?

A. Buy
B. Don't buy
C. Lose
D. Win

20-95 C
Hard
Goal: 5

What is the value or perfect information?

A. $1.00
B. $0.998
C. $1.998
D. Cannot be computed

Answers to Fill-In Questions

Chapter 20. An Introduction to Decision Making under Uncertainty

20-35 acts

20-36 outcome

20-37 payoff

20-38 probabilities

20-39 value of perfect information

20-40 certainty

20-41 state of nature

20-42 expected monetary value

20-43 opportunity loss

20-44 opportunity loss

20-45 maximin

20-46 decision tree

20-47 regret

20-48 maximax

20-49 payoff table

20-50 decision tree

20-85 S3

20-86 S1

20-87 S2

20-88 S1

20-89 S2

McGraw-Hill/Irwin
Test Bank to accompany STATISTICAL TECHNIQUES IN BUSINESS AND ECONOMICS, Eleventh Edition, by Lind, Mason, & Marchal.

We hope this manual and the text are error free and easy for you to use. Invariably, however, if there are errors, we would appreciate knowing about such errors as soon as possible so that we can correct them in subsequent printings and future editions. Please help us by using this postage-paid form to report any that you find. Thank you.

Attention: R. Hercher

Name______________________School__________________________

Office Phone__________________________

Please fold and seal so that our address is visible, and mail.

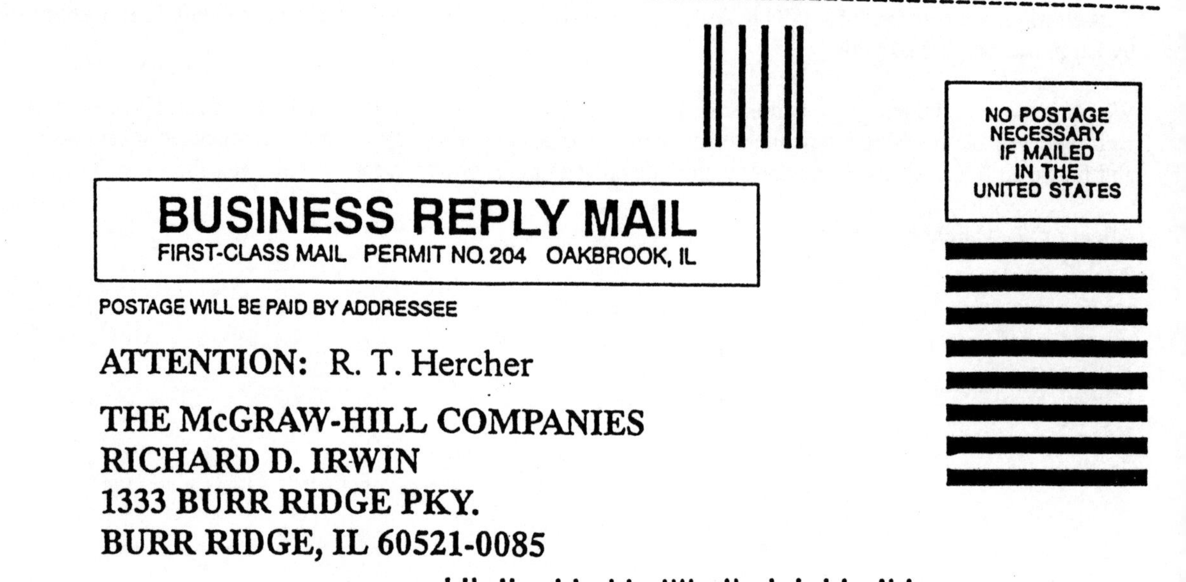

NO POSTAGE
NECESSARY
IF MAILED
IN THE
UNITED STATES

BUSINESS REPLY MAIL
FIRST-CLASS MAIL PERMIT NO. 204 OAKBROOK, IL

POSTAGE WILL BE PAID BY ADDRESSEE

ATTENTION: R. T. Hercher

THE McGRAW-HILL COMPANIES
RICHARD D. IRWIN
1333 BURR RIDGE PKY.
BURR RIDGE, IL 60521-0085

(fold)

(fold)

McGraw-Hill/Irwin
Test Bank to accompany STATISTICAL TECHNIQUES IN BUSINESS AND ECONOMICS, Eleventh Edition, by Lind, Mason, & Marchal.

We hope this manual and the text are error free and easy for you to use. Invariably, however, if there are errors, we would appreciate knowing about such errors as soon as possible so that we can correct them in subsequent printings and future editions. Please help us by using this postage-paid form to report any that you find. Thank you.

Attention: R. Hercher

Name________________________School______________________________

Office Phone______________________________

Please fold and seal so that our address is visible, and mail.

NO POSTAGE NECESSARY IF MAILED IN THE UNITED STATES

BUSINESS REPLY MAIL

FIRST-CLASS MAIL PERMIT NO. 204 OAKBROOK, IL

POSTAGE WILL BE PAID BY ADDRESSEE.

ATTENTION: R. T. Hercher

THE McGRAW-HILL COMPANIES
RICHARD D. IRWIN
1333 BURR RIDGE PKY.
BURR RIDGE, IL 60521-0085

(fold)

(fold)

McGraw-Hill/Irwin
Test Bank to accompany STATISTICAL TECHNIQUES IN BUSINESS AND ECONOMICS, Eleventh Edition, by Lind, Mason, & Marchal.

We hope this manual and the text are error free and easy for you to use. Invariably, however, if there are errors, we would appreciate knowing about such errors as soon as possible so that we can correct them in subsequent printings and future editions. Please help us by using this postage-paid form to report any that you find. Thank you.

Attention: R. Hercher

Name________________________School____________________________

Office Phone______________________________

Please fold and seal so that our address is visible, and mail.

NO POSTAGE
NECESSARY
IF MAILED
IN THE
UNITED STATES

BUSINESS REPLY MAIL
FIRST-CLASS MAIL PERMIT NO. 204 OAKBROOK, IL

POSTAGE WILL BE PAID BY ADDRESSEE

ATTENTION: R. T. Hercher

THE McGRAW-HILL COMPANIES
RICHARD D. IRWIN
1333 BURR RIDGE PKY.
BURR RIDGE, IL 60521-0085

(fold)

(fold)

McGraw-Hill/Irwin
Test Bank to accompany STATISTICAL TECHNIQUES IN BUSINESS AND ECONOMICS, Eleventh Edition, by Lind, Mason, & Marchal.

We hope this manual and the text are error free and easy for you to use. Invariably, however, if there are errors, we would appreciate knowing about such errors as soon as possible so that we can correct them in subsequent printings and future editions. Please help us by using this postage-paid form to report any that you find. Thank you.

Attention: R. Hercher

Name________________________School______________________________

Office Phone______________________________

Please fold and seal so that our address is visible, and mail.

NO POSTAGE
NECESSARY
IF MAILED
IN THE
UNITED STATES
BUSINESS REPLY MAIL
FIRST-CLASS MAIL PERMIT NO. 204 OAKBROOK, IL
POSTAGE WILL BE PAID BY ADDRESSEE
ATTENTION: R. T. Hercher
THE McGRAW-HILL COMPANIES
RICHARD D. IRWIN
1333 BURR RIDGE PKY.
BURR RIDGE, IL 60521-0085

(fold)

(fold)